PRAISE FOR *SALTED AND CURED*

"Even without recipes, this is a most delicious read! Jeff Roberts is not only passionate about salumi today, but he is also a skillful writer who deftly brings together the complex threads of his subject. Woven among the players, the history, animal welfare issues, and so much more are some great stories. I relished them all."
— **Deborah Madison**, author of *Vegetable Literacy* and *In My Kitchen*

"*Salted and Cured* is a story of immigrants in America. Not only did different immigrant communities arrive with their own butchery and curing traditions, but they adapted their techniques to their new corners of America. Whether you're a gastronaut or a delicatessen denizen, Jeff Roberts is your man! He is your best guide to the people and places where you'll find cured meats that resist the industrial meat system that deadens our taste buds, robs places of flavor and wealth, and condemns animals to the horrors of confinement."
— **Richard McCarthy**, executive director, Slow Food USA

"It is surprising how much intelligence, sensitivity, practicality, resilience, and love for the community and the land are captured in traditional products such as charcuterie. Within these pages, we are fortunate to come to understand how a product born out of necessity has become a symbol of identity, one that tells the stories of countless people and *peoples*."
— **Carlo Petrini**, founder, Slow Food

"Charcuterie is truly the preservation of time and place. Roberts focuses on the modern American artisans of meat through a global lens that honors the fabric of history that is woven with cultural food traditions. This book will forever change your perspective of the landscape of American cured meats."
— **Adam Danforth**, author of *Butchering Beef* and *Butchering Poultry, Rabbit, Lamb, Goat, and Pork*

"Not too long ago, salting a ham and hanging it to dry was considered a simple act of economy and faith. Today, it is in many ways a revolutionary act, one that flies in the face of our industrial food production system. In this fascinating and richly reported book, Roberts introduces us to the renegade butchers, farmers, chefs, and charcutiers of America who wave their hams like freedom flags, who spread the salt gospel through their communities and across the nation, and who quietly tend to the fermented funk of their salamis like monks in prayer, all in the name of change."

— **Camas Davis**, founder, Portland Meat Collective

"While guiding us through the history of preserved meats, culminating in today's neo-artisan food movements, *Salted and Cured* never lets us forget that we need art *and* science — and probably a little love — to create truly transcendent food. Jeffrey Roberts has created a testament to a craft, once a necessity, that survived commodification and is blossoming again. Get yourself some handmade meat snacks and prepare to dive in."

— **Gordon Edgar**, author of *Cheddar*

"*Salted and Cured*, Jeff Roberts's lively tour of the world of American preserved meats, is an informative and entertaining overview of new traditions rooted in deep history. The tale begins with a brief history of pigs and meat preservation, brings the pig and its enthusiasts to the United States, and then reveals, region by region, the evolution of the art and craft of cured meats in the United States, from the Atlantic, across the Midwest, to the Mountain States and the Pacific. At its best, our culture takes the old and delicious and generates innovative, bold, and delectable formats. *Salted and Cured* brings to life the story and world of salumi. Much to read and learn, much to eat and enjoy!"

— **Kathy and Herb Eckhouse**, La Quercia Cured Meats

"I love this book! It is a chronicle of America's unique relationship with pork. Jeff Roberts weaves together the stories of so many local and regional producers inspired by so many varied traditions that what emerges from the pages is a picture that is uniquely American. A great read for anyone interested in drilling down into the meat of both our emerging cuisine and our varied heritage."

— **Mateo Kehler**, cofounder, Jasper Hill Farm

"Always the educator, Jeff gives us a gift with *Salted and Cured*. He clarifies the mystery of why we love cured and fermented foods by digging into the culture and history of salumi."

— **Emilio Mignucci**, vice president, Di Bruno Bros.

SALTED

&

CURED

Savoring the Culture, Heritage, *and* Flavor

of America's Preserved Meats

JEFFREY P. ROBERTS

CHELSEA GREEN PUBLISHING
WHITE RIVER JUNCTION, VERMONT

Project Manager: Angela Boyle
Developmental Editor: Michael Metivier
Copy Editor: Eileen M. Clawson
Proofreader: Rachel Shields
Indexer: Peggy Holloway
Designer: Melissa Jacobson

Printed in the United States of America.
First printing March 2017.
10 9 8 7 6 5 4 3 2 1   17 18 19 20 21

Our Commitment to Green Publishing
Chelsea Green sees publishing as a tool for cultural change and ecological stewardship. We strive to align our book manufacturing practices with our editorial mission and to reduce the impact of our business enterprise in the environment. We print our books and catalogs on chlorine-free recycled paper, using vegetable-based inks whenever possible. This book may cost slightly more because it was printed on paper that contains recycled fiber, and we hope you'll agree that it's worth it. Chelsea Green is a member of the Green Press Initiative (www.greenpressinitiative.org), a nonprofit coalition of publishers, manufacturers, and authors working to protect the world's endangered forests and conserve natural resources. *Salted and Cured* was printed on paper supplied by Thomson-Shore that contains 100% postconsumer recycled fiber.

Library of Congress Cataloging-in-Publication Data
Names: Roberts, Jeffrey P.
Title: Salted and cured : savoring the culture, heritage, and flavor of America's preserved meats /
  Jeffrey Roberts.
Description: White River Junction, Vermont : Chelsea Green Publishing, [2017] | Includes
  bibliographical references and index.
Identifiers: LCCN 2016052766 | ISBN 9781603586603 (hardcover) | ISBN 9781603586610 (ebook)
Subjects: LCSH: Meat — Preservation. | Meat — Preservation — United States. | Meat — United States
  — History. | Dried meat — United States — History.
Classification: LCC TX612.M4 R625 2017 | DDC 641.4/9 — dc23
LC record available at https://lccn.loc.gov/2016052766

Chelsea Green Publishing
85 North Main Street, Suite 120
White River Junction, VT 05001
(802) 295-6300
www.chelseagreen.com

Dedicated to my grandparents—
Maria (Mary) and Pietro (Peter) Veleno, and
Jeannette and Jacob Rothenberg

CONTENTS

ACKNOWLEDGMENTS

I am indebted to dozens of chefs, charcutiers, and salumieri who talked at length about their craft, sometimes roads less traveled, and perspectives on fermentation and dry-cured meats. In addition to the list of people interviewed, I thank Caroline Abels, Janet Fletcher, Lisa Harris, Corin Hirsch, Josiah Lockhart, Chris McDonald, Corrie Quinn, and Eric Zander for taking time to read and comment on the initial proposal. My good friends and colleagues Illtud "Bob" Dunsford, Kevin O'Donnell, Mirco Marconi, and Bob Perry offered timely feedback, while Tom Slayton jogged memories of the "Boar's Head Carol." Thank you as well to the photographers and the many businesses that generously provided wonderful images. To developmental editor Michael Metivier, editor Ben Watson, copy editor Eileen Clawson, proofreader Rachel Shields, and publisher Margo Baldwin, who have traveled now with me through cheese and cured meat, thank you for all the support and patience.

Finally, to my wife, Cari Clement, who more than once asked, "What's growing in the fridge, and is it contagious?" words cannot express my gratitude for your caring, love, and interest through a very long haul. I promise not to have hip surgery and recovery again while undertaking another book.

Introduction

Go hang a salami; I'm a lasagna hog.

— A PALINDROME

America's contemporary food scene is anything but quiet! The food revolution continues its loud and delicious transformation, a cornucopia jam-packed with the pleasures of fermentation: thousands of craft beers, hundreds of handmade breads, caves of artisan cheese, unique bottles of spirits, and, now more than ever, grottoes and space-age "caves" full of meats — charcuterie, salumi, and country hams — curing both in restaurants and in the countless new cured-meat operations that have appeared across the country over the past two decades. Building on the success of craft beer and artisan cheese, and buoyed by increasingly appreciative and sophisticated consumer demand, chefs, food professionals, and entrepreneurs are fashioning hundreds of new, delicious dry-cured meats. What a time in America to enjoy great eating.

And yet sometimes our contemporary fascination with, and desire for, the latest unique food or flavor overlooks a long history of necessity and struggle for survival that is often the foundation of extraordinary tastes and unique cultural expressions. For thousands of years the practice of salting and dry curing was an essential technique to preserve fresh meat resources and survive winter months. It allowed the salted and cured foods to function as a pantry when food was scarce. By enabling our forebears to preserve a wide variety of fish, meats, fruits, and vegetables, curing foods using various combinations of salt, saltpeter (potassium nitrate) or nitrates and nitrites, smoke, air- and even freeze-drying resulted in a remarkably diverse array of great-tasting foods.

The arrival in North America of English and Scotch-Irish colonists, French and German settlers, and subsequent waves in the nineteenth century of eastern and southern European immigrants, led to a transplanting of traditions and helped create ethnic identities through food and culinary ideas. In both rural and urban communities, we could identify nationalities by churches and synagogues, languages, and food, including approaches to curing meat. Since refrigeration and refrigerators did not became widespread until after 1900, traditional ways to preserve foods remained a significant part of America's food landscape through the mid-twentieth century. After World War II, however, a combination of factors reduced small-scale production of dry-cured meat and overall consumer interest. From shifts to industrial-scale manufacturing to changes in convenience and taste preferences to health and safety concerns, domestic handmade production disappeared in many places.

As far as pork, the main meat used for dry curing, is concerned, beginning in the 1970s, federal guidelines and health advisories from medical advocates and organizations directed Americans to forgo high-cholesterol foods and eat more chicken and fish. To address these changes hog farmers bred pigs with less fat, and the American Pork Council launched its successful promotional campaign to tout the value of lean pork, "the other white meat." And we gobbled up this substitute for poultry, despite its noticeable loss of taste and texture. In 2015 we slaughtered 115.5 million hogs, and at the time of this writing, in 2016, the forecast aims for 116.5 million.[1]

But many Americans now realize our country's contemporary industrial food system, while providing seemingly inexpensive food at the checkout counter, has detrimental consequences for animals, people, and the environment. America forfeited much on the altar of abundant, convenient, and inexpensive food with destructive consequences: Diets of highly processed foods impacted our health; the meat industry's widespread use of antibiotics contributed to a rapid evolution of virulent drug-resistant pathogens; long-distance food miles to satisfy our insatiable desire for out-of-season produce required huge outlays in energy and a corresponding low investment in the people who grow and raise our food; we chose to overlook legitimate welfare concerns for food animals; and we compromised air, soil, and water resources. Ultimately, as a country we sacrificed just plain good taste and decided against, as many of our mothers taught us, "everything in moderation."

The consequences of industrialization and consolidation over the past six or seven decades led many Americans and most foreigners to consider the United States a food wasteland. But we did not lose all our farmers and food artisans. We did not lose our ability to smell and taste nor the faculties to distinguish good food from bad. For decades authors such as Julia Child, James Beard, M. F. K. Fisher, and Marion Nestle and such journalists as R. W. Apple Jr., Marian Burros, Craig Claiborne, Clementine Paddleford, and Ruth Reichl have argued for a different understanding of food as nourishment and cultural identity. Increasingly since 1970, as the tsunami of McDonald's burgers and Domino's pizzas has washed across the country, restaurateurs and chefs — for example, Dan Barber, Rick Bayless, Emeril Lagasse, Danny Meyer, and Alice Waters — have taken to their cutting boards to ride in a different direction.

The relatively recent advent and intersection of many tectonic shifts in the food landscape were owed in part to these chefs and writers; organic foods; heritage animals and plants; fermentation; artisan cheese and craft beer; spirits and cocktails; organizations such as Slow Food International (in 2000 at an event in New York City, its founder, Carlo Petrini, argued for an international society for the preservation of good microbes); farm to table; farmers' markets and community supported agriculture and restaurants; and efforts to promote good diet and health, to name a few. These created an environment of discovery for consumers and producers alike. In part connected and fueled by the internet, these overlapping dynamic, delicious developments helped support and expand each trend.

The shift back toward better tasting pork in particular began in the late 1990s and accelerated after September 11, 2001, when Americans reembraced comfort foods, together with family and community recipes that reminded us of happier times. The aromas, flavors, and textures of comfort food helped reassure us about the future.[2] Realizing life is too short to deny ourselves the pleasures of good food and a welcoming table, we turned to foods such as mac and cheese, meat loaf and hamburgers, and iceberg lettuce with pink Thousand Island dressing that found their way from our kitchens and diners even to fancy white-tablecloth restaurants, with bacon taking center stage as one of the iconic foods that defined the shift.[3]

Over the last fifteen years, the bacon renaissance contributed to an important shift in hog breeding and meat production. Although a very small fraction of the country's total output, whole-animal purchasing and successful dry-cured experiments by chefs led to demands for better tasting pork. In turn, the change sparked the reintroduction of important hog breeds: Berkshire, Duroc, Large Black, Mulefoot, Old Spot, Ossabaw, and Tamworth. In many parts of the country, because feral hogs are so destructive to farms and forests, open hunting exists, and fresh and cured wild boar showed up on menus as well! The greater availability of traditional hog breeds and grass-fed meat in general created a need for more skilled butchers and culinary innovators in the kitchen. As consumers sought out exciting new culinary ideas, chefs purchased whole carcasses to cook extraordinary fresh cuts, made delicious sausages and pâtés, utilized offal, and with salt and time, aged and cured charcuterie, country hams, and salumi. Using the entire animal — snout to tail — brought down cost and created more sustainable enterprises for farmers and chefs. Dozens of new businesses — from Seattle to San Diego; Salt Lake City to Norwalk, Iowa, and Indianapolis; Washington, DC, to Lititz, Pennsylvania — opened to make dry-cured meat products. And while the United States once lost thousands of the butcher shops and the artisanal dry-cured meat products that defined neighborhoods and regions, some small-scale businesses managed to stay afloat and continue to make these historic products. Today important centers of artisan production remain, and their presence celebrates places and people, from Italians in the Bronx, San Francisco, and Seattle to country ham craftsmen in Kentucky and Virginia to Chicago and Cleveland's Czech and Polish butchers.

Paralleling the expanding interest in cured meats was the appearance of important books about the craft and traditional practices to transform pork into delicious and safe products. I highly recommend seeking out books by Francois Vecchio, Michael Ruhlman and Brian Polcyn, Jane Grigson, Elias Cairo, Steve Coomes, and Jamie Bissonnette, to name a few recognized authors. These recent publications, coupled with dozens of internet sites and classes on butchering and curing, contributed to the development of new businesses, consumer knowledge, and elevation of product quality and safety. Today consumers can find excellent American-made cured meat almost everywhere, from local pubs and restaurants to internet marketplaces, producers, and local retailers. Even large national manufacturers have developed new "limited edition" product lines to utilize better quality hogs and conform more closely to traditional practices to fulfill demand.

❧

One of my ancestors' gifts to me is a lifelong interest in great food and drink and the people who grow and produce them. My mother's family is Italian-American, with roots in the region of Molise, formerly the southern tip of Abruzzo. My mother and grandparents spoke Italian when they were together. My brother and I picked up words . . . although not the ones children are allowed to speak. During my first visit to Italy as an adult, while not understanding the language, I felt it in my bones, as the culture slipped quietly, perhaps loudly, into my soul. I sensed through taste and smell so many dimensions of myself, often without words to describe my emotions. Whether in the blood or genes, the smells, tastes, celebrations, laughter, and sharing are constant memories for me . . . and salumi was certainly a part of these experiences.

Around 1900 my father's family arrived in New York from Romania. My grandfather owned a business in New York City and commuted from his home in New Rochelle, northeast of the city. Although she was a Romanian Jew, my grandmother believed her children should have the freedom to explore, and food was a place for discovery and celebration. One of my father's favorite childhood memories and one he eagerly shared with my brother and me was Walter's Hot Dog Stand in Mamaroneck, New York. Opened in 1919, Walter's served dogs made from beef, pork, and veal and cooked in butter with the rolls toasted on the grill! In the 1950s, on our summer swim excursions from Mount Vernon, Walter's was a must-stop. Years later my aunt told me that, while their home was kosher, she, my father, and my uncle could all enjoy the fruits of Walter's magic. What heartbreak when we moved away and Walter's became a memory for me, although one in which I can still smell the dogs, butter, and mustard.[4]

I thank and salute both families for bringing me to places of such wonderful food; their roots nurture this book.

❧

Salted and Cured is not a "how to make cured meat" recipe book. Rather, I invite readers to take a historical journey in space, time, and taste, from China to classical Greece and Rome, across Europe to North America and contemporary producers. The book provides a brief overview of practices from ancient civilizations to colonial American settlers and nineteenth- and twentieth-century immigrants to industrial production. The narrative links the reemergence of curing to the contemporary food landscape, including agriculture, animal breeds, diet and health, and safety and regulations. While most chapters are organized geographically, each section weaves stories of specific businesses with broader cultural and historical change, trends, and events.

I did not attempt a comprehensive survey of businesses, in part because data and evidence is elusive. Locating today's artisan cheese companies, which I did in my first book, is easier because of how they are licensed and regulated at the state level. In contrast, since city or county health departments inspect businesses that produce limited quantities of dry-cured meats to use or sell on premises, the task of identifying them is daunting. Not until a company wants to market to restaurants or other retailers does the USDA become the regulator and inspector. The individuals and businesses in *Salted and Cured* represent a cross-section of contemporary dry curing. I acknowledge that many noteworthy, well-established companies do not appear in these pages, but I believe the people profiled reflect the breadth of today's charcuterie, country ham, and salumi artisans. Whether they are mentioned or not, I applaud all of these businesses as another dimension of America's rediscovery of great fermented foods.

While focusing on dry-cured pork products, let's not forget ways in which we preserve beef, lamb and mutton, and goat. Corned beef and pastrami occupy iconic places in America's culinary culture for both the Irish and Jews. Lamb prosciutto appears today on many menus, while *violino di capra*, or goat prosciutto, with origins in the northern mountains of the region of Lombardy, Italy, has appeared in the last few years.

Our culinary journey begins with the first chapter's overview of hog natural history and domestication and the deeply intertwined relationship with human evolution. Discoveries in Indonesia of thirty-five-thousand-year-old cave paintings of a babirusa, or pig-deer, highlight the animal's importance to local inhabitants. Paralleling the evolution and domestication of hogs are elaborations of complex cultural expressions of their importance to the rise of civilizations. The introduction of new preservation techniques also changed the manner in which we articulated the value of hogs to human life. Whether we consider the Chinese, Greeks, or Romans, locating adequate food resources was a daily challenge, and pigs played an essential role in both human survival and cultural evolution. Consequently, I've woven language and religion into the narrative about natural history and domestication.

Next we investigate a brief history of how immigrants to the United States brought different traditional cured pork practices with them. In my opinion, the history of cured meat illustrates the growth of the country's settlements and westward movement. Subsequent chapters explore in detail the contributions of immigrants and the contemporary landscape of dry curing. As we encounter different types of cured meat, the stories describe and explain their characteristics. Rather than separate chapters devoted to such critical issues as sustainability, animal welfare, or breeds, I've incorporated descriptions and explanations throughout about changes in animal husbandry, regulatory scrutiny, the role of chefs and restaurants, and the broader connections to fermentation.

Join me on a journey of survival, necessity, great taste, innovation, appreciation, and slow knowledge.

CHAPTER ONE

From the Silk Road to the Forum Suarium

To me, life without veal stock, pork fat, sausage, organ meat, demi-glace, or even stinky cheese is a life not worth living.

— ANTHONY BOURDAIN

Bourdain sums it up for many of us — we eat to live and yes, live to eat. And for much of human history, hogs have been a mainstay of our diets and culture, both contributing to our survival and enjoyment and sometimes provoking our distaste and even prohibition. Our historical and contemporary cultural manifestations of hogs embrace both the sublime (two-thousand-year-old Gallic copper coins imprinted with hams) and the ridiculous (pink flying pigs dressed in tutus). Each reflects a moment of hog history in which we viewed the animal's value sometimes as essential to life, sometimes as a movie caricature. In the novel *Animal Farm*, George Orwell bestowed his fictional pigs with intelligence, aggressiveness, and dogmatism, traits perhaps found in hogs but certainly attributable to some human swine. Whether we consider the practical and delicious place of meat in our diet or extraordinary cultural expressions, hogs have shared close relationships with humans for millennia. Even an absolute rejection of pork on religious grounds reflects powerful human sensibilities and reactions to their place on the planet.

An Abbreviated Natural History of the Hog and Its Early Domestication

Paleontologists have discovered fossil remains of forty-million-year-old prehistoric pigs in Asia, Africa, and Europe. One descendant, the omnivorous *Daeodon shoshonensis* (formerly known as *Dinohyus*, or "terrible pig"), living about twenty million years ago, was more than six feet tall and weighed thousands of pounds. Over millions of years these beasts evolved in many directions and populated most places on Earth. Scientific evidence shows wild pigs or boars, *Sus scrofa*, originated in Southeast Asia and subsequently radiated north and west; when they reached Europe, their numbers took off. Today's domestic pig, *Sus scrofa domesticus*, a subspecies of wild boar, is related to hippos, South American peccaries, warthogs, giant forest hogs, and numerous South Pacific island hogs. Excellent swimmers, pigs settled on these islands where geography and genetic isolation contributed to the evolution of smaller animals adapted to a limited environment.

As they evolved, wild pigs developed certain physical characteristics to help them survive, attributes passed down to and shared by their domesticated cousins. Without sweat glands pigs can only regulate body temperature, especially heat, through their noses or adaptive behavior practices. By living in forests and adjacent grasslands, wild pigs take advantage of water, mudholes for wallowing, and cooler temperatures to survive; domestic pigs famously create their own wallows for the same purpose. Although they have four toes, all pigs walk on just the two middle ones and have long legs ideal for running to escape danger. They tend to have large heads, small eyes, and elongated snouts with disk-shaped noses, one of nature's most efficient devices to dig, root, or plow in the ground. With excellent senses of hearing and smell, pigs rely less on eyesight to forage for food and avoid danger. Wild hogs have prominent, often razor-sharp tusks that are actually extended or stretched canine teeth. When cornered, wild boars are extremely dangerous, their tusks becoming lethal weapons. Although domesticated pigs have little or no tusks, if they become feral, their canines will reappear.

Hogs are also very fecund; in one year a wild sow may have one to two litters, with an average of five to six piglets per birth, while domesticated sows deliver two to three litters with an average of ten offspring at a time.

This reproduction rate, combined with a piglet's ability to grow rapidly to sufficient weight, made hogs an ideal meat source for humans for at least five thousand years. Cows, goats, sheep, and other potential food animals have much longer gestation periods and give birth to only one or two off-spring at a time.

Among many hog adaptations is their ability to eat almost anything; although not exclusive to pigs, this is a somewhat unusual mammalian trait. Cows, sheep, goats, camels, and similar ruminants have herbivore digestive systems that enable them to feed primarily on grasses, grains, and other vegetation. The first stomach, called a rumen, contains a host of microflora — bacteria, yeasts, protozoa — that break down cellulose and fatty acids for digestion. What cows eat transfers directly to milk; if they graze on onion grass, the milk smells and tastes exactly like onion. On the other hand, cows that feed on a variety of lush grasses, herbs, and flowers create highly prized milk with unique aromas and textures, the perfect raw material for great cheese.

In contrast, humans, chickens, rats, and hogs have simple stomachs that enable us to dine on a diversity of plant and animal foods. In the forest, pig ancestors enjoyed a smorgasbord of mushrooms, insects, tubers, fruits, nuts, maybe an occasional snake, carrion, and for island dwellers even shellfish. A hog transforms everything it eats into meat and, depending on diet, quantities of fat; because pigs cannot digest fat, whether from nuts or grains, it is distributed throughout the animal's muscles (this is known as marbling) and deposits layers on backs, bellies, and hind legs.

Most contemporary archaeology points to hogs as humankind's first domesticated food animal, appearing some twelve thousand to fifteen thousand years ago in the Fertile Crescent and on Cyprus. In China the evidence shows hog domestication about 6000 BCE along the Yellow and Yangtze Rivers. In 1989 archaeologists made significant discoveries at Hallan Çemi, an 11,000 BCE village in southeastern Turkey. They found bones of wild deer, goats, sheep, and pigs, the remnants of the community's hunts, evidence of their prowess as hunter-gatherers. In *Lesser Beasts*, his thorough description and analysis of global porcine history, Mark Essig maintains that as people harvested trees the number of deer and hog bones should have declined over time, as these animals were forest dwellers. But surprisingly, the scientists found the bones of young, mostly male pigs, implying that settlers bred and slaughtered hogs. Essig points out that as these hunter-gatherers transitioned to pastoral settlements they no longer walked away from their garbage and other waste. Wild pigs recognized potential foodstuffs in these communities; as omnivores pigs converted everything they ate from the village — meat scraps, grains, and human waste — into fats and proteins. It would seem obvious that humans purposely domesticated these animals. Essig, however, argues, "Wild boars, in adapting to the new niche created by human settlements, evolved in ways that made them capable of living in close proximity to people. Pigs, in other words, domesticated themselves."[1]

Ultimately, proximity, familiarity, and access to food contributed to the animals' domestication. While detailed histories of evolution and domestication go beyond the scope of this book, I recommend the early work of Charles Towne and Edward Wentworth and the contemporary scholarship of Mark Essig, Barry Estabrook, Jeffrey Weiss, and Peter Kaminsky, whose books articulate current research and hypotheses about domestication. Today, with new research tools for DNA and mitochondrial analysis, scientists are able to describe how domesticated and wild hogs interbred frequently over several thousand years, a process that constantly renewed genetic diversity and even gave rise to new breeds.

A Brief Introduction to Preservation Techniques

Clearly, one significant challenge to early humans was how to manage quantities of meat, poultry, fish, and other perishables beyond what people could eat immediately during one or two meals. The development of methods to preserve meat and foods such as grains, milk, and other perishables helped steer humans on our evolutionary path. Sometimes our contemporary fascination and desire for the latest unique food or flavor overlooks how a long history of necessity and struggle for survival are the foundations of extraordinary tastes and unique cultural expressions. As mentioned in the introduction, the practice of salting and dry curing was an essential preservation technique to manage fresh meat resources and to survive harsh winter months. These preserved foods served as a pantry when food was scarce. Our forebears preserved a remarkably diverse array of great-tasting foods using different combinations of techniques.

Because food preservation was critical to human survival, air- and sun-drying most likely preceded salt and dry curing, all dependent upon favorable geography and climate. In Asian, Egyptian, and Middle Eastern deserts, air- and sun-drying methods sufficed; strips of meat would dry quickly in these arid, hot environments. Archaeological evidence from early cave dwellings in Africa and the Middle East reveals soot deposits on ceilings and walls from fires used to keep people warm, cook food, and provide protection. Prehistoric humans hung meats from the ceiling to dry and smoke.

The Quechua, Aymara, and Inca peoples, living in South America's Andes Mountains and taking advantage of the high-altitude cold and dry atmosphere, utilized freeze-drying methods to preserve potatoes centuries before high-tech machinery created foods for long-distance hikers. Variations of jerky, derived from the Quechua word *ch'arki*, meaning dried, salted meat, were found throughout the Americas. In similar fashion Inuit and other arctic dwellers preserved wild salmon by hanging butterflied fish in cold, dry winds. Some two thousand to three thousand years ago in North America, Native peoples cut strips of bison, venison, elk, llama, and moose meat to air- and sun-dry. Many tribes pulverized the jerky and added fat, dried berries, and flavorings to produce pemmican, a lightweight, energy- and protein-dense food. They later taught these techniques to Europeans. Robert Peary took pemmican on his expeditions to the North Pole, while Roald Amundsen and Ernest Shackleton carried it to the South Pole.

Although definitive evidence does not exist for dates of its initial discovery, humans, whether nomadic or sedentary, later developed salt curing as a technique to preserve what they gathered and hunted or their first harvests. A fundamental necessity for early salt-curing practices was access to the mineral resource, and therefore, the technique appeared in different places around the world. These sources included evaporated ocean water, prehistoric deposits, saline pools, and myriad other sites. Since humans and other mammals require salt to live, our ancestors knew where to find adequate supplies. At certain times and places, eating meat was as much about salt requirements as the other physical needs for proteins, fats, and other nutrients.

The word "cure" stems from the Latin word *curare*, "to take care of." Beyond a method to preserve food, cure relates to healing or restoring health, a medical remedy, or the means to correct something troublesome or detrimental. The linguistic intersection of food and medicine expresses clearly that ancient peoples both understood and nurtured a close physical relationship between what they ate and human health.

Most important for our focus on dry-cured meat, by 3000 BCE China and Middle Eastern civilizations used salt curing for a variety of foodstuffs. The practice of preserving meat with salt appears to have originated in Asian deserts:

> *Saline salts from this area contained impurities such as nitrates that contributed to the characteristic red colour of cured meats. As early as 3000 BC in Mesopotamia, cooked meats and fish were preserved in sesame oil and dried salted meat and fish were part of the Sumerian diet. Salt from the Dead Sea was in use by Jewish inhabitants around 1600 BC, and by 1200 BC, the Phoenicians were trading salted fish in the Eastern Mediterranean region. By 900 BC, salt was being produced in "salt gardens" in Greece and dry salt curing and smoking of meat were well established. The Romans (200 BC) acquired curing procedures from the Greeks and further developed methods to "pickle" various kinds of meats in a brine marinade.[2]*

On a trip to China in 1986, as our party passed through rural villages, I saw whole dried corn cobs, cascades of chiles resembling Mexican ristras, and bundles of odd-looking mahogany-colored pods, all hanging under roof eaves to dry in the sun. The dark red-brown pods were *lawei*, a southern China cured-meat specialty that resembles Native American jerky. During the lunar calendar's twelfth month, the ancient Chinese made numerous gifts to their gods, including large quantities of sacrificial animals, poultry, and fish. To preserve the leftovers, the populace, especially in southern provinces with short winters, created lawei. The cured meat took many forms: pork (*làròu*), sausage (*làcháng*), even chicken (*làjī*) and fish (*làyú*). "Historical records show that more than 2,000 years ago, Confucius charged every student some làròu as a tuition fee," a reflection of its culinary value and financial worth.[3] For làròu, làjī, and làyú, the meat was cut in strips, marinated in salt and spices, and then hung to dry. In "Guangdong, Sichuan and Hunan, smoking the meat is an indispensable final step to infuse it with an appetizing color and fragrance. Làcháng, the fatty sausages often used in southern cooking, are prepared in a slightly different way — seasoned sliced pork is stuffed into a pig's small intestines and hung to dry."[4]

Early humans made sausages from cleaned, cooked intestines stuffed into stomachs. The use of intestines and stomachs reflected a need to utilize the entire animal. The stomach was large enough to accommodate other ingredients, such as grains, spices, and other offal. Haggis, Scotland's national dish, is a combination of ground sheep offal, oats, fat, spices, and other items stuffed into the animal's stomach and boiled. The organ's resiliency and strength made it possible to thoroughly cook the pudding.

In ancient Rome, while the elite ate the best cuts of pork, the poor enjoyed different types of fresh and smoked sausages; in Latin, *botulus* (or *botellus*, for a small sausage). Named after its origin in the southern region Lucania (today's Basilicata), Lucanian sausage is one of the earliest documented botuli. *De re coquinaria* ("On the Subject of Cooking"), a late fourth- or early fifth-century CE compilation of Roman recipes, describes one for Lucanian sausage that contained pounded pork spiced with pepper, cumin, savory, rue, parsley, bayberries, garum (a Roman fish sauce), fat, and pine nuts. After being thoroughly mixed, the concoction was forced into intestines and smoked.

From the Romans to the present, we find recipes very similar to Lucanian sausage, from French boudin to blood sausage, mortadella to frankfurters. The technique of finely pounding, mincing, or emulsifying meats into sometimes nearly liquid compositions, combined with other ingredients, created savory dishes — the original pudding — that solidified when stuffed by medieval European cooks into different-size casings and then boiled or steamed. Linguists suggest the term "pudding" came from the French "boudin," whose origin in turn was the Latin "botellus."

The process of dry-curing sausage differs from that for hams, but each must achieve a similar end point of safety. If preservation techniques are not applied, sausage and ham spoil, and if done improperly, these meats are potentially dangerous. Whether we consider whole muscles such as ham or the chopped, ground, minced, or otherwise cut-up meat of sausage, all must be treated with salt to cure, killing off bacteria and other harmful microorganisms. Through osmosis, salt draws water from bacteria cells, drying them out until rendered harmless. Dry-cured sausage (in contrast to fresh sausages like boudin and Lucanian sausage) was mixed with salt and often saltpeter (potassium nitrate), both of which kill microbes such as bacteria.

In addition to the word "pudding," another noteworthy bit of Roman historical and linguistic lineage relates to ham-curing practices. The word "prosciutto" comes from the verb *prosciugare*, which in Italian means "to dry from the inside out." Prosciugare is a combination of the Latin *pro* (before) and *exsuctus* (past participle of *exsugere*) "to suck out [the moisture]." Hence, it means to dry up, all dried up, or lacking juice. The exact historical sequence of ham curing in Europe remains hidden. We know that 2,200-year-old Greek curing techniques guided later Roman practices, while the *Larousse Gastronomique* argues that Gaul was the origin of cured ham somewhere between 200 and 100 BCE. Whether true or not, cured hams were certainly known and consumed by Romans. Roman aristocracy enjoyed both cooked hams (prosciutto *cotto*) and cured hams (prosciutto *crudo* [raw]), certainly as early as 160 BCE, if not earlier.

Roman senator Marcus Cato the Elder described how to salt hams in *De agri cultura* ("On Farming") ca. 160 BCE. The techniques he described are still the basic recipe used today to make both prosciutto di Parma and prosciutto di San Daniele. For centuries regional ham producers worked with the four seasons, each approximately three-month period providing critical temperature and humidity differences to stimulate salt penetration and enzymatic transformation deep in the muscles. Farmers or a *norcino*, a traveling butcher, would slaughter hogs in November or December, and the process to cure the hams began. Except for the hog's exposed exterior and skin, the ham muscles are sterile unless diseased or damaged in some way.

To preserve the whole muscle, therefore, requires specific salting techniques; after trimming, the exposed flesh is covered with dry salt, while the skin receives a wet salt. After salt was applied, the hams were hung in caves, where cold temperatures and wind helped retard spoilage, as the salt began its penetration into the meat. Hams would be washed and sometimes re-salted, and hung to dry for about three months. Prior to the last aging phase, a producer coated each ham with *sugna*, a mix of spreadable fat, salt, pepper, and occasionally rice flour, to protect them from excessive drying and hungry insects. During the final step the hams hung in a cool cellar, and as temperatures and humidity changed, the magical alchemy occurred as the ham slowly dried. Depending on the size of the ham and variations in weather, it could age for twelve or more months. Although techniques to produce Parma and San Daniele prosciutto differ, both regions reflect a fundamental reliance on climate and geography. The unique characteristics of wind, temperature, humidity, and geology (at least before the twentieth-century introduction of refrigeration removed a key variable from the production of both regional hams) contribute to distinctive differences in terroir.

An Evolution of Cultural Expressions

Although in many cultures access to pork and other meats depended on wealth and social status, for several thousand years pigs fed humans in Asia, Europe, and, once introduced by the Spaniards, in the Americas. In general, aristocrats and more well-off citizens enjoyed tender, quality cuts of meat, while the poor ate what they could find. For Chinese peasants the essential place and role of rice and pork assumed powerful cultural significance. From centuries of depravation and the value of rice as a belly filler, the Chinese still greet each other by saying *"Chi fan le mei you?"* (Have you eaten [rice] yet?) The importance of rice was matched by the dominant status of swine: "The Chinese character for 'home' is formed by placing the symbol for 'pig' under the symbol for 'roof': home is where the pig is."[5]

The ancient Romans took their pork seriously — on their plates, in cultural expressions, and language. For centuries Rome fed its citizens quite well; even the poor had meat on occasion. The city had a variety of designated food markets (*forum venalium*), one of which was the *Forum Suarium*, the pork market. While they enjoyed other meats, recipes for pork dominated cookbooks, and Romans used almost every part of the pig. More Latin words for pork exist than for any other meat: sellers of live pigs (*suarii*); ham (*pernarius*); dried pork (*confectorarius*); and fresh pork (*porcinarius*).[6] Roman treatises on agriculture detailed how to breed and raise hogs, the best feed regimens, and how to ensure the finest tasting meat and fat. The result was the presence of two distinctive hogs, one found south of Rome that resembled a wild pig, with lots of tough bristles. The other was a large, smooth, sometimes white animal that lived in sties, on farms geographically close to Rome. Their diets were designed to nurture both size and flavor. The white hogs fed the elite and because of their powerful physical presence were sacrificed on altars to the Roman gods.[7]

After the fall of Rome in 476 CE, the white pig favored by the aristocracy disappeared, and the formerly domesticated black hogs reverted back to their wild ancestors. My colleague Mirco Marconi, professor at the Slow Food *Università degli Studi di Scienze Gastronomiche* (University of Gastronomic Science), teaches a master's seminar on cured meat. He postulates that in the late sixth century a semiopen domesticated farming system emerged in the Po River Valley in which semiwild hogs enjoyed both farmland and forest. The hogs resembled earlier breeds, small in stature, in dark brown to black colors, with long bristles and longer front legs than hind ones.

When I asked Professor Marconi about why contemporary Italian prosciutto is sliced thin, he described a significant change in animal genetics that began in the 1870s. Clearly, a group of Italian hogs evolved over hundreds of years, but according to him, these resembled the older, wilder breeds, and therefore, the animals had less fat and tougher meat. According to Professor Marconi, prior to 1870, most prosciutto had to be cooked to tenderize the hams.[8] In the late nineteenth century the introduction of English and Danish breeds changed the nature of prosciutto production in both Parma and San Daniele.

One tangible cultural expression that reveals the value of hogs and hams to early Romans occurred during the reign of Emperor Caesar Augustus (27 BCE–14 CE). The Gallic city of Nemausus, a colony of Marseilles, issued the "hams of Nemausus" coins, "commonly known as 'boar's feet' . . . struck on copper planchets [in] the form of a ham with a projection ending in the foot of a pig."[9]

Following the linguistic trail closer to the present day, we encounter "the proof is in the pudding," a twentieth-century variation of an early seventeenth-century expression. In his *Remaines of a Greater Worke, Concerning Britaine*, William Camden wrote, "All the proofe of a pudding, is in the eating," meaning you had to taste and eat the pudding to know if it was good. Unfortunately, sometimes an undercooked pudding or sausage might sicken you from botulism. To bring it full circle, this potentially fatal illness, caused by the bacterium *Clostridium botulinum*, takes its name from a late nineteenth-century German word, *Botulismus*, that means "sausage poisoning." And that German word stems from the Latin "botulus," "sausage." These words and phrases, all with Roman origins, show the extent of that civilization's influence on European meat preparations for 1,500 to 2,000 years.

Another expression familiar to us today comes from late nineteenth-century America, when to live or eat "high on the hog" referred to how the wealthy ate pork cuts, such as loin, from above the belly. The poor could afford trotters, hocks, belly, jowls, and most types of offal and pickled pork. These wealth and social contrasts around access to food still exist today in myriad forms, from high-end white tablecloth restaurants to the critical value of local food banks to aid hungry Americans, and from Wagyu beefsteak to feedlot steers for inexpensive hamburger meat.

Crossbreeding for Different Purposes

Long before Gregor Mendel's nineteenth-century experiments with peas and the first scientific understanding of genetics, farmers and horticulturalists knew crossbreeding might produce an extraordinary new hybrid steer, hog, or peony, or maybe a dud. Depending on geography, climate, and markets, farmers bred pigs for litter size, adaptability, disease resistance, foraging ability, and many other traits. From the late eighteenth through the nineteenth centuries, European breeders were responsible for several important new hogs that changed hog production and ultimately cured meat in Italy and the United States.

In Italy a key new breed arrived in the late nineteenth century: the British Large White, more commonly referred to as the Yorkshire Large White.

In 1761 agriculturist Robert Bakewell became interested in a local tribe of hogs known as the Leicestershire breed and molded them into a large, useful hog that became popular in England. It is very likely that some, if not most, of the best Yorkshire hogs today came from these hogs. The first Yorkshires in the United States were brought into Ohio around 1830.[10] Antonio Zanelli, an agronomist and professor at the Istituto Tecnico Agrario of Reggio Emilia, is credited with introducing the Yorkshire to Italy in 1873. Today the Large White Italiana, a descendent of the Yorkshire, is the Italian strain and one of the three pigs sanctioned by the Consorzio del Prosciutto di Parma and Consorzio del Prosciutto di San Daniele.

The Danish Landrace became the second hog to transform Italian production. The Danes are among the world's highest per capita consumers of pork, in part because they love bacon. In 1896, after several decades of crossbreeding trials, Danish hog experts established the first registered Landrace herd with very specific characteristics for lean bacon and other products. "They truly appear to be a breed developed very systematically and carefully to produce some of the world's greatest pork products for exacting home and export markets."[11] After World War II the Danish Landrace was exported to Italy, but not for bacon production. It became the Italian Landrace:

> *The original stock was brought to Italy from Scandinavian sources, but selection has been toward meat characteristics and away from extremes for the best in bacon production. One can always find selection within a breed to be directed more toward the requirements of the host country, and Italians do not put the emphasis on bacon that is placed there by northern Europeans.*[12]

The last hog authorized by both regional consortia in the prosciutto triumvirate is Duroc, an American development from the early nineteenth century, when an initial Red Hog was bred in New York and New Jersey. The Red Hog, most likely from New York Red Durocs and Jersey Reds, was renowned for large litters and rapid weight gain. As the National Swine Registry describes its evolution:

> *In 1823, a red boar from a litter of ten, whose parents were probably imported from England, was obtained by Isaac Frink of Milton in Saratoga County, New York, from Harry Kelsey. Kelsey owned a famous trotting stallion, Duroc, and Frink named his red boar in honor of the horse. This boar was known for his smoothness and carcass quality.*
>
> *His progeny continued the Duroc name and many of them inherited his color, quick growth and maturity, deep body, broad ham and shoulder, and quiet disposition. The Duroc was smaller than the Jersey Red, with finer bones and better carcass quality.*[13]

Today the Duroc Italiana is the principal sire to the Large White Italiana and Italian Landrace to produce the heavy hogs needed for prosciutto di Parma and prosciutto di San Daniele, both of which are Denominazione di Origine Protetta ("Protected Designation of Origin"), or DOP, products. Looking at the fresh hams and the finished prosciutti from both regions, you are struck immediately by their large size, marbling throughout the muscles, and extensive fat cap. Without these essential characteristics, what we understand, taste, and celebrate as some of the world's finest cured hams might not exist. Another distinguishing feature for prosciutto di Parma: the hogs enjoy whey from Parmigiano-Reggiano cheese-making creameries, and many connoisseurs believe and claim they can taste the difference!

Some might argue that since the foundation of contemporary Parma and San Daniele prosciutti is three foreign heritage hogs, the unique place of both regional products is compromised. I do not agree with this point of view. If anything, we recognize and understand the long history of hog evolution, in which hundreds if not thousands of different *Sus scrofa domesticus* pigs have come and many have gone. As farmers learned more about crossbreeding, many characteristics changed to fulfill different agriculture and food needs. The ability of a domesticated pig to adapt to new conditions meant a steady improvement of meat quality. For centuries, whether in Rome or other cities, people recognized and celebrated the quality of Parma and San Daniele prosciutti. The introduction of American, Danish, and English hogs offered a better raw material for the Parma and San Daniele prosciutto maestros to create world-renowned *capolavori* (masterpieces).

Over centuries pigs raised in different places with unique climates, foods, and husbandry conditions developed different traits that sometimes required different preservation processes. By the medieval period in Europe, although we find *Sus scrofa domesticus* across the continent, these hogs differed genetically from earlier Middle Eastern types. While domesticated, these pigs were allowed to roam the forests and often resembled their wild brethren far more than you would expect to see in an enclosed barnyard.[14] "In medieval times, hams were made all over Europe. Every cottager kept a pig, which was killed in autumn and preserved to provide food through winter."[15]

However, because of different climatic realities, dry curing hams in Northern Europe or the British Isles was the exception. Since cold and damp conditions made drying difficult, salting in combination with smoking or cooking hams and other preservation techniques were the principal methods. Schwarzwälder Schinken, or Black Forest ham, is the only dry-cured ham made in Germany and at that for just the last two hundred years. Because temperature and humidity conditions were better in the southern Black Forest region, pigs were raised elsewhere. Whether salted in brine or with dry salt and spices, these hams are made from deboned legs. After salting and resting stages, the hams are cold smoked over different combinations of pine, fir, juniper, and other evergreens to produce a deep brown to black surface. In total the process takes about three months to create a soft, moist, fully flavored meat.

In the British Isles cold, damp fall and winter seasons led to similar preservation techniques of salt and smoke. Regional variations existed, and depending on where they once lived, when the first English settlers arrived in the New World, their transplanted methods and techniques reflected these differences. As we next explore the history of hogs and curing in North America, many centuries-old practices repeat themselves again and again.

CHAPTER TWO

From the Old World to the Americas

The boar's head in hand bear I,
Bedeck'd with bays and rosemari.
And I pray you, my masters, merry be
Quot estis in convivio (As many as are in the feast)

Chorus
Caput apri defero (The boar's head I offer)
Reddens laudes Domino (Giving praises to the Lord)

— "BOAR'S HEAD CAROL," FIFTEENTH-CENTURY
ENGLISH CHRISTMAS CAROL

While at the University of Rochester, I was a member of the men's chorus, and each December, the university sponsored a Boar's Head Dinner, at which we sang this carol. Ancient English and Scandinavian traditions included the sacrifice of a boar to celebrate the yuletide season. The roasted head, complete with an apple or orange in the mouth, arrived in a processional march with minstrels singing the carol.

The "Boar's Head Carol" reminds me of the several-thousand-year history of human interaction with hogs. In the United States that history begins more than five hundred years ago with Columbus, the revolution wrought by his accidental stumbling onto the Caribbean islands, and the subsequent arrival of Spanish explorers. The Columbian Exchange, a term coined by Alfred Crosby, reflects a global movement of food and agriculture, ideas, technology, people, and diseases, with the Americas and Spain as the linchpins. Like it or not, for better or worse, we deal with the consequences of the Columbian Exchange every day.

Among many Western Hemisphere foods we celebrate globally today are cashews, chiles, chocolate, corn, peanuts, pineapples, potatoes and sweet potatoes, tomatoes, turkeys, and vanilla. In turn, many international ingredients over time came to the Americas: chickens, coffee, hogs, rice, steers and dairy cows, sugar, and wheat. Potatoes and sugarcane transformed the United States. Europeans initially deemed the lowly spud poisonous (a member of the deadly nightshade family), fit only for animals. When finally accepted as food, it led eventually to the rapid growth of Berlin and a population explosion in Ireland from 1750 to 1840. The subsequent Irish Potato Famine of the 1840s and early 1850s created an enormous outflow of emigrants, many of whom came to the United States. Those settlers and their descendants changed the tenor of American history.

After conquering a number of Caribbean islands, the Spanish introduced sugarcane and enslaved the indigenous Taino people to cultivate the crop. A combination of warfare, disease, and slavery wiped out these Native people and threw open the door to the African slave trade. With the discovery of rum distillation from molasses, the movement of slaves accelerated to satisfy a global demand for sugar and liquor. Subsequent colonization of North and South America brought more African slaves to both continents. In the United States the history of African-Americans within the larger white population reflects discrimination, tragedy, and suffering and, on the other hand, resiliency, strength, and accomplishment. Today most people worldwide no longer see how two foodstuffs could transform and reverberate throughout millions of lives, countless places, and five centuries.

While clearly not on the same level of human consequence, the arrival of pigs, especially to North America, caused fundamental changes to the landscape, agriculture and the environment, how we eat, and the country's growth as a nation. Meat preservation and specific contributions of new immigrants are part of America's history and culture.

Consider the impact of Spanish conquistadors and explorers. In 1493, on his second voyage, Columbus brought the first pigs to Cuba, ones related to the Iberian (*Ibérico*) hogs he obtained from Spain's Canary Islands. Within a few years the island was overrun with pigs. Spanish explorers often traveled with hogs, leaving boars and sows on an island, knowing they would multiply and be available for hunting in a year or two. On their conquests in Mexico and South America, Hernán Cortés and Francisco Pizarro took pigs with them to feed themselves and the troops.

Some Ibérico pigs were dropped on an island close to the Georgia coast, about twenty miles south of today's city of Savannah. Here, isolated from the mainland, they flourished and returned to a feral state. Of all the pigs in the United States today, the Ossabaw, named after the island, may be the most genetically pure example of an imported European hog and one of the most endangered breeds. The Livestock Conservancy explained how DNA and mitochondrial DNA research findings suggest the Canary Islands as their original home. While more research is needed, the conservancy described the Ossabaw in the following manner:

> Its history as an isolated island population has meant that the Ossabaw is the closest genetic representative of historic stocks brought over by the Spanish. Second, the presence of pigs on Ossabaw Island provides scientists with an exceptional opportunity to study a long-term natural population. Third, the Ossabaw breed is biologically unique, having been shaped by natural selection in a challenging environment known for heat, humidity, and seasonal scarcity of food.[1]

In his book *Pig Perfect*, Peter Kaminsky spins a remarkable tale of ancient hogs and the unique characteristics of Ibérico pigs and their amazing transformation into Spain's many varieties of *jamón* (the Spanish word for ham), especially Jamón Ibérico de Bellota. Kaminsky saw the potential value of Ossabaw hogs as the perfect breed for an American-style jamón and pursued a handful of farmers and chefs committed to a different American food system. Although small-scale production began in the 1980s, we have a long way to go before supply equals demand.

It was Hernando de Soto who introduced pigs to what became the southern mainland of the United States. In 1539 he landed in present-day Tampa Bay, Florida, and over the next two years traveled through what became Georgia, the Carolinas, Alabama, Mississippi, and Arkansas. De Soto came ashore with hogs obtained from Cuba. The pigs accompanied the expedition, often disappearing into the forest, where they reverted to wild forms — lean, long-legged "razorbacks." The wild animals multiplied and fed both the Spanish troops and Native American tribes, who developed a real taste for pork!

Eventually, the arrival of settlers into the American South changed the equation. Initially, hunting for wild game was the preferred way to put meat on the table. But timber clearance and the impact of farming pushed game farther away from settlements. The English hogs brought by settlers to Virginia were often managed by letting them run free in fields or woods. A daily bucket of corn or other grains ensured the animals returned every night. At the same time animal husbandry took place in the forest; domestic pigs bred with wild hogs, with many genetic outcomes.

From New England to the Mid-Atlantic to the coastal South, the task to manage these hogs amid all the other new frontier challenges was often daunting. Far easier, whether in city, small settlement, farm, or forest, was to allow the animals to roam freely. Forests were the key for all areas of the nascent country. Trees provided ideal foods, called mast, at the end of the summer into fall — diverse varieties of nuts, especially acorns, hickory nuts, and beechnuts. Colonial virgin forests proved to be the perfect feeding ground for pigs across newly settled lands. However, the initial practice of letting hogs run wild met with varying degrees of appreciation and success and, in some cases, predictable consequences; as pigs multiplied rapidly, farmland, towns, and villages — even New York City — were overrun. Semiwild pigs conducted such rampages in New York colonists' grain fields that every owned pig taller than fourteen inches had to have a ring in its nose. On Manhattan Island a long, solid wall was constructed on the northern edge of the colony to control roaming herds of pigs. After the wall was removed, its imprint remained as Wall Street in southern Manhattan. And the pig population of Pennsylvania colony numbered in the thousands by 1660.[2]

By 1700 in the New England and Mid-Atlantic colonies, herd management practices were firmly in place, especially finishing the animals on Indian corn. Native American tribes, including the Abenaki, Penobscot, Iroquois, Mohegan, and Powhatan, introduced colonists to a number of corn varieties and recipes for using the grain. Beyond making corn bread, hoecakes, succotash, and eventually whiskey, corn and its shocks fed thousands of hogs. Imagine a farmer's delight when his hogs grew robust and fat from eating corn. "[T]he typical farmer owned four to five hogs, which not only supplied salt pork for the family, but helped initiate the barreled-pork trade of the next century."[3]

From the early to mid-eighteenth century, these same colonies and Virginia established significant export trade in barreled and salted pork and beef, especially to the Caribbean. With the discovery of rum distillation, the demand for food to feed the slaves multiplied, while distillers in Connecticut, Massachusetts, and Rhode Island needed access to sugar and molasses as raw material. Barreled and pickled pork often provided the currency for these transactions.[4] From north to south, seventeenth- and eighteenth-century farmers and city dwellers also preserved meat by smoking. Records from seventeenth-century Williamsburg, Virginia, show most likely this was accomplished in chimneys or adjacent small boxes, but after 1700 small workable smokehouses appeared.

In the eighteenth and nineteenth centuries, Dutch, German, and Swiss immigrants arrived in Pennsylvania; most were Amish, Mennonite, and other Brethren escaping religious persecution, as the colony welcomed many different religious groups. Since farmers in Europe owned only small farms, they raised appropriately sized livestock such as pigs. Lancaster County, Pennsylvania, however, offered more space, and the new farmers diversified their livestock with steers and dairy cows. The Amish, Mennonite, and Brethren farmers followed European practices and traditions from their former countries, slaughtered both beef and hogs, and built smokehouses across the state.

Perhaps the best-known sausage from the region and the period is Lebanon bologna, coarsely grown beef that ferments in a barrel and is then seasoned with spices and stuffed into large casings. The sausage is slow-smoked, often for days, until it turns dark brown to black and is redolent with smoke and spicy aromas.[5] Like Italy's mortadella and Germany's Thuringer, Lebanon bologna is known as a cervelat, a dry or semidry sausage that is preserved by curing, drying, and smoking, rather than cooking. Because the preservation process involves fermentation, Lebanon bologna and similar sausages are characteristically pungent.[6] Today Lancaster County celebrates its Pennsylvania Dutch (German) heritage in part through the Lebanon bologna.[7] Sadly, few artisan producers remain, although a few large companies such as Seltzer's Lebanon Bologna date their histories back to the turn of the twentieth century.[8]

As illustrated in the previous chapter, the language of cured meat often derives from Latin and that includes the term "cervelat." The sausage, the national dish of Switzerland, is also found in Alsace-Lorraine and adjacent regions in Germany. "Cervelat — also sometimes spelt Servelas or Zervelat (all deriving from the Latin word for brain [*cerebrum*]) — was traditionally made of pork and brain. The brain element was later dropped."[9] The two-thousand-year-old language of European cured meat continues today, although brains definitely disappeared much earlier from recipes.

In the early to mid-eighteenth century, as settlers moved west so did pigs. Loaded wagons often had a wooden crate suspended under the carriage to carry the piglets. At the end of the Revolutionary War, a number of veterans received bounty land awards in the newly acquired land west of the Appalachian Mountains. Movement from Georgia, the Carolinas, and Virginia was through the Cumberland Gap into Kentucky and Tennessee. In the north New Englanders traveled down the Ohio River and its tributaries or across Lake Erie into Indiana and Illinois.

The federal land programs created extraordinary opportunities for East Coast farmers to buy land, and pigs drove their success. The settlers brought hogs, more like the wild boars of Europe than contemporary heavy ones. While the forests were still vast and flourishing, they lived their lives for several decades in the Ohio Valley woods and were often known as wood hogs. William Hedgepeth detailed the many names given to these pigs: piney woods rooter, stump rooter, wood wanderer, landpike (after the fish), prairie racer, mountain liver, acorn gatherer, bristle bearer, alligator, wound maker, and, of course, razorback.[10] Each name suggests its geographic influence, as well as how settlers viewed pigs: occasionally with admiration, more frequently with derision and scorn.

Sometimes farmers trained their hogs with a small supply of grain at the end of the day, so the animals knew to return. Others sent out riders carrying Indian corn to herd the animals back to the farm. Regardless of approach, by all accounts the populations of hogs exploded: "When the first livestock census was taken in 1840, the four and one-half million people of the seven states from Pennsylvania to Mississippi, and from Tennessee northward, had ten million hogs."[11]

Prior to the arrival of canal and river transport and railroads, hogs, cattle, and sheep walked from these key producing states to East Coast cities (turkeys even sashayed to Boston). As early as 1655 New England hog drovers moved animals to slaughter. From the early to mid-nineteenth century, thousands tramped across the Appalachian Mountains from Kentucky and Tennessee on their way south to feed plantation owners and slaves or east to Baltimore, Philadelphia, and New York to sustain urban dwellers or be processed for export.[12]

Cincinnati became one of the most important cities in nineteenth-century American hog history. The rapid increase of the hog population across the Ohio River from the city allowed it to take advantage of the waterway's links southwest and then down the Mississippi to New Orleans. As early as 1803 beef and pork moved downriver to Louisiana. "In 1818, Elisha Mills opened the first modern-day pork-packing plant in Cincinnati, stuffing the meat in brine-filled barrels for preservation. Salt pork quickly became a U.S. food staple."[13] The hogs, fattened on mast, were driven from Kentucky and Tennessee to the Ohio. However, before slaughter, they were fed a diet of corn to harden their fat. While hogs grew large because of mast's high fat content, their fat became very soft, almost runny. A few weeks of eating corn, which solidified the fat, made processing into bacon, lard, and other products possible.[14] "The availability of pork byproducts brought other industries to the booming city. Small companies sprang up to process pork byproducts into soap and candles, including a little company called Proctor and Gamble that has branched out quite a bit since its founding in 1837."[15]

Access to salt and a workforce, many of them German, with skills as butchers and wurst (sausage) makers, contributed to the city's prominence as the leading hog processor. "In 1833, more than 85,000 pigs were processed in Cincinnati, and by 1844, 26 different meat-processing plants were located here. Cincinnati was the biggest city in the West by 1850 and quickly earned the nickname 'Porkopolis.'"[16] By the 1850s the city processed upward of half a million hogs a year. Without refrigeration the city slaughtered and processed in the late fall, and travelers took note of the River Styx–like atmosphere:

> *Huge quantities of these useful animals are reared after harvest in the*
> *corn-fields of Ohio, and on the beech-mast and acorns of its gigantic*

forests. At a particular time of year they arrive by thousands — brought in droves and steamers to the number of 500,000 — to meet their doom, when it is said that the Ohio runs red with blood!

There are huge slaughterhouses behind the town, something on the plan of the abattoirs *of Paris — large wooden buildings, with numerous pens, from whence the pigs march in single file along a narrow passage, to an apartment where each, on his entrance, receives a blow with a hammer, which deprives him of consciousness, and in a short time, by means of numerous hands, and a well-managed caldron system, he is cut up ready for pickling.*[17]

But without demand Porkopolis might have never been. Considering the essential place of food preservation for a growing nation, salted meat was absolutely fundamental to America's rapid economic ascension and its westward expansion. Demand rose everywhere for pork. In the South, while most farming was oriented to cash crops, especially cotton and tobacco, several areas within the region imported food, including significant amounts of preserved pork, from either outside their borders or neighboring states.[18] New Orleans became the principal entrepôt for salted and barreled pork from Cincinnati for local use, maritime provisions, or export. The abundance of cheap pork established a powerful food tradition throughout the South for both African-Americans and whites that still exists today.

The Cincinnati Board of Trade established a grading system for barreled pork:[19]

1. Clear pork: Highest grade with only the sides of large hogs. For New England markets.
2. Mess pork: Hams and sides. Used principally by the navy and commercial maritime.
3. Prime pork: Sides, shoulders, and jowls from lighter-weight hogs. Maritime use and southern market.
4. Bulk pork: Literally anything else, including head and feet. Shipped to New Orleans, destined for slave food.

Throughout the eighteenth and nineteenth centuries, barreled pork, salt pork, fat back, and bacon were ubiquitous meats found on the plates of miners, explorers, slaves, and soldiers; in other words, preserved pork fueled America. Some evidence suggests the expression "scrape the bottom of the barrel" has its origins in the fact that when pork supplies ran low, one scraped the barrel for whatever leftovers remained.

The arrival of both railroads and the Civil War ended Cincinnati's dominance as the nation's meat packer. The war cut off the Mississippi River, and Chicago's already extensive railroads changed the supply system dramatically. Beginning in 1862 the federal government authorized several homestead acts that enabled a prospective farmer to lay claim to land through the Great Plains and beyond. Again, the presence of hogs provided sustenance and some cash for farm families; only now, corn fed the animals, not mast. The westward movement of corn was matched by a similar march of hog raising. Farmers still grew a few pigs for the family, but most were destined for the Chicago stockyards and points east.

Philip Armour Sr., farmer and former gold prospector, sold millions of dollars' worth of meat to the Union army, by which he established Armour & Company. Gustavus Swift, a New England butcher, founded Swift Brothers and Company in Chicago. Both men transformed the entire meat industry from the original farm suppliers to include transport, slaughter and processing, and refrigerated railcars to move fresh meat. Their companies were the foundation of Chicago's predominance at the center of America's meat universe, and they dominated the meat landscape. For example, around the turn of the twentieth century, the Swift company slaughtered and processed two million cattle, four million hogs, and two million sheep a year.

The story of cured meat in America is about not only hog production but also the immigrants who arrived with knowledge and skills from their countries of origin, how they applied them and adjusted to a new society, and how they innovated to re-create traditional products. Butchers catered to fellow countrymen with dry-cured, smoked, and pickled meats reminiscent of the old country, even though they often contended with the impacts of different climate and geography on their traditional methods. Not until well into the twentieth century did we have real climate controls; often cool cellars sufficed to ferment great-tasting and safe cured meats.

Beginning in the 1840s the arrival of hundreds of thousands of German immigrants to the States changed the country's food scene dramatically. Beyond wurst, they brought strong traditions and skills as brewers; within a few years lager breweries appeared wherever Germans settled. The Yuengling family established its brewery in 1829 in Pottsville, Pennsylvania, while the Schell family opened its business in 1860 in New Ulm, Minnesota; both breweries are still family owned. German butchers opened small shops and sold fresh meat and hundreds of different fresh and cooked wursts; many, if not most, cooked types were smoked. Although most of the small companies disappeared decades ago, several large ones remain today: Milwaukee's Usinger's Famous Sausage was founded in 1880 by Frederick Usinger and is still family owned. Other brands include Oscar Mayer, Kunzler, Karl Ehmer, and Schaller & Weber, the latter featured in a subsequent chapter.

In almost two hundred years, beginning in 1820, more than five and a half million Italians came to the United States. From 1880 to 1920 alone, four million immigrants entered the country. The majority came from Italy's southern provinces — Abruzzo, Molise, Puglia, Basilicata, and especially Calabria, Campania and the city of Naples, and Sicily — its most impoverished regions.

After landing at New York's Ellis Island and enduring its "rite of passage," Italians headed to cities, in part because it was easier to make a living there than by farming. Like newcomers before them, they faced discrimination and barriers to advancement. Many were illiterate and did not speak English; they distrusted authority and identified themselves by region; and Roman Catholicism differed from the by-then-established Irish Catholicism. Whether settled in cities or in towns, close family ties and regional connections helped bond and protect these newcomers.

Among other occupations, Italian men became dockworkers and laborers, miners and railroad workers, while women, if they were allowed by a patriarchal family, worked in the textile and needle trades. A small percentage, arriving with skills — barbers, carpenters, or masons, or speaking English — enabled communities to begin a slow evolution to stability and prosperity. In cities especially, street or pushcart vendors sometimes transitioned into owning small shops, often a delicatessen or butcher shop. German and Italian butchers had excellent reputations with New York City residents, in part because of their attention to cleanliness and quality animals.

As Simone Cinotto describes in his book *The Italian-American Table*, coffee shops, restaurants, and delis helped create identity, familiarity, and community. The food stores offered the products of home, and shop owners and importers became important neighborhood businessmen. Many delicatessens produced salamis and other cured meats and even made mozzarella, sometimes from fresh milk, later from locally produced curd. Although most disappeared years ago, a few three-generation family-owned delicatessens still exist today.

Other eastern European immigrants from arrived 1880 to 1925 — Czechs, Hungarians, Poles, Romanians, and Slovakians — and opened similar butcher shops to those of the Germans and Italians. Important urban centers such as Buffalo, Cleveland, Cincinnati, Chicago, Milwaukee, and St. Louis contained sizable eastern European populations. Many Jewish immigrants opened kosher butcher shops to meet religious requirements. New York, with a population of two million Jews, had thousands of kosher shops and delis across the city. The shops made a variety of pickled or brined meats — corned beef, pastrami, and tongue — while other delis crafted beef salamis and frankfurters. In 1905 a Russian Jew established the renowned Hebrew National Kosher Sausage Factory on Manhattan's Lower East Side.

Through World War II many neighborhoods and towns with a noticeable ethnic identity nurtured their butcher shops and other small businesses. The postwar migration to suburbs and the parallel population shift away from rural farms and villages often spelled the demise of many businesses. Postwar Americans, after fifteen years of the Great Depression and war, demanded everything from new homes and cars to convenient and inexpensive foods. As tastes changed and foods disappeared, we lost much of the cultural identity of places and the histories behind the people who made them.

Published in 1906, Upton Sinclair's *The Jungle*, an exposé about the exploitation of immigrants in the United States, is best known for its graphic depictions of the country's meatpacking industry. The book details the horrors of animal slaughter; unsanitary conditions; production of sausage and other processed meats, containing among other things, dead rodents and their waste; and a "devil-may-care" attitude on the part of the packers. The public outrage, coupled with President Theodore Roosevelt's revulsion, led to the 1906 Pure Food and Drug Act, the precursor of today's Food and Drug Administration. Over the past 110 years, additional legislation at every level of government has created new mandates to manage safety threats, although some apprehensions about traditional practices lacked the support of strong scientific evidence.

Beginning in the 1950s federal food safety regulations and concerns about imported European cured meats established new requirements for producers, and many small operations went out of business. We are quite fortunate that a number of them survived and helped set the stage for the late twentieth- and early twenty-first-century renaissance. The introduction in the 1980s of Hazard Analysis Critical Control Point (HACCP), aimed initially at the seafood industry, today is one of the regulatory bedrocks for food producers. Over the past several decades, especially since September 11, 2001, federal and state food requirements have grown more stringent and expensive to implement.

The 2011 Food Safety Modernization Act added layers of new regulations, review, monitoring, and inspection. The new law established a wide range of standards, many of which impacted farmers, food producers of all sizes, and ultimately customers, who pay for increased business expenses. In some instances small artisan food producers, including those of cured meats, closed shop because they could not afford the costs to retrofit an old facility or build a new building.

Cured meat businesses receive inspections from different government entities, depending on the type of operation. If a company produces only to sell direct, local inspectors from city or county offices of public health monitor compliance. A cured meat enterprise can obtain a "retail exemption" if the butcher shop, restaurant, or delicatessen sells direct to customers, whether packaged to go, served on a charcuterie board, on a take-out sandwich, or offered at a farmers' market. Many city and county officials inspect hundreds of diverse food businesses to ensure public safety. Their work requires knowledge of food processes, familiarity with the science of microbiology and with fermentation, and other critical skills; all require time and experience to learn.

The United States Department of Agriculture (USDA) becomes involved in meat processing when a company manufactures products for wholesale. Daily meat fabrication procedures and processing cannot occur unless the resident USDA inspector is in attendance. In actuality, the company hires its own on-site USDA inspector and compensates the individual, even though the person works for the agency.

As more small-scale cured meat businesses opened, owners struggled with many inspectors' lack of knowledge or their interpretations of regulations that did not fit the law. Depending on location, an inspector has the tools and expertise to inspect a cured meat business. However, in some instances, a charcuterie shop, desiring to sell direct to consumers and eligible for an exemption, is the first of its kind. Consequently, a local inspector, not understanding cured meat, the science, and the safety requirements, by interpreting the regulations forcefully, slows or halts its opening. These are not isolated instances, as we shall see.

To be fair the food world has changed dramatically since 2000, and an individual inspector's knowledge, technical skills, and understanding of food and cuisine is in many cases still running to catch up. In several instances local officials confiscated a business's cured meat, arguing it was unsafe, although they lacked medical or scientific evidence. At Healthy Living Market in Burlington, Vermont; Denver's Bonanno Concepts; and Farmstead in Providence, Rhode Island, inspectors either confiscated the items or poured bleach over them.

With willingness by regulators to support and work with companies, whether they are start-ups or ones with previous issues, the problems are resolvable. Of the three mentioned above, Farmstead closed, and award-winning owners Kate and Matt Jennings opened a new restaurant and market in Boston. However, they decided against a new fermentation program, not just because of the previous experience. They realized the amount of time, labor, and money to establish a new endeavor on solid regulatory ground was not worthwhile. Today Matt contracts with Joshua Smith, owner of New England Charcuterie in Waltham, Massachusetts, to produce diverse cured meat for Townsman, their new place in Boston.[20]

Likewise, Rick Gencarelli, who began a small in-house charcuterie effort at Shelburne Farms in Vermont, found the costs of a comprehensive fermentation program were not sustainable when he moved to Portland, Oregon. He started with a food truck, named Lardo, in a city with six to seven hundred trucks, all vying for attention and parking places. Its success led to an opportunity for a brick-and-mortar restaurant, where he initially worked with basic brine and smoke. Since the first Lardo in 2012, his empire grew fat (pun intended), from one place to seven establishments, including a commercial kitchen. At the same time Portland's changing food scene offered opportunities to relinquish some fermented products. He could save money purchasing from the city's renowned artisan producers; Olympia Provisions, for example, for cured meats, or kimchi from Korean experts.[21]

I've organized the book's chapters to further investigate the history and culture of dried cured meat from our early seventeenth-century settlements to the contemporary renaissance. The constant evolution of hogs over the past two thousand years and centuries of crossbreeding, whether intentional by breeders or simply from natural procreation between domestic and wild hogs, informs the narrative. The role of human ingenuity across millennia to preserve food, stave off starvation, and, in the process, create extraordinary foods, remains a cornerstone. Today we have the luxury of choice, along with technologies from refrigeration to chemical extenders and myriad mechanical methods, to ensure we don't starve. The growth and presence of artisan cured meat contributes to a deeper understanding of farming and animals, diet and nutrition, and human-animal relationships.

CHAPTER THREE

A Tale of Three Smithfields

During the Vietnam War I was stationed at the Oceana Naval Air Station in Virginia Beach and later aboard the USS *Independence*, whose home port was Norfolk, Virginia. An occasional dinner out introduced me to foods typical of eastern Virginia but unknown to me as a native New Yorker. I recall vividly a fast-food joint on Virginia Beach's Atlantic Avenue that sold deep-fried battered chicken gizzards, hearts, and livers, accompanied by white bread and coleslaw . . . oh man, what an amazing feast with some cold beer, overlooking the ocean. It could make you forget that tomorrow you were back in uniform.

I also remember, in the spring, summer, and fall, making my way along the coastline toward the Virginia–North Carolina border to a place called Sandbridge, where on a Saturday morning net fishermen would pull in catches of porgies, butterfish, and an occasional striped bass or red drum. Some enterprising folks brought along a grill, charcoal, and cold beer, and the beach became the scene of some of the simplest, tastiest food delivered to your beach blanket.

But the highlight was a small restaurant that served Smithfield country ham as steaks or layered in warm biscuits. I recall walking through the doorway and smelling the warm aroma of tangy ham. As I sat down the waitress already knew me well enough to bring a glass of unsweetened ice tea. Most often I ordered the country ham platter with biscuits, slaw, and occasionally baked beans or succotash. Sometimes they offered a ham steak with eggs, toast, and some of the best home fries or grits ever. However they prepared it, the Smithfield ham burst with melting fat and sweet, slightly salty, chewy, fragrant meat. While growing up and attending college, I read about country ham, probably in a *New York Times* article, but until I arrived in Virginia, it was only a story. The actual ham surpassed anything words could convey. Years later I wonder if my fascination with dry-cured ham may have started in that little restaurant.

This "country" style of cured ham traces its history to Virginia's town of Smithfield, founded in 1634 along the banks of the Pagan River as it flows into the James River, opposite Newport News. The colonists brought English hogs and released them into the forests, where they grew rapidly and turned feral. Both settlers and Native Americans hunted the now wild pigs, also known as razorbacks.[1] Whether domesticated or wild, hogs and abundant game provided significant food resources for Virginia's colonists.[2] But if colonists were to survive the winters, they had to preserve as much meat as possible. Enter salt and smoke. The Native Powhatan people harvested sea salt from the tidal flats and salted and smoked both fish and game. Their techniques meshed with British traditions, and cured, smoked ham became a staple throughout the South.[3] In 1779 Captain Mallory Todd conveyed the first Smithfield hams to Bermuda. The shipment established the Todd family as the first commercial curing business in Smithfield.[4]

But it was the mighty peanut that transformed both the hog and Virginia's fortune and reputation. In the pre-Columbian era, peanuts, native to South America, were grown as far north as Mexico. Spanish explorer Hernán Cortés found them sold in Tenochtitlan (the site of today's Mexico City) and took the peanut back to Spain, where in turn explorers and merchants introduced them to West Africa and Asia. The climate in West Africa was ideal for growing peanuts, and when Africans were enslaved and brought to colonial America in the early eighteenth century, peanuts accompanied them and became an important foodstuff for slaves, poor people, and hogs. The first commercial plantings of peanuts occurred in Sussex County, Virginia, in the 1840s, about fifteen miles west of Smithfield. After harvesting, farmers allowed the hogs to root up the remaining peanuts and vegetation. The sandy soil of the Western Tidewater was ideally suited to grow peanuts, and by the 1870s the counties of Southampton, Sussex, Surry, and Isle of Wight in southeastern Virginia were the state's principal growing region; the abundant goober gave local pigs a reputation for outstanding size and quality.

In 1874 P. D. Gwaltney Sr. and O. G. Delk opened a peanut business in Smithfield with an adjacent smokehouse to cure a few hams. After buying out his partner, Gwaltney expanded his ham business; as it turns out, during the nineteenth century the entrepreneur was well known as the "Peanut King" and used his surplus goobers to fatten pigs and then cure the hams. His quality products and marketing ability led to Queen Victoria's insistence that only Smithfield hams be served on her dinner table — the palace ordered six every week! Her dedication reflected a worldwide reputation of the quality ham made by Smithfield's numerous small companies, ones we would identify today as artisan operations.

The hams' popularity and reputation led other businesses, not located in town or even Virginia, to label their hams "Smithfield." In addition, the Todd business, now the E. M. Todd Company, the town's large processor, was purchased in 1916 and moved to Richmond, where it expanded operations but continued to label its products "Smithfield." Since ham production identified as Smithfield was a significant economic force in the Tidewater region, inaccurate if not false labels presented a real challenge. In 1926, with lobbying from the Gwaltney Company, the state legislature passed a food origins law stating that any ham with a Smithfield label had to originate from peanut-fed hogs grown in Virginia or North Carolina and "cured, treated, smoked, and processed in the town of Smithfield." By defending the brand, now a "protected product," the legal buttress enabled companies to expand markets without fear of competition from imitation hams and reinforced consumer confidence.

Smithfield Packing Company

Until the 1960s Smithfield took pride in the number of small companies located in and around the town, one of which was the Smithfield Packing Company, opened in 1936, and our first Smithfield tale. During the 1950s the demand for Smithfield labeled hams from peanut-fed hogs exceeded the supply from Virginia and North Carolina. Moreover, the amount of peanuts for hog feed diminished as farmers utilized more efficient harvesting equipment and no longer invited the animals onto their farms. A more efficient harvest left almost no peanuts to forage and growers wanted to avoid the animals uprooting their fields. In 1966 the peanut-fed requirement was removed from the statute; North Carolina and Virginia companies could expand hog production without using peanuts as feed.

The legal change occurred almost simultaneously with the nationwide acceleration in the 1970s to raise hogs in efficient industrial settings or factories. Smithfield Packing Company became an aggressive leader in the expansion and consolidation of pork processing and cured ham production. Among other companies merged into Smithfield were Gwaltney, E. M. Todd, and V. W. Joyner & Co. (bought by Swift in 1926) in 1983 and Iowa's John Morrell in 1995. Today, while hams originate from all over the country, as well as North Carolina and Virginia, the requirement that they be cured in Smithfield remains. Since the 1980s Smithfield Packing, now Smithfield Foods Inc., became the nation's and then the world's largest producer and processor of hogs. The Smithfield Hog Production Division, located in Warsaw, North Carolina, annually manages sixteen million animals produced nationwide by 2,000 farmers, including approximately 1,250 in-state growers. The company's 973,000-square-foot Tar Heel plant slaughters and processes approximately thirty-two thousand pigs a day.

In an ironic twist of the pig's tail, in 2015 China's Shuanghui Group purchased Smithfield Foods and all of its subsidiaries, a reflection of the growing international appetite and demand for pork, driven principally by China's rapidly emerging middle class.

In 1978 China's meat consumption of eight million tons was one-third the size of the United States' consumption of twenty-four million tons. But by 1992 China had overtaken the United States as the world's leading meat consumer — and it has not looked back since. Now China's annual meat consumption of seventy-one million tons is more than double that of the United States. With US meat consumption falling and China's consumption still rising, the trajectories of these two countries are determining the shape of agriculture around the planet.[5]

For a growing number of American consumers, the presence of industrial animal production; assembly line slaughterhouses; underpaid and exhausted African-American, Indian, and Latino workers; and computerized processing speaks to the worst of America's food system.[6] Whether because of husbandry practices, inhumane growing and slaughter practices, uncompassionate treatment of employees, or poor food safety, the system makes many people uncomfortable.

S. Wallace Edwards & Sons

This brings us to Surry, a small town about twenty-five miles northwest of Smithfield, the county seat of Surry County and the home of S. Wallace Edwards & Sons, a well-known country ham producer whose family roots extend back to at least the mid-nineteenth century. Our second tale of Smithfield, that of Edwards country ham, weaves together a rural family farm, a ferry, ham sandwiches, and the founding of Colonial Williamsburg.

Born in 1896 on a rural farm in Isle of Wight County, Samuel Wallace Edwards was the oldest of eight children. At the turn of the twentieth century, still prior to the advent of electricity and refrigeration, farm families preserved food for the winter out of necessity. Wallace's mother, Emma, homeschooled her children, raised hogs that ran free in meadows and woods where acorns were plentiful in the fall, and taught Samuel how to cure bacon and hams in a backyard smokehouse. With ten mouths to feed in his family, we can imagine the number of hams the young man put up every fall and winter.

Enter the ferry. From the seventeenth century to the early twentieth century, small ferries plied the James River between the settlements of Surry and Jamestown. These unmotorized ferries became obsolete with the arrival of the automobile and highways, but no river crossing existed for cars between Richmond and Newport News, a distance of nearly eighty miles. In the 1920s Captain Albert F. Jester, who ran a passenger and mail boat from Smithfield to Newport News, decided to establish a motorized ferry between Surry and Jamestown to carry cars, at that time mostly Model T Fords. In 1925, when the ferry service began, one boat captain was his son-in-law, S. Wallace Edwards.

For ferry travelers, while crossing the James River offered a convenient rest, many were hungry, since restaurants or rest stops for automobile travelers didn't exist in most rural areas. Wallace Edwards saw a chance for some extra money and made sandwiches from the family's cured hams. Word spread quickly about the delicious food served aboard the ferry, and every day Wallace's wife, Orieta, made sandwiches that he sold easily to ferry riders. In 1925 the ferry business consumed fifty-five country hams; the following year he built another smokehouse to manage the demand, and the S. Wallace Edwards country ham business was born.

The revival and restoration of Williamsburg in the late 1920s and '30s and the subsequent creation of Colonial Williamsburg as a tourist attraction increased ferry traffic across the river. Orieta and Wallace Edwards left the onboard sandwich enterprise and set up a cured ham operation in Surry, a couple of miles from the ferry dock, conveniently located on Highway 31, which ran straight through town. The company built distinctive large wooden smokehouses, with pyramidal roofs with the four hip rafters jutting through the top, reminiscent of teepees. I can imagine crossing the river, seeing the smokehouse peaks in the distance as we approach, discovering whiffs of hickory smoke, and finally the aromas of smoke and pork. No wonder travelers stopped!

Wallace indeed designed his structures as a tribute to the Native Americans who taught the early settlers how to cure meat and fish. The commemoration may well be accurate, but other explanations add contrasting dimensions. For millennia Europeans salted and smoked fish and meat, and documentation of smokehouses in England goes back at least to the thirteenth century.[7] The knowledge and experience to cure fish and meat was widespread but it was the purview of farmers and tradesmen, and this may explain the different interpretations for Virginia's smokehouse origins. The majority of the first English settlers in Jamestown were upper-class individuals who lacked survival skills in an unfamiliar land, including knowledge of curing. Whether the native Powhatan introduced these skills or it was a combination of their influence and the subsequent arrival of small numbers of Italians, Germans, and Spaniards, a cottage industry of cured and smoked bacon and hams sustained the nascent colony in the seventeenth century.

Smokehouses, or "smoak" houses, were essential structures on rural farms throughout colonial America. Smoking meat, especially pork, required skill, patience, and artistry; if the smoke temperature was too hot, the meat would cook or the fat would melt, neither of which preserved the ham. As a general rule, cold-smoke temperatures range between 60°F and 80°F and not above 100°F. After the first stage of salting the hams, farmers hung them from the rafters to catch smoke from very slow-burning fires. Smokehouse designs varied but generally drew air from the bottom of the walls, and since most structures did not have a flue, the smoke escaped through cracks between boards or cedar shakes. Buildings with pyramidal or conical roofs, often with extra beams studded with nails and pegs for hanging more hams, concentrated and held the smoke to maintain the maturation process. These smokehouses also protected the hams from pests and were locked to secure them from thieves.

In a *Colonial Williamsburg* journal article, Michael Olmert describes early references to these structures in eighteenth-century Virginia, several of which were in the Tidewater region:

> *In 1716, there's a mention of a smoak house on a plantation in York County, Virginia, the earliest known use of the term. A Hanover County plantation listed for sale in the* Virginia Gazette *on January 7, 1742, points to its "new fram'd Smoak-house, 8 Feet Square." In 1732, "a Smoak house eight foot square" with a "planked Dore," is ordered for the glebe of Newport Parish, Isle of Wight County, Virginia.[8]*

Olmert further explains the number of smokehouses in Williamsburg:

> *Everyone needed a smokehouse. At Colonial Williamsburg, of the eighty-eight original structures that survive, twelve are smokehouses. And an additional fifty reconstructed smokehouses dot the backyards of the Historic Area, many built atop the foundation footprints of likely smokehouses. At the Governor's Palace, the Wythe House, and the Peyton Randolph House, reconstructed smokehouses are still used to cure and flavor pork.[9]*

Records for early seventeenth-century Virginia do not document specific structures for smokehouses; however, since smoking was an essential process for meat and fish preservation, colonists might have hung hams in chimneys or other makeshift apparatus. For Wallace Edwards the pyramid-shaped structure describes a lineage from early Virginia settlements into the twentieth century. Beyond its practical benefits and aesthetic appeal, the shape resembled the small A-frame structure he used to smoke hams on the farm. Today his grandson, Sam Edwards III, has sections of the original smokehouse on display.

From its start in the 1920s, the business grew as Wallace introduced bacon and sausage while continuing to refine his ham cure. The addition of new smokehouses increased production and expanded retail and wholesale sales. He developed and branded Edwards Wigwam country ham, another tribute to Native Americans, a unique long cut and long shank ham — meaning the entire hind leg — that became its most-sought after product. To meet demand they constructed a slaughterhouse, and through the 1940s the company processed five hundred hogs weekly and employed eighty workers from the community.

Orieta and Wallace's son, Sam Jr., born in 1930, began work at a young age and learned how to cure pork from his father. In the 1950s, after his father retired, he joined the business full time and faced the first of many evolving challenges for small-scale curing businesses. The postwar American drive toward inexpensive convenience food was felt in the community as local curers looked for ways to streamline long-established processes and reduce costs. Sam Jr. resisted the shift; he saw these changes as a significant threat to hundreds of years of traditional culture, the loss of which would affect his family, his business, and his community.

While opposing many of the changes, he could not ignore the value of new opportunities and the significant competition. Sam initiated a series of renovations to modernize Edwards' facilities, fulfill new USDA regulations for food safety, and, most importantly, improve product consistency. For example, temperature and humidity levels vary from year to year and may occasionally swing dramatically. Without mechanisms to mitigate these fluctuations, the curing process might result in inconsistent ham quality. Edwards added temperature, humidity, and airflow control systems to manage environmental conditions. The innovations augmented the father and son's deep knowledge, refined skills, and exquisite sensory capabilities; now they had tools to adjust the "climate" of the entire cure.

In 1956 Sam III was born and as a fourteen-year-old was already taking on responsibilities in the company. After graduating from college in 1978, he returned to the family business to manage sales. In the 1960s the family closed its slaughterhouse and invested once again in improvements to upgrade the salt, smoke, and aging rooms to emulate the four seasons; each incremental step enhanced quality. The company's success led to a print catalog and wholesale distribution nationwide. The arrival of Edwards cured meats in such restaurants as the Williamsburg Inn and the Greenbrier in West Virginia added to the brand's cachet and market recognition.

The art of "controlled spoilage" fundamentally engages and relies on sensory ability and perception. All five senses are deployed to make great bread, beer, cheese, and cured meat. Of the five, a refined sense of smell is paramount. Smell is the first sense to develop in a mammalian fetus. Without an acute sense of smell, babies — whether human, feline, or canine, for example — cannot find nourishment from their mothers. Humans are born with highly evolved sensory abilities; we are "hardwired," but since our survival doesn't depend on smelling danger or food, most of us lose a significant part of this capacity over time.[10] For food producers an ability to smell, to detect one part per billion, can make the difference between a good batch and a bad one. The process of becoming an expert artisan producer of cheese or cured meat takes years, and part of the training takes place in your nose.

A master cheese maker, charcutier, or cure master, walking into an aging or smoking room, smells the air and knows if the process is proceeding accurately. In Italy a *salumiere* inserts a thin *ago d'osso di cavallo*, a horse bone needle, into a prosciutto and then smells it; the needle picks up the aromatics. After thousands of prosciutti a master recognizes not only an off aroma but also the level of maturity and readiness in the ham. Likewise, for the Edwardses, a complex, rich smell, sometimes described as a sweet, applelike aroma; bronze to mahogany color; and firm texture are hallmarks of the Wigwam ham.

In the 1970s and 1980s, the Edwards Company faced the tidal wave of change wrought in part by Smithfield Foods and other meat conglomerates with their appetite to gobble up competition. Extensive crossbreeding programs with Yorkshire, Duroc, and Landrace hogs created a commodity pig. While the development of this faster-growing, larger, leaner hog certainly met America's desire for affordable, less fatty pork, the opposite was true for Edwards. The animals' small fat layer and almost no marbling through the muscles created significant challenges in aging much larger hams for nine to twelve months without resulting in a desiccated leg. Rather than simply buy what was available, the Edwardses visited slaughterhouses to locate the best quality hogs. The strategy enabled them to maintain quality into the twenty-first century.

Sam Jr. adjusted the length of time large hams were in salt to extend the smoking and slow-drying stages. In 1984 they introduced Edwards Petite

Ham, a boneless, fully cooked, two- to three-pound product aged four to six months. The smaller size met the eye of American consumers looking for affordable, convenient, and delicious meals. Over the past thirty years, the product line comprised Wigwam, aged ten to twelve months, and Virginia and petite hams, both aged four to six months, plus an array of smoked bacons and sausage. All the hams are available bone-in or boneless and cooked or uncooked.

A few years ago the renaissance in better quality hog breeds caught Sam Edwards's attention. New York–based Heritage Foods USA approached Sam III with a proposal to process Berkshire hogs it would supply from farmers following humane and sustainable practices. The idea blossomed into the wonderfully named Surryano line introduced in 2008. The linguistically creative name paid tribute to Spain's Serrano hams and the long history and tradition of Edwards in Surry. The purebred Berkshire hogs are certified humanely and pasture raised, and some are even finished on peanuts. They make several varieties of Surryano hams, including the long-leg, long-ham style; all are dry cured, hickory smoked, and aged a minimum of four hundred days, while a selected handful mature at eighteen months.

Demand quickly outstripped supply, and Sam lobbied for more pigs. But to increase production from small farms takes time, and demand from chefs, restaurants, and cured meat producers for Berkshire, Tamworth, and other heritage breeds totally swamped availability. In addition to increased demand from these consumers, the "buy local" movement for similar animals intersected and drove demand even higher. For many growers scaling up production was a lot easier said than done. If hogs are on pasture and not eating the commodity corn/soybean ration and not receiving antibiotics that function as growth stimulants, they take more time to reach an appropriate weight and fat-to-meat ratio. In addition, a farmer needs more land, both pasture and forest, to allow grazing and foraging. The bottom line: It takes time to scale up the operation.

In 2016 sustainably raised heritage breeds constitute a tiny fraction of America's hog production; figures vary from 1 to 3 percent. And clearly, we want to avoid a rapid expansion of production, since the only method available to do so is what these growers reject. Until the end of 2015, the Edwards heritage country hams represented about 15 percent of total production, and the company was utilizing some Large Black hogs in addition to the Berkshires. Toward the end of 2015, Heritage Foods offered Sam about 1,500 heritage hogs, a welcome jump in supply.

After demand took off for Surryano ham, in 2013 Sam embarked on another project with roots deep in Virginia's colonial past. The inspiration came from two men: David Shields, a Southern food historian, and Craig Rogers, the shepherd of Border Springs Farm in Virginia's Piedmont region. Evidence shows that together with cows and pigs English settlers brought sheep for wool and meat, and a rack of lamb or mutton stew found its way onto many early Virginia tables. After pork and beef Virginians chose lamb and mutton to eat.

Rogers and Shields describe Virginia as "the leading sheep producing state" during the colonial period. "Thomas Jefferson and George Washington were famous sheep farmers, with Jefferson even keeping some sheep on the White House lawn."[11] Craig Rogers urged Sam to use legs and shoulders from his farm and apply the same curing and aging techniques used for country ham. In 2014 they debuted the dry-cured, hickory-smoked lamb ham to rave reviews, and Sam had another traditional meat in the Edwards repertoire.

Then disaster struck on January 19, 2016, when a huge fire destroyed the processing plant. Fortunately no one was injured, but Sam Edwards estimated they lost between twelve thousand and fourteen thousand hams, many of which were twelve to eighteen months old, including batches of the Surryano hams. For a company that sells upward of fifty thousand hams a year, the economic impact will reverberate for months. The company had an offsite cold storage facility, but the processing plant and the heritage hams are gone. The family lost irreplaceable heirlooms; the one item recovered was the original brass key to Wallace Edwards's smokehouse. In addition, suddenly Heritage Foods had 1,500 hogs it committed to buying from small growers in the Midwest; fortunately, other country ham producers purchased the pork, so the impact on farmers was mitigated.

Given the family's long history and presence, the value of the company to the local economy, and the identity of Edwards Country Ham to the cultural fabric of Surry, the impact on the community goes beyond the obvious financial impact. With several hundred years of family relationships and marriage, lifelong friendships, and intrinsic knowledge of place, the loss is physical, emotional, and psychological, with some consequences unknown.

Sam and I talked months after the fire about the loss of another community, in many ways an equally important population: the microflora inhabiting the walls, the wooden racks, even the ambient air of the aging room. In the 1950s the family built several rooms, and over sixty years of continuous use with the ebb and flow of outside air, with nature's inoculations of welcome molds and bacteria, distinctive qualities emerged that contributed to the distinctive aroma and flavor of Edwards Country Ham, what we may identify as an Edwards' terroir.

We tend to associate the idea of terroir with growing grapes and making wine. A diverse array of physical characteristics — for example, soil, geological substrates, climate, the age of vines, and sunlight — coupled with well-established cultural and human values, marks unique places around the world. Similarly, for handcrafted beer and artisan cheese, an extraordinary range of yeasts, bacteria, and molds define individual sites and are conditioned by the geography and climate of a place. Microflora may vary from one side of a hill to another. Examples include Belgian Lambic beers, Trappist washed-rind cheeses, and cave-aged cheddars. Likewise, well-defined terroirs exist for Edwards and some other country ham and cured meat operations.

While Sam Edwards vows to return to business as soon as possible, it depends on how quickly he can overcome the financial, insurance, and legal hurdles. After he constructs the new plant, Sam intends to introduce wooden racks from the off-site cold storage facility in the hopes they will inoculate the structure with colonies of good microbes to kick-start the development of terroir. Replacing or perhaps rejuvenating these unique microcommunities will take time, perhaps decades, with no guarantee of exactly the same aging personalities. Establishing the right balance takes time, and it may take years to complete the biology of the aging rooms.

Johnston County Hams

The final story of three Smithfields takes us to North Carolina, where we find Johnston County Hams, whose tradition of dry-aged country hams is still alive. The town lies southwest of Raleigh, about halfway to Goldsboro. In 2012 I met Rufus Brown, manager and part owner, at the American Cheese Society annual meeting in Raleigh. He was sampling different types of Johnston County country hams at an event hosted by **culture** magazine, whose tagline is "the word on cheese." While obviously a cheese lovers' publication, **culture** is an equal opportunity "controlled spoilage" magazine that celebrates all things fermented, including dry-cured meat. Rounding a corner among the many food purveyors, surrounded by guests packed solidly wall to wall, I nearly ran into the hoof of a huge cured ham. It was one of several beautiful, dark, aromatic country hams suspended on holders; behind them stood a friendly, athletic man, knife in hand, expertly carving translucent slices that glowed as he offered them to me with great pride. As he sliced, Rufus described a bit of the company's history and his vision for the future to diversify the business by curing hams from heritage hogs, one of which I savored as he spoke.

Holy flying pig! One of the hams came from a Mangalitsa hog, until the late 2000s an unknown breed in the States. In the early nineteenth century Austro-Hungarian breeders crossed several varieties of Romanian and Serbian hogs to create the Hungarian Mangalitsa, known as the "wooly pig," which, because of its very curly hair, thrives in cold climates. The Mangalitsa is a lard hog, its thick, firm fat prized by bakers, butchers, and chefs. With the demise of the Austro-Hungarian Empire and global shift away from lard, the breed nearly disappeared. In the 1990s work in Europe to save the animal slowly increased its numbers, and some stock arrived in the States around 2009.

And here was a Mangalitsa country ham, a rare breed cured in an increasingly difficult-to-find traditional American country style. What a remarkable coincidence, a delicious intersection of efforts to resurrect important heritage hogs, preserve genetics, and encourage increased traditional production, all wrapped in a thin slice of ham. If ever an argument could be made for strategies to influence sustainable agriculture, appropriate stewardship of land and nature, and humankind's creativity, I held it in my hand and savored an elemental reason to nurture such unique animals and defend millennia-old preservation techniques.

Rufus manages the company, whose origins date back to 1946, when Johnston County Frozen Foods opened in Smithfield, North Carolina. Back then the business was a freezer locker doing custom butchering for local farmers, residents, and hunters and some pork curing. US Highway

301, a principal north-south road from Florida to Maryland, bisected the town and funneled tourists traveling in both directions into the downtown, where they found the small country ham shop. The flow of visitors created steady demand for country hams, and the owners needed help to expand production.

Enter the Brown family, whose roots extend back into the early nineteenth century in Virginia's mountain communities of Tazewell and Bluefield. The Browns, like other farm families, "put up" a diverse variety of food, from pickled vegetables and dried grains to cured ham and lots of rendered lard. After serving in World War II, Rufus's father, Jesse, became a master butcher, opened a small meat store and smokehouse, and quickly earned a reputation for quality hams. The appetite for smoke and cure also included Rufus's uncle J. Brit Brown, who owned the Country Ham House in West Graham, a mile or two west of Bluefield.

In 1967, after Johnston County hired Jesse, the family left Virginia's mountains for Smithfield's flat landscape, where he managed Johnston County Hams for the next thirty years. His arrival was an essential ingredient to the future of the business. Prior to his hiring, Johnston used a two-stage curing process: a salting stage at 38°F and 80 to 95 percent humidity, after which the hams rested for two days for every pound of weight; stage two was at 80°F and 60 percent humidity. The hams aged between one and six months to dry. When all conditions were right, the process produced excellent hams. But Jesse found some hams spoiled and determined an additional step, a new second stage called equalization, was needed to create the best hams. During this period the hams are washed, dried, and then rested at 50 to 55°F and 60 percent humidity for at least a month before moving into the warmer maturing environment. Equalization ensured deeper salt penetration and required less salt to accomplish. Depending on an overall curing process, contemporary producers use similar traditional parameters to accomplish the three-stage practice.

Jesse Brown introduced another curing practice that differentiates Johnston County Hams from Smithfield and Virginia products. Many of us know North Carolina's west-east split over barbeque sauce — a fierce loyalty to either tomato- or vinegar-based sauce, respectively — and the arguments, sometimes stretching across multiple generations, about which is superior. Oddly, in Virginia a similar east-west division exists around smoke, although perhaps not accompanied by a contentious debate. Historically, eastern Virginia producers such as Edwards, Gwaltney, and Todd cold smoked hams anywhere from one to thirty days. Cold smoke adds flavor and color and helps protect the ham from insects. However, families and businesses in Virginia's mountains and such places as the Shenandoah Valley, at higher elevations and with cooler, drier weather, didn't use smoke at all, relying on salt and sometimes borax to manage the curing and safety concerns. When Jesse Brown took over at Johnston, he smoked its hams over hickory for only eight hours to achieve color, though it turns out that historically few if any North Carolina hams were smoked. For a period of time, Jesse used black pepper as an insect repellent. Although it does not flavor the ham, black pepper works to keep the bugs off.

The arrival of Interstate 95 in the mid- to late-1960s in North Carolina had a significant impact on the business. The highway, bypassing Smithfield just a mile or two to the east of town, meant travelers could make trips much faster, but they no longer stopped to buy hams. Almost simultaneously with the arrival of I-95 appeared the new technology of vacuum packaging for a variety of foods. Adopting the innovation, Jesse opened new markets for Johnston County that saved the company. Rather than making efforts to attract business from the interstate, they could ship and distribute vacuum-sealed hams safely to grocery stores, food services, and other large-volume users. In the 1970s and 1980s, the company's important investments in packaging equipment paid off with increased business far beyond North Carolina.

For example, in the 1970s a food distributor saw a Johnston ham that resembled a Portuguese cured ham, called *presunto*. He convinced Jesse the large Portuguese populations in southeastern Massachusetts and Rhode Island were potential markets. The company designed a presunto-style ham, and for several decades a Johnston North Carolina–Southern New England ham "train" fulfilled demand from the Portuguese communities.

Other country ham establishments took the same direction to increase their markets and also introduced smaller cuts and even cooked hams. However, Johnston made an interesting decision not to portion its hams into various cuts but to vacuum wrap the entire leg, and for many years this feature distinguished them from other country ham producers. Eventually, shifts in American diet, taste, and even kitchen appliances and size caught up with traditional country ham. After World War II, as soon as families could afford it, they traded their icebox for a refrigerator; or the new house in the suburbs was equipped with the latest model, and the need for a shelf-stable ham diminished. Or perhaps, as Rufus explained, the very large pots needed to cook a long-leg ham just disappeared!

In their place Johnston and other country ham producers developed smaller-size hams; instead of a whole bone-in leg at thirteen pounds, you could buy a half, weighing about six. In addition, the company marketed hams aged for three or six months. The younger one offered a softer texture and less salt; the older ham was drier, saltier, and firmer, the result of additional aging time during which it lost water. Cooked hams appeared often with a brown sugar glaze, ready to eat or bake. Slices and spiral-sliced hams were welcome party attractions that required little work.

Jesse's innovations in curing and packaging contributed to Johnston County's sterling reputation, and eventually he was crowned the "Ham King of the South." In 1983 three local businessmen bought the company from the original owners, and in 1989 Rufus joined the business full time.

But looking at the big picture, a far more important challenge than I-95 emerged in the same decades: the rapid expansion and transformation of industrial hog production. Small businesses like Johnston either adapted or closed. The vertical integration often meant the loss of local suppliers, with commodity hogs the only substitute. Rufus described the company buying pork in the 1970s and 1980s from the Midwest, principally from Indiana. With ongoing concerns about quality, Jesse turned to the Lundy Packing Company in Clinton, North Carolina, to supply Johnston with hogs from local farmers. In 1950 Burrows Lundy established the first USDA-inspected slaughterhouse in the state because he wanted to ship pork nationwide. Lundy set up buying stations across North Carolina to which small growers brought animals. His success spurred interest and the growth of small hog farms in the region, and by 1985 the packing house handled six thousand hogs a day.

For a period of time, Jesse Brown enjoyed the access to local hogs. However, by the 1990s Lundy's rapid expansion degraded the quality of the raw hams Johnston needed to produce country hams to his standards. For example, Lundy continued to expand its capacity as hog production grew.

From the mid-1980s it grew to handling nine thousand animals daily. In 2000, Premium Standard Foods purchased the company and again capacity increased; then in 2007 Smithfield Foods bought Premium!

The problem wasn't with the slaughterhouse, but it had everything to do with the national movement toward leaner hogs, "the other white meat," and simply how we raised, slaughtered, and distributed pork products. Throughout the 1980s and 1990s, a handful of companies vertically integrated the cycle from birth to table and consolidated the *industry* (my italics to highlight the application of industrial technologies and practices) through mergers and acquisitions. However, the bigger, leaner hogs produced large hams with little fat marbling through the muscles. For Jesse and Rufus the heavy hams presented significant problems in the curing. For their style of curing with less salt, hams either spoiled or lost too much weight to make them profitable. By the 1990s Johnston experienced a decline in meat quality from industrial hog growers. Inferior meat translated into substandard hams.

I recall a conversation many years ago with Allison Hooper, cofounder and owner of Vermont Creamery, about aging cheese. At the time, the creamery focused on fresh and bloomy-rind cheeses that took only a few weeks to mature. Allison pointed out that most consumers cannot smell or taste flaws in fresh, young cheeses. However, as it ages, whether it's two months or two years, small problems in a cheese, or in our situation, country ham, become large, significant ones. Both cheese and country hams lose weight as they mature; if cheddar and country ham begin with excellent raw material and are well made, the loss of water concentrates their aromas and flavors and transforms textures into truly delicious foods.

The challenge for Johnston was twofold: where to obtain better quality hogs and how to adjust the curing process to create outstanding country ham. The extraordinary growth and vertical integration of Smithfield Foods (Smithfield Hams is a subsidiary) to embrace every aspect of hog production, slaughter, fresh and cured processing, and distribution resulted in the loss of thousands of small farms and artisan businesses in North Carolina, Virginia, and beyond. Raw ham from a vertically integrated operation generally means fairly standardized taste and texture without distinctive qualities. Left behind were small curing operations such as Edwards and Johnston County. To stay in business they bought commodity hogs to provide enough hams and other cuts to cure. It's a wonder that Edwards and Johnston survived.

To replace Lundy, Johnston bought Duroc hams and loins from the J. H. Routh Packing Company in Sandusky, Ohio; at the height of Johnston's relationship with Routh, they used seventy thousand to eighty thousand hams a year; by 2015 they processed half that number, with 90 percent made from commodity hogs, all of which are still smoked over hickory wood. The other 10 percent represent the important diversification reflected by Brown, Edwards, and other cured pork producers.

Rufus described his interest in locating heritage breed animals and how he read about a fellow named Heath Putnam in Washington State. Motivated by his taste for great pork, Putnam and his wife learned about Mangalitsa hogs while in Hungary at the Pick Salami and Szeged Paprika Museum. He decided to bring them to the States rather than travel back to Hungary to eat woolly pig meat. In 2007 Putnam was able to legally import sows and boars and in 2008 delivered the first Mangalitsa hog to Thomas Keller at the French Laundry in California. Over the past several years, as breeding stock increased and more animals became available, Putnam and other growers found ready markets, all at the top end of the culinary world. While some restaurants created charcuterie along with fresh products, Rufus wanted to explore the Mangalitsa for curing hams. Beginning in 2009 he received shipments of Putnam's Mangalitsa pork, and about a year later, they began to show up at several well-known restaurants, including the French Laundry and several John Besh places in New Orleans.

Although it's a small percentage of its overall production, Johnston County now offers a high-end line of Curemaster's Reserve hams: country ham, mangalitsa ham, and mangalitsa shoulder. Rufus selects each ham individually for size, color, aroma, and age; yes, he does a smell test, using a stainless steel needle — no horse bone needles here — to insert into the ham to assess aroma and quality. The best become Curemaster's Reserve. Although the company prides itself on its modern stainless steel facility, these top-quality Curemaster products reside and age in a small wooden attic. The USDA allows the use of the attic as a grandfather clause exception. Here, like the now destroyed wood aging room at Edwards in Virginia, the legacy of well-worn decades guide and shape each item. Smoke and pork aromas permeate every board, and well-established colonies of bacteria and mold add their unique qualities as well. In my opinion, the attic is a small national treasure and directly a result of Jesse and Rufus's stewardship over sixty years; it cannot be reproduced or even moved. It represents one of a few singular examples of terroir related to curing meat still extant in the United States.

Beyond the reputation for both traditional and new variations of country ham, Johnston County attracted at least one individual who needed a different kind of help. In 2010 Sam Suchoff, a chef and restaurateur from North Carolina's Research Triangle region, opened the Pig restaurant in Chapel Hill. As its name suggests, the place was about all things porky — hot dogs, barbeque, and other items. Sam was buying antibiotic- and hormone-free hogs, pasture raised on roots, grubs, nuts, and seeds from small-scale farmers in the eastern part of the state and transforming them into a diverse array of products. The problem was what to do with the hams. Sam and Rufus had worked together previously on a farm project, so he approached Rufus about curing the hams, and the result was Lady Edison country ham. Today Johnston County has eighteen to twenty thousand pounds of the ham aging beautifully in Smithfield.

In 2014 and 2015 in Denver, I had an opportunity to showcase Lady Edison at a cured meat tasting for the international Slow Meat conference, organized by Slow Food USA. At both events Lady Edison was a beautiful example of great pork meeting great talent! The 2015 session also featured a Johnston's Mangalitsa ham; for most attendees this might have been the first time they heard about the animal, or tasted its ham. The event highlighted the serious interest from producers, farmers, and consumers to encourage greater collaboration for sustainable farming practices, humane slaughter, complete use of the entire animal, and development of truly outstanding cured products.

Contemplating the lineage represented by Sam Edwards, Rufus Brown, and Sam Suchoff, I am struck by how a simple country ham ties contemporary America to some of its first European settlers. A process born of necessity thousands of years ago kept our forebears alive when most people did not have many choices about what to eat — they ate to survive. But these preserved meats did not just feed us, they nurtured cultural identities that still exist in our country. Today we have diverse, global choices about what we eat. But the lowest common denominators of food do not support and cultivate small farm families and artisan food producers. For these individuals to succeed, we must eat what they produce to save them — not a new idea but a very relevant one in the meat community. For me, enjoying a well-aged cheddar or Parmigiano-Reggiano paired with great country ham or prosciutto is one of life's singular culinary experiences . . . and don't forget the great craft beer or wine.

CHAPTER FOUR

Hams of Many Generations

*Much smoking kills live men
and cures dead swine.*

— GEORGE DENNISON PRENTICE

Ge
eorge Prentice's quote humorously introduces us to a northern
European practice that contributed to the creation of a uniquely
American cured meat, Southern country hams. While the history of
smoke for curing stretches back millennia, its application, coupled with
recipes, different hogs, diet, and weather conditions, fashioned a distinctive
food that sustained Southern families for generations. Across the region
grocers and country-store owners often accepted freshly slaughtered hogs
as currency for goods, and many applied their expertise to preserve and
transform the hams. Country stores alongside rural dirt roads would offer
typical salt- and sugar-cured smoked hams, and the best alchemists became
renowned for their prowess.

But the advent of automobiles, parkways, and then superhighways doomed
these artisans, and only a handful of talented country ham producers are left.
Let's consider histories of two remarkable Kentucky family businesses.

Col. Bill Newsom's Aged Kentucky Country Ham

Imagine some of the first European settlers arriving in Virginia's wilder-
ness during the 1630s, numbering just a few thousand immigrants. Now

visualize the countless descendants populating the state's Tidewater counties and areas of North Carolina, Kentucky, and Tennessee, and you begin to grasp the breadth of the Newsom family's impact through 380 years of American history. But the story begins even farther back, in fifteenth-century England with William Newsom, the patriarch of a family whose subsequent progenies carry us to Kentucky and the Col. Bill Newsom Kentucky ham. A short genealogy is perhaps in order.

Various thirteenth- and fourteenth-century records identify early residents of the county of Lancashire, England, with names similar to Newsom. "William Newsom (or Newsham) may have been the first resident of Newsham Hall in Lancashire, England, and was Lord of the Manor. 'Newsham' was pronounced by the 15th Century English similarly to how 'Newsome' is pronounced today in the United States."[1]

Six generations later, in 1584, William Newsom Sr. was born at Newsham Hall. His son, William Jr., was born in 1614, a few years after the first permanent settlement at Jamestown. The prosperous Lancashire farm family raised livestock, including hogs, and various grains. In 1635 the twenty-one-year-old William departed London on the ship *George* for Virginia; he "signed [the] ship's register as 'William Neesum, farmer.'"[2] He landed in James City County, directly across the James River from Surry, and purchased land southeast of Jamestown in Rich Neck. Young William arrived with considerable financial resources and proceeded to establish a farm. Although records are nonexistent, we can surmise that William, like his Lancashire forebears, smoked meats for his family's survival. His experience, paralleling Jamestown's practices, thus intertwines with the earlier stories of Williamsburg and S. Wallace Edwards.

Michael Olmert, pointing out the absence of documentary or archaeological evidence from seventeenth-century Tidewater, suggests, "If they're smoking meat at Jamestown, they're doing it in ephemeral sheds or barns, not in purpose-built structures. Or the task may have been done as it often was in England, in smoking closets tucked away inside chimney flues."[3]

William Newsom, his son William III, and other offspring married into seventeenth-century Tidewater families and remain identified in the region to the present. William Newsom III was one of the wealthiest and most influential men in James City County, and his descendants provide the link to Col. Bill Newsom and Kentucky ham, as his family members migrated to

North Carolina in the late seventeenth and early eighteenth centuries and then farther west in the 1790s after the Revolutionary War.

The Newsom settlements in North Carolina coincide with the appearance of smokehouses throughout the colonial South. "A new class of building is regularly appearing in the backyard landscape: the smokehouse, alternatively spelled 'smoak' house. Typically, these are cubical structures of wood, eight to fourteen feet square, with steep pyramidal roofs for holding in the smoke among the hanging cuts of meat."[4]

The western migration over the Cumberland Gap through the Appalachian Mountains brought settlers into southeastern Kentucky and eastern Tennessee. The Gap, made famous by Daniel Boone, was the gateway for the Newsom family arriving from North Carolina. Nancy Newsom Mahaffey, the current owner of Col. Newsom's, easily traces her forebears from father Colonel Bill Newsom to grandfather Hosea Cleveland Newsom (1885–1933), who opened the store and smokehouse in 1917, to great-grandfather William Hosea Newsom (1839–1915), and finally, great great-grandfather Hosea Newsom (1798–1843). This last Hosea was the first Newsom ancestor connected directly to Col. Bill's ham business; part of the North Carolina Newsom branch, he arrived in Kentucky, probably through the Gap, after receiving a Revolutionary War land grant for his service during the war.

> There were about 1400 acres in the original land grant to Hosea and Martha Newsom about 1823, south of Princeton KY. [The] plantation like most other plantations of this period, was self-supporting. . . . A big ash hopper was constructed not far from the house where lye was obtained by pouring water over the ashes. Lye was necessary for making soap, hominy, for removing hair from hogs, and was necessary for general cleaning and scrubbing. Meat, vegetables and fruit were cured in preparation for long winter months.[5]

Perhaps you're wondering, what's the point of reading the names Hosea and William repeatedly throughout the Newsom genealogy? If we use the Newsom kinfolk as an example, Col. Bill Newsom's Aged Kentucky Country Ham reflects a five- to six-hundred-year family history and practice that nurtured a way of life difficult to find in contemporary America.

We must remember that the use of salt, smoke, and time were essential practices to sustain life; if you wanted to eat in the winter or when food was scarce, you learned to preserve it.

In recounting the successive generations of Newsoms, I celebrate a tradition, a process, and a family whose roots rest in ancient practice. The stories of S. Wallace Edwards and Johnston County reflect similar Virginia bedrock to that of Newsom. Those companies got bigger, a difficult decision in the mid- to late twentieth century, trying to stay in business and still produce extraordinary country ham. Col. Bill and Nancy Newsom made a different choice. They emphasized traditional curing practices, welcomed the vagaries of weather, stayed small, and, by doing so, expressed their personalities. Nancy said curing a ham "starts inside of you; it's who you are. The ham develops a soul."[6] As noted above, in 1917 her grandfather, Hosea C. Newsom, opened a general store in Princeton that sold a diverse array of goods, many linked to a specific season: spring seeds and plants, followed by summer and fall vegetables and fruits, and crowned in the winter with a few country hams. Pictures of the old store show H. C. in front of a window proclaiming groceries, while another depicts a long first floor flanked on both sides by display cases and a sign advertising garden seeds.

Because the area was mostly rural, farmers gathered for the annual fall or early winter slaughter ritual and cured their own hams; therefore, the store sold a limited quantity of bacon and ham. The Newsom family certainly followed the same seasonal custom in late November or early December. H. C. inherited a hundred-year-old salt and sugar curing recipe developed by his great-grandfather, James Newsom in North Carolina, who bequeathed it to subsequent generations. Talk about a sense of history! Until the store's opening, the heirloom Newsom achievement was enjoyed only by family and friends as they ate H. C.'s bacon and ham . . . but not the recipe or method. He guarded the secret recipe and process and taught his son through a hands-on, learn-by-doing education.

Sadly, H. C. Newsom died at an early age in the early 1930s from cirrhosis of the liver, a result of working with pesticides that contained lead arsenate. His son, William "Bill" Newsom, later Col. Bill, took over the store when he was just eighteen years old, and for the next thirty years, except during his World War II service, he operated the country store, continued to sell seeds, and cured country ham. After verifying the 1798 recipe, Col. Bill adjusted the amount of salt in the cure and continued to smoke the hams in his father's nineteenth-century smokehouse.

In 1963, the same year the state of Kentucky bestowed on Bill Newsom the honorary title of Kentucky Colonel, he built a new cinder-block smokehouse with a capacity of 1,000 to 1,500 hams. As Steve Coomes points out in *Country Ham*, changes in lifestyle, arrival of refrigeration, and the new interstate highways altered the way people lived and shopped.[7] Dozens of country stores with small curing businesses watched customers disappear. At the same time and for similar reasons, Bill Newsom saw fewer farmers curing hams. But while supply diminished, local demand for quality remained, and Col. Bill's new smokehouse helped fulfill customer interest. To help replicate the terroir of the old smokehouse, Nancy said her father brought some original wood boards to the new facility to inoculate the space with the legacy molds.

The smokehouse incorporated USDA regulations that disrupted many old practices and techniques. Historically, Southerners buried hams in salt boxes in cold rooms or buildings. As Rick McDaniel describes it, "The hams and shoulders would be placed in a 'meat box' or curing trough and buried in salt for four to six weeks to draw out moisture. Salt boxes ranged in size from a few feet long for a small farm to a massive, twenty-foot-long cypress salt trough. . . ."[8] The new requirements disallowed the salt box. Prior to 1963 Col. Bill cured his hams in salt boxes used by his father and smoked them in the same wood building.

Over time the boards and the molds transformed the building and helped continue the family's regional recognition for distinctive, quality country hams. But it was James Beard's writing and accolades in the mid-1970s that brought wide public attention to Col. Bill and a dramatic increase in demand. Nancy and her family returned to Princeton about the same time, and she went to work helping her father manage the growing business in country hams. But the local store hit hard times with the arrival of a Walmart in the late 1970s that sold seeds, plants, and other items at prices everyone but the Newsoms celebrated.

Nancy considered the growing domestic interest in their hams and read the changing national mood around food better than most. She launched a gourmet business based around gift baskets packed with Newsom hams and local preserves and candy. Her sixth sense about authenticity and products with the family's high standard of excellence kept them going.

In 1987 the Newsom General Store burned down, although the hams were safe in a different building. Col. Bill wanted to walk away, but Nancy said they were coming into the fall season and they had hams to sell. Her father essentially said, "You do it," and she did. As soon as the holidays concluded, she and her workers turned to curing the next year's batch of a thousand hams. Looking back, Nancy feels the fire was a blessing in disguise; she had to traverse a painful period, but the Princeton community, her workers, and their customers offered support, and they sold every ham.

I am impressed by the amalgam of tradition and exquisite intuition and sensory ability that go into curing a simple country ham, requiring extraordinary skill and patience. While Nancy never met her grandfather, she described H. C. with great affection and respect for how he managed the business as well as his deep, intuitive slow knowledge of dry-curing country hams. Nancy, her father, and her grandfather practiced the simple and yet magical alchemy of transforming a raw cut of meat into an extraordinary food. She embraces this amazing history with no idea what the future holds; rather, on a conscious and perhaps unconscious level, beyond her dedication to family is a powerful commitment to preserve a tradition, a process, and an elegant food that fundamentally is a simple expression of survival. In hindsight I see a parallel to a Buddhist's sense of the present moment. What Nancy practices every day rests on the fleeting, perhaps ephemeral gifts of nature, climate, and place, always changing, never the same, but always present.

Nancy and her crew of five to six people hand-massage approximately 350 fresh hams a day with a mixture of salt and brown sugar but no nitrates. Sugar (sucrose) serves several important purposes in cured meat. First, it adds flavor, and second, it counteracts the harshness of salt. If caramelized, the sugar provides a surface color characteristic of aged ham. Both brown and white sugars can be used; the sugars most frequently used are sucrose, cane sugar, dextrose, and invert sugar.[9]

Federal regulations require a country ham to lose a minimum of 18 percent of its weight to be labeled a country ham. To ensure they meet this criterion, Nancy selects a few hams at random to track through the initial steps. She calculates the amount of salt for each batch from the gross weight of the day's delivery.

Next, in a practice called lacing, the salted hams are stacked tightly on oak shelves, the first layer butt end out, the next by shank end, then another layer by butt end; when complete, the stack is eighteen to twenty feet high. Over a period of weeks, the entire stack comes down, and each ham is washed, re-salted, and stacked again. The process is repeated several times to ensure uniform salting, and the changing distribution ensures all hams share similar compression from the weight of the meat that contributes to water loss and even salt penetration.

This procedure reminds me of how cheddar cheese is made: the adjustable pile is quite similar to the cheddaring process, in which slabs of curd are stacked, then moved and restacked, to remove whey from the bundle. As each stack grows larger, additional amounts of watery whey drip out. Similarly, during the lacing process salt is further distributed through the hams, while each repositioning sets up different weights and aids in water extraction.

After the final washing they place the hams in netted bags; at this stage the butts are a gray color. Had Newsom used nitrates or nitrites, the flesh would retain a pink to reddish-brown color. Depending on the dynamics of spring weather, the bagged hams are suspended in the smokehouse, with its twenty-foot-high ceilings, for three to four weeks. In contrast to that used by Edwards and Johnston County, this equalization stage is accomplished strictly with ambient air. Ideally, Nancy looks for cool, dry days to fire up the smoker with a mixture of hickory wood and sawdust, contained in an old cast-iron kettle sitting in the middle of the room. I imagine a cross-section of the black patina, the layers of smoke inside the kettle, might resemble a tree's growth rings, layers of ash and soot now fossilized, also an expression of a year's weather.

As this step is completed, the smoke transforms the ham's surface into a deep, luminescent mahogany as it awaits its final stage, the heat and humidity of a Kentucky summer. While each point in the process is critical to the final product, the next several months require Nancy's constant diligence and vigil. She conducts daily weather checks and, with intuition gained from decades of experience, determines ambient airflow to adjust for temperature and humidity. During the summer months the hams lose 26 to 36 percent of their weight. While nature decides how long the hams must hang, Nancy is their unique guide and conductor from raw ham to a Newsom Aged Kentucky Country Ham.

Will Nancy's ability to read the weather and adjust the daily air and humidity flow fall victim to changes in our climate? I don't have an answer, except to say the continued fluctuations with hotter summers will require even greater diligence to maintain product integrity and excellence. If anyone can manage, I'd put my hickory chips on Nancy.

For the past twenty-five years, demand for Newsom ham far outstripped supply. In 2008 Nancy built a new smokehouse to expand production; today they make three thousand hams annually and are still unable to meet customer requests. The process remains the same: all hand-produced utilizing Hosea's inherited recipe, under Nancy's watchful eye and nose. For several decades the company bought conventionally grown pork from Missouri. In the mid-2000s Nancy introduced limited edition Kentucky hams from pasture-raised Berkshire, Gloucester Old Spot, Large Black, and Red Wattle heritage hogs. In 2010 she added a long cut and long shank ham from pastured Duroc/White cross hogs. While most Newsom hams age eleven to twelve months, Nancy sets aside a small, exclusive batch to mature for seventeen months.

Consider the centuries-old traditions embodied in Nancy Newsom Mahaffey and her remarkable focus to produce hams fully dependent on nature. Add the living microflora communities embedded in the smokehouse walls and their singularity in a world of sameness. Contemplating the value of Nancy and her commitment, I am reminded of Japan's Living National Treasures. In 1950 the country created a program to acknowledge and celebrate keepers of important intangible cultural properties, including unique, traditional skills; for example, in ceramics or textiles.

These craftsmen with decades of experience, many of them multigenerational artisans, create the finest, minutest nuance in a tea bowl or a samurai blade. These subtleties carry meaning and valuable cultural identity and are not something learned from a book. To express such characteristics requires patience, openness, refinement, and concentration. To see and experience a bonsai oak, maple, or wisteria created by not one master but several generations speaks to deep cultural reservoirs, slow knowledge, and pride in craftsmanship.

In my opinion, Nancy Newsom Mahaffey embodies these same qualities. In 2002 Kentucky awarded Nancy the honorary title of colonel in recognition of her legacy and contributions to the state's history and community.

While applauding this wonderful honor, I think a recognition received in 2009 epitomizes the international community's acknowledgment of Nancy as a "living treasure." That year the Fifth World Congress of Dry Cured Hams in Aracena, Spain, invited her to attend, and she brought a seventeen-pound heritage ham. It is still there, hanging in a vitrine in the Museo del Jamón, identified as one of the world's greatest hams.

¡Cumplido! 褒め言葉 *Homekotoba!*

Broadbent's

What do you do when you have a ninety-year-old award-winning ham business but want to retire to the farm, and the children want to move on? Well, you could sell it to a husband and wife who build furniture and know nothing about running a country ham enterprise but admire their neighbor in Cadiz who makes a good product. Does this sound like a winning strategy? Absolutely!

The Broadbent family traces its colonial history to early eighteenth-century Virginia, when the first individuals arrived from Lancashire, England. Clearly, given both the Broadbents and the Newsoms, we see a deep geographic link between country ham and the same region in England. After the Revolutionary War, family members moved west across the Appalachian Mountains, and by the early nineteenth century, settled in Trigg County in southwest Kentucky around the village of Cadiz, close to the border with Tennessee. As subsistence farmers they planted enough to feed themselves through the coming winter. Learning from Native Americans, they grew the Three Sisters — corn, beans, and squash — with each plant part of a dynamic synergy to nurture its neighbor. These vegetables were easily stored and provided a well-balanced diet as well. In the early winter after slaughtering hogs, local farmers preserved various cuts and parts for the next year in separate smokehouses or sometimes multipurpose structures, part of which were used for smoking.

In 1909, using a traditional family recipe of salt and sugar, Anna and Smith Broadbent established a pork-curing business on their farm to sell smoked bacon, country ham, and sausage to friends and neighbors as gifts for Christmas. While the hams were darn good, the couple really didn't see curing as a business. Their sons, Robert and Smith Jr., graduates of the

University of Kentucky (UK), became farmers and prominent leaders in the state's agriculture and business communities. Smith grew and developed hybrid seed corn, while his twin brother raised livestock.

At that time farmers could ship their homemade country hams without much regulation, and one recipient, Barry Bingham Jr., a Louisville newspaper and media owner, prized the Broadbents' gifts of country ham. On a hunting trip with Smith Broadbent Jr., Bingham proposed they establish a country ham business. Robert, with his experience as a hog grower, would handle the farm and slaughter operation while Smith III cured the hams and other products in a Cadiz facility. Bingham took on the responsibility of marketing and selling the hams in Louisville and beyond.

Just as the Newsom family discovered, new requirements in the early 1960s no longer allowed for the shipment of mail-order hams without USDA approval of sanitary standards. To meet the regulations, Smith engaged faculty from the university to help design and build a curing and aging facility. In 1963 the new company, Broadbent-Bingham, put up its first hams and a year later sold the inaugural batch. But business was slow, and then, tragically, in 1966 Barry Bingham died in an automobile accident. Smith bought Bingham's share of the company, renamed it Broadbent's B&B Food Products, and launched a mail-order catalog. A year later, with encouragement from a UK professor, Smith entered a ham in the Kentucky State Fair competition and received the Grand Champion award. (He repeated the success seven more times, the last one the year prior to selling the business.)

In 1974 James Beard lauded the company in a much-repeated quotation: "It was only lately, while in Kentucky, that I became acquainted with these superb hams. There's a company called Broadbent-Bingham that sells cured and aged country hams. If you visit them, you can also buy extraordinarily good ham hocks, thick ham steaks and hams, all cured the same way. I carried back a cooked ham for Thanksgiving which was much admired by all who tasted it."

With an award-winning state fair track record and positive press, the company grew steadily, until it produced about three thousand hams annually. In 1999 Smith Broadbent III sold the business to Beth and Ronny Drennan from Fredonia, about fifteen miles northwest of Princeton, where they both grew up, Ronny on a local dairy farm and Beth in town.

Can you imagine the prospect of buying a company with more than thirty years' success and recognition from a luminary like James Beard? What will long-time customers think? To be honest, they didn't know what to make of the sale and feared the worst.

For years the Drennans ran Country's Inn furniture, a successful, well-regarded pine furniture company in Kuttawa, a village about fifteen miles southwest of Fredonia. As small business owners they understood the value of quality products and sound financial practice and sold furniture to stores throughout the state. While living on his family's dairy farm, Ronny experienced an annual hog slaughter and his father's curing of bacon and ham. But all the hams were sold to make extra money, and as Ronny relates, it wasn't until he was an adult that he ate country ham.[10]

But home curing was clearly not the same as a commercial, inspected operation, so Smith taught Ronny the art and science of curing ham, bacon, and other pork products. Together in January 1999 they put up Ronny's first hams, and in August he entered a group in the state fair and didn't win anything. Now, considering that at the previous year's competition Smith won several first-place ribbons, Ronny was determined to understand what happened. He caught up with the judge, who described and explained how he evaluates hams in the different classes. It turns out a ham's taste and flavor, which I assumed were of primary importance to judges, are considered in just one of the six competition categories.

Ronny described the six competitive classes, based on different-size hams and whether the curing began before or after January 1 of a given year. Judges look for presentation and appearance. Does the ham conform to an overall set of features: a classic teardrop shape and plumpness; the artistry and workmanship to trim the ham or how it is presented; color, mold, and fat-to-lean marbling; and finally, aroma! The judges evaluate aroma carefully; sometimes a nuance might be all that separates first and second prizes, or even the grand champion. I was relieved to learn they have a "Best Taste" or "Cut Class," in which the judges get to taste the hams. Hallelujah, they do get to eat a sliver!

Ronny listened mightily. At the end of 1999 and in January 2000, he applied his new knowledge and understanding to another crop of hams, and in August his efforts paid off, with not only four first prizes but the Grand Champion award as well.

As Sandra Myers related to Kentucky readers:

> *Those who bemoaned the sale of Broadbent B&B Food Products two years ago can now rest easy.*
>
> *After all, the names Trigg County and Broadbent are synonymous with Kentucky's most famous country ham, and it's a well-known fact that curing a good country ham is an art that few can master.*
>
> *However, traditionalist [sic] can now be [sic] put their worries aside, as new owners Ronny and Beth Drennan have more than proven their ability to serve up good country ham.*
>
> *It all happened Thursday at the South Wing banquet hall at the Kentucky Fair and Exposition Center in Louisville when their firm's 2000 Grand Champion Ham was auctioned during the 37th annual Kentucky Country Ham Breakfast for a hefty $37,000.*[11]

The morning following an announcement of the year's Grand Champion the Kentucky State Fair has a wonderful tradition of a ham breakfast and auction at which the winning ham goes under the hammer and the proceeds go to the highest bidder's favorite charity. Over the years Beth and Ronny's grand champions sold for several hundred thousand dollars each. But hold on to your hams: In 2014 the Broadbent ham sold for a hot two million dollars. Later the same year Ronny and Beth also won Grand Champion at the National Country Ham Association annual meeting. What a tribute to a couple of furniture makers, who now stand among the best country ham artisans in the United States.

Beth points out the strong relationship between Ronny's skills as a furniture maker and his ability to trim hams. In an interview conducted by Steve Coomes, Beth described his talent:

> *Other people tell him he should have a workshop on trimming hams, and he says, "Come on down and I'll show you how to do it." I think that when we were doing furniture he got really good at details. He was picky then, and those same details make his hams look so neat.*[12]

When Beth and Ronny took over the business, Broadbent handled 3,000 to 3,500 hams annually. Today the company cures approximately 12,000 a year, and the growth reflects several important changes. Until the 1970s or 1980s, Smith bought a limited number of hams from his brother Bob, given his farm size. The emergence of commodity pig production enabled Smith to increase production, but the size of the old curing and smoking facility basically limited expansion to around the three thousand threshold.

Until the late 2000s the Drennans ran their business from Cadiz, but increasingly they realized distance and travel time, plus limited curing capacity, put a brake on any future growth. In 2008 they opened a modern facility in Kuttawa that quadrupled ham output and significantly expanded the bacon lines. Today bacon accounts for more than 50 percent of the business. They purchase hams from Premium Standard Farms, a Smithfield subsidiary in Milan, Missouri. As Beth and Ronny said emphatically, as much as they would like to buy local pork, "Nobody wants hogs next to them."[13]

In my opinion, the Drennans' ability to work with a standard hog and create award-winning hams reflects an extraordinary degree of skill, attention to the smallest details, and commitment to the highest level of excellence. It starts with the cure developed by Smith Broadbent Sr., an unusual blend of salt, sugar, nitrite, and dried honey. Until talking with Ronny I had never heard of dried honey, and this from someone who collects and consumes honey from around the world. It turns out the product is simply dehydrated honey, although other ingredients may be added to keep it pourable. For the cure the dried honey and sugar help balance saltiness, especially as the ham ages and loses weight.

The Broadbent process is similar to practices of other country ham producers, from salting, smoking, and equalization to aging. The new facility enables them to process hams year-round using climate-controlled rooms to re-create seasonal changes. After the "winter" stage in which the hams rest at 38°F, they move into the "spring" or equalization phase at 50°F and finally into a "summer" season of 70°F or higher. After emerging from the equalization stage, the hams dry for a week or two and then are smoked for five to seven days to attain a beautiful pecan-brown color. Ronny reminds me that the smoking step is purely cosmetic and doesn't add flavor to the hams. He also points out that when you have twelve thousand hams to process and cure, control of variables contributes to consistent aroma, texture, and taste.

Ronny feels the Broadbent "sweet spot" for aging is eight to nine months, although some hams age out at twelve to eighteen months, principally for restaurant use. They cure some hams for fewer months to create a softer, milder, and less salty product. During the salt and equalization stages, he monitors their shape and trims a small number of hams as needed to smooth them; these are the state fair entries. In this manner Ronny achieves a consistent style as he whittles each ham into its perfect dimensions. Regardless of how much trimming is done, the final state fair competitors have a consistent color.

But other options for Broadbent are on the pork horizon beyond a commercial hog. In 2015 Patrick Martins, owner of Heritage Foods USA, introduced Berkshire and Red Wattle hogs to the Drennans, and they started to cure a group of hams in October. The first limited edition hams were available in July 2016 after aging nine months, and then year-old ones were ready in October. Stay tuned! Beth and Ronny are committed to working with these hogs, and given their great success with the other breeds, these should be extraordinary.

The other possibility may stem from research conducted by Bob Perry, special projects manager for the Sustainable Agriculture and Food Systems group at UK's College of Agriculture. In 2008 I met Bob during an event for the Slow Food USA board, at which he carved a beautiful country ham made from a crossbreed 50/50 Ossabaw and Farmers Hybrid hog grown by West Virginia's Woodlands Pork, called "Cross-a-baw" and fattened on mast. The ham was spectacular, and I found it difficult to pull away to attend to other obligations.

The history of the Farmer's Hybrid hogs dates to the mid-1940s and Iowa's dominance in reproducing crossbred animals. Collaborations between the Farmers Hybrid Company and Iowa State University geneticists developed a unique hog, bred for its hardiness, meat quality, and reproductive characteristics. However, the takeoff of commodity production with crosses of Duroc/Yorkshire/Large White hogs left Farmers Hybrid with few customers, and it closed in 1999.[14] A handful of growers continued to work with the Farmers Hybrid genetics, and some eventually reached West Virginia.

The Cross-a-baw ham introduced me to Bob Perry's work in researching heritage breeds, known as the "Saving Endangered Hog Breeds" project.

Over several years his research team examined the genetics of eight distinct breeds and different feed protocols, to test and evaluate yields and taste characteristics for each ham. Among the eight breeds studied were American Guinea, Hereford, Mulefoot, and Ossabaw.[15]

At a Slow Meat conference in Denver in 2015, Bob brought a thirty-six-month-old Hereford hog country ham. None of us guessed the ham's age because the thick fat surrounding it made the ham look as if it had been aged for just a few months. The link to the Broadbent story is that the company was responsible for curing hams from all eight heritage hogs. In my opinion, and given the response from the Slow Food audience, the Hereford was an amazing example of where the future of country ham and the preservation of heritage animals might exist.

The next step is to recruit and support farmers dedicated to growing these animals. The challenges are many, including ensuring the right genetics, adequate and affordable feed, proper slaughter and butchering, conscientious use of the entire hog, and development of a large enough market to fairly support farmers and processors.

The history of the Kentucky Country Ham Producers Association offers an indication of the challenges facing cured meat producers and of the incredible success of Beth and Ronny at the helm of Broadbent's. In 1982 Smith Broadbent organized the association to help promote the state, and at one point the group accounted for thirty-five producers. Today eight Kentucky companies are left, a reflection of increased federal inspection requirements and associated costs, business mergers, and lack of family interest to continue, among others.

Another critical factor is a loss of small-scale, farm-based curing; in many ways, without the experience gained on a farm, the idea of buying a curing business is outlandish. Beth and Ronny have shown it can be done, but not many people like them exist. If we are to change the way America raises, processes, and eats pork, then people like the Drennans and companies like Broadbent are essential players. But we must consider the place of country hams in the universe of dry-cured, preserved meat. Until the twentieth century, dry curing, pickling, cooking, and smoking hams were the available preservation techniques. With most farmers putting up meat, no one looked to country ham as a major money maker; it was simply part of the culture of farming and rural life. The few farms and general stores selling hams made a little money, but the food was viewed through a different cultural lens.

After 350 years of production and local use, country ham occupies a defining place in Southern foodways and cuisine. And yet, since we continue to lose small producers, the question is one of balance. Do we run a risk of elevating a country ham to a pedestal similar to what prosciutto or jamón are on, with their associated price tags? What happens when we shift the ham from its cultural and historic roots? Do we lose these fundamental expressions of tradition, culture, and contemporary practice because our celebration of their uniqueness and willingness to pay more alters the historical and social equations? I'm not sure I have an answer, but the inquiries are important.

CHAPTER FIVE

Le Bon Temps Roulé

I figure that about 80 percent of the boudin purchased in Louisiana is consumed before the purchaser has left the parking lot, and most of the rest is polished off in the car. In other words, Cajun boudin not only doesn't get outside the state; it usually doesn't even get home.[1]

— CALVIN TRILLIN

For more than thirty years, my travel experiences have introduced me to food and cuisine in China, Kenya, Italy, and Scotland, to name a few countries, and in the States, so many cities and rural communities I won't attempt a list. I am grateful for these many opportunities and very fortunate that New Orleans (NOLA) has been a frequent destination. If we are what we eat, then visits to New Orleans and the rest of Louisiana have transformed parts of me into an oyster, boudin sausage, beignets with powdered sugar, shrimp, crawfish, red fish, muffuletta, gumbo, and jambalaya, with a cap of Creole cream cheese. I'll leave it to you to decide about the transformed parts.

Woven between my impressions are the writings and intellect of John Folse, a German-American whose family arrived in Louisiana in the mid-eighteenth century. In 2002 I met John in Washington, DC, at an American Cheese Society annual meeting, where he spoke about Bittersweet Plantation, his new company making Creole cream cheese, a historical New Orleans dairy product. Over the years our paths crossed (although not enough times), including a visit when he guided me through Cajun country. One of the country's most creative chefs, writers, restaurateurs, and specialty food producers, he runs a multifaceted business dedicated in multiple ways to educating a global audience about food, especially the history and culture of Cajun and Creole cuisine.

John helped me understand the extraordinarily diverse, rich overlays of people, ingredients, and techniques that today we call Louisiana foodways. Without recognizing the presence of Native Americans, the French, the Spanish, Africans, Germans, English, and Italians, you cannot comprehend and appreciate the centuries and layers of influence and blending. I do not for a moment profess to understand this complex history, but I can smell and taste it and through these experiences better appreciate a European and African history dating to 1700 CE and that of Native Americans to 10,000 BCE.

Although Louisiana does not have a historical culture and tradition of dry-cured meat, food preservation was nevertheless essential to survival. With a climate of high temperatures and humidity, the seasonal stages needed to make fermented sausage or country ham just do not exist. But historically, Louisiana's Native Americans and immigrants faced the same challenges in preserving food every fall to carry over into the next growing season as people in cooler, drier climates did.

Most of us not living in Gulf Coast areas don't appreciate how upside down the region's climate can be. For example, if you visit the New Orleans Crescent City Farmers Market in December, as I did in 2015, produce vendors have first-of-the-season fresh Creole tomatoes and great strawberries for sale! In Vermont those fruits have foreign labels on them around Christmastime. On the other hand, in early May 2013 during a visit to this great city market, I noticed the last of the tomatoes were disappearing because it's just too hot for them to survive the summer.

New Orleanians, Cajuns, Creoles, and other South Louisiana residents slaughtered pigs and, regardless of the season, had to use the fresh meat immediately. One adaptation was from traditional French *boudin blanc* and *boudin rouge*, fresh white or red pork sausage, the latter flavored with pork blood. The sausages mixed leftovers from the slaughter with rice as a filler, which then, whether fresh or smoked, could be boiled, panfried, or grilled. "Boudin is made from the parts of the hog that can't be preserved — liver, hog jaw, belly, heart, kidney and, sometimes, blood. All the good stuff is ground and mixed with rice, green parsley, green onions, onions, and other secret spices then squeezed into a sausage casing."[2]

As in most agricultural and rural areas, neighbors helped each other to slaughter hogs. Historically, farmers who could afford to own hogs might solicit grains and food scraps from nearby friends and relatives, who then received a portion of the pig after slaughter. In South Louisiana the communal slaughter and processing, called a boucherie, was a time for celebration, with eating, drinking, music, and dancing.

In Louisiana and other Gulf Coast states, people ate fresh sausage immediately and preserved the larger cuts of pork generally by pickling, also called brining. For preservatives farmers often combined rock salt ("corns" of salt, hence "corned" beef) and potassium nitrate (saltpeter), perhaps mixed with cloves, allspice, onions, and bay leaves for flavor. They packed the meat into barrels layered with the curing mix, and as the salt drew water from the muscles, it created its own brine. Just as with corned beef, another preserved meat, the pickling or brining process tenderized the pork. But local supply in Louisiana could not fulfill demand, and the primary source for pickled pork during the early to mid-nineteenth century came from the Ohio Valley. Kentucky and Tennessee pork, processed in Cincinnati, went down the Ohio River to the Mississippi and on to New Orleans. None of it was fresh; most of it was pickled pork, although occasionally a few country hams arrived.

Beyond pickling, alternate ways to preserve meat depended on adapting traditional European methods to Louisiana's particular climate. While Native Americans used smoke and fire to dry fish and meat, the arrival of the first German immigrants in the 1720s contributed to technical changes in meat preservation and pork recipes.[3] Coming from Alsace-Lorraine, the new arrivals were familiar with both French and German styles of curing, and their bilingualism eased the transition into French-controlled Louisiana. The Germans settled on the east bank of the Mississippi River, northwest of New Orleans, in what became known as Côte des Allemands, "the German Coast."

Several decades later, with the arrival of Acadians from Nova Scotia, intermarriage occurred frequently with the earlier German settlers. Some Acadians traveled through South Carolina on the way to Louisiana, where they encountered golden rice, the ancestor of American long-grain rice, and brought it with them. As the Acadian/German residents moved south into areas of the Atchafalaya River basin, they started to cultivate rice. Today we are blessed with the historic marriage of rice and fresh pork, the offspring of which is Cajun boudin. I highly recommend tracking down Bob Carriker's

Boudin: A Guide to Louisiana's Extraordinary Link and his food website to end all boudin sites: boudinlink.com.[4] As Trillin's quotation attests, boudin is best wherever you are in Louisiana. You'll discover regional differences, passionate debates, family disputes, variations in grind and amounts of rice, with or without liver, and spices all over the map. In my opinion, you're in for a treat wherever you stop.

The marriage of rice and pork is a French and German food duet, but the Germans in Louisiana introduced centuries-old meat preservation techniques using salt and smoke. If you consider a map of today's Louisiana landscape and use Interstate 10 as a rough east-west dividing line, Cajun foodways differ on either side of the highway. To the north are the prairie Cajuns, often descendants of the earlier French and German intermarriages, who built smokehouses to preserve different types of pork: Andouille sausage and Tasso ham; chaurice, a spicy sausage used to make gumbo; sometimes boudin; and other smoked sausages.[5] Today the parishes of Acadia, Evangeline, and St. Landry are considered the epicenter of Cajun smoked meat. South of I-10 we find fresh fin and shellfish — crab, crawfish, oysters, shrimp, and red fish, with an occasional alligator (tastes like chicken!) — from bayou waters or the Gulf of Mexico. Here, the sausage is fresh, and prior to refrigeration folks ate it the day it was made.

While Andouille and Tasso occupy central places in many South Louisiana dishes, they are best known as essential flavor ingredients in gumbo and jambalaya. Andouille has its origins in France, where peasants made a spicy, heavily smoked sausage stuffed with hog small intestines and tripe. While this recipe was carried over to Louisiana, today practitioners make either a coarse-grained or cubed pork sausage from smoked or unsmoked pork shoulder. Recipes vary but generally include liberal additions of red and black pepper and garlic. After curing for twelve to forty-eight hours, the sausages are heavily smoked. "Each family had its own recipes for making Andouille as well as different techniques for smoking, all of which were highly guarded and rarely shared. Because pork is the main ingredient in Andouille, it was at the boucherie, or the butchering of the hogs each winter, that most all of the Andouille was made."[6]

The name Tasso "ham" is somewhat of a misnomer, since the pork comes from the shoulder, rather than the hind leg. Clearly identified with Cajun cooking, the meat is heavily spiced, dried, and smoked. After cutting the seven- to eight-pound shoulder into slices, producers dredged each strip in a salt, sugar, and saltpeter cure. A few hours later they washed and dried the meat; then they coated each slice with varying amounts of cayenne, garlic, paprika, and cumin. Tasso is ready once the strips are smoked and air-dried. Although its name origins are obscure, the process relates to Native American air-drying techniques, noted earlier with the Quechua, whose ch'arki became jerky. Originally Tasso was made from beef, but after the Civil War, pork became the predominant meat.

For the most part Louisiana cooks use Andouille and Tasso to add layers of flavor and spicy heat to gumbo and jambalaya. In addition, both meats find their way into New Orleans' classic red beans and rice, or New Year's black-eyed peas and rice, or with collard greens. Today the spice mixtures also carry over into contemporary New Orleans restaurant charcuterie and even some salumi.

An alternative method to salt and smoke is confit, a technique dating to at least the medieval period, often used to preserve meat. Many of us know of duck confit, in which a thigh and leg cook slowly in their own fat; once complete, the fat is spooned over the meat and allowed to cool. The duck fat or pork lard creates an oxygen barrier, and properly stored, a confit keeps for months. Toby Rodriguez from Grand Coteau, Louisiana, introduced me to *saucisse de graisse* or grease sausage; the language suggests the French introduced the technique and terminology in Louisiana. Toby's grandmother kept a crock of cooked sausage covered with lard. He has loving memories of her welcoming him home from school with a snack of grease sausage. She would slice it lengthwise, cook it up in lard, and serve saucisse de graisse with white bread. The remaining fat went back in the crock. What a simple yet sophisticated technique and one that, given Toby's enthusiastic description, was delicious.

The blending of ideas, techniques, traditional recipes, ingredients, and spices drove the creation of many fresh, smoked, or cooked sausages and other pork foods. Coupled with physical and often social isolation, Cajun food evolved without the interference of outside attention. The foods remained hidden. Not until Paul Prudhomme, from St. Landry Parish, popularized Cajun and Creole cuisines did the outside world recognize their distinctive characteristics and qualities.

When we consider food preservation, including cured meats, across the American South, the impact of refrigeration cannot be overlooked. In the "Cold" episode of Steven Johnson's documentary series *How We Got to Now*, he documents the transformative role of cold, ice, freezers, and refrigerators.[7] From movie theaters to Pillsbury frozen peas to office buildings and ice cream, late nineteenth- and twentieth-century inventions altered every Southern and Southwestern state and region from the Carolinas to Louisiana to Southern California. After 1945 inexpensive home refrigerators and room air conditioners made it possible for millions to live comfortably in these regions; among other outcomes were major population shifts from the north to the south.

The advent of refrigerators and walk-in cold boxes with temperature and humidity controls greatly increased the number of ingredients and techniques available to restaurants everywhere. In the South doors opened for imaginative chefs and meat processors to experiment with cured meats previously beyond their physical capability. In the late twentieth century, as national interest expanded to include craft beer, artisan cheese, and then cured meat, New Orleanian butchers and chefs introduced charcuterie and salumi to their menus. Post–Hurricane Katrina, new restaurants, often with innovative curing programs, contributed to the rebuilding.

To explore both the traditional and new charcuterie and salumi in Louisiana, I needed a knowledgeable guide and was fortunate to have met Seth Hamstead. In 2013 I was in NOLA for a Slow Food USA national meeting and arrived early to spend some time with Richard Sutton, owner of the St. James Cheese Shop. Richard and I knew each other through the American Cheese Society, and I conducted a couple of cheese seminars for him at the store. We planned another food event in 2013 and broadened it to include more fermented foods — cheese, bread, cured meat, and beer. That day we drove around the city to visit the vendors whose products we featured that night: baguettes from Bellegarde Bakery; NOLA Brewing beer; and cured meat from Cleaver & Co., owned by Seth. The evening event was a smash hit and a testimony to the breadth of fermented foods and beverages now produced in the city.

When I organized the cured meat tasting for Slow Meat 2015 in Denver, I asked Seth for one of his products. That's when I learned he had sold the business, but he provided two dry-aged bresaola made from a grass-fed Red

Angus/Brahman steer from New Iberia, Louisiana. And he volunteered to help organize my trip when I visited New Orleans in fall 2015. Originally from Chicago, Seth has an interesting, varied background. After receiving a BA in chemistry from Tulane, he went back to the Windy City, where he taught chemistry. He shifted gears, worked nearly ten years as an economic consultant, and returned to Tulane to earn an MBA. He applied these skills to business consulting but fortunately along the way was bitten by a meat bug.

In 2011 he opened Cleaver & Co., a full-service butcher shop and small curing program, with Kris Doll managing the curing cabinet. The company bought heritage hogs from Louisiana and Mississippi farmers, as well as beef, duck, rabbit, and an occasional lamb and goat. One reason for selling the shop was a new business venture, Continental Provisions, with Bellegarde Bakery, Cleaver & Co., and St. James Cheese Company. The joint venture operates a retail stall in the French Market to sell cheese, charcuterie, bread, and sandwiches. In early 2016 Seth became the financial officer for Liberty's Kitchen, a nonprofit organization using food to help at-risk kids.

Cleaver & Co.

The first of our stops was Seth's now former company, Cleaver & Co., located in the Uptown area. Unfortunately, the new owners, Daniel Sinclair and his nephew Nathaniel Wallace, were not available. Part of what made the new Cleaver story intriguing to me is that Daniel owns Stirling Wakefield Wagyu Beef in St. Francisville, north of Baton Rouge, where he and Nathaniel raise the steers. They approached Seth initially to sell beef, but instead he negotiated a sale of the store to them. So now Cleaver & Co. has Wagyu beef to accompany its Red Wattle and Tamworth pork.

We talked instead to Becky Mumaw, a lively, engaged ex-farmer and butcher-in-training. Becky and her former partner owned a small farm, named Clawhammer, in upstate New York. She related that despite great animals, a community supported agriculture program, New York City restaurant customers, and gross sales in 2014 of half a million dollars, they only made a four thousand dollar profit, an experience that highlights the difficulties of making a small farm financially viable, even with access to a substantial customer base. Afterward, Becky left for points unknown, and while visiting a friend in New Orleans, she decided to stick around.

She found a job with Nathaniel and Daniel and was thrilled to work with a group of dedicated farmers.

She mentioned Home Place Pastures in Como, Mississippi, as the source for the shop's pork and explained how she gravitated to the farm's mission because it reflected the philosophy at Clawhammer. Later I dug a little deeper and discovered that Como is way up in the northwest corner of Mississippi, not far from Memphis. I wondered why Cleaver would go 350 miles to obtain pork, until I read about the farm, owned by the same family since 1871. Today brothers Marshall and Jemison Bartlett, the next generation of young Bartlett family farmers, operate the farm with help and guidance from their parents, Meg and Mike.

Faced with changes in the pork industry, supermarkets, and agriculture in general, the Bartletts embarked in the direction of heritage hogs and sustainability. They emphasize four principles — ethical treatment, land stewardship, economic sustainability, and community involvement — as the foundation of the farm and the business. While the country has numerous small farms with similar commitments and philosophy, something struck me about Home Place. All of the keystones are important, especially ethical treatment of animals and sustainability, but I think what caught my eye was their statement about land:

> *Land Stewardship: Our land has provided our family's sole livelihood for [five] generations. It takes care of us, and we take care of it. Period. Any activity that detracts from the health of our soils and watershed detracts from the health of our family and our community; we farm accordingly.*[8]

Given our country's challenges with maintaining clean water and healthy soil, this commitment emphasizes the foundational value of land and good soil to grow crops and raise animals. Farm systems in which animals may graze, forage, and root around in turn fertilize the soil and contribute to both being healthier. Home Place Pastures also supplies pork to a number of other NOLA butchers and restaurants for their charcuterie boards.

As Seth, Becky, and I talked, we considered the place of responsibility, honor, and respect for farmers, butchers, and consumers. Seth and Becky argued that greater transparency by farmers, butchers, chefs, and restaurateurs would contribute to stronger consumer confidence. In turn, we agreed consumer trust and deeper understanding about the food system means a willingness to pay a little more for good food grown and raised humanely with close attention to the environment.

Becky, reflecting on her farm and butcher experiences, described the extraordinary conundrum of how to explain to consumers where meat comes from. More than once, while in New York and now in New Orleans, customers asked, "It's muscle? Meat is muscle?" She feels strongly that for the future of small-scale meat farmers and ranchers, all of us must do a much better job of educating consumers about the basics of food. Perhaps the focus on children through school gardens, great-tasting school lunches, better nutrition, and accessibility will eventually change the equation. It is equally important to Becky that more women develop an interest in butchering and curing meat. The challenge becomes how to attract, train, accept, and advance women butchers without the nonsense idea that they cannot manage the tasks.

Seth, on the other hand, decried how standards, in this case not legal protocols but rather ones imposed by major food retailers, often obscure the science behind them. Years ago a question arose about the use of nitrates and nitrites as preservation agents, and some advocates argued consumers should be aware the chemicals might cause cancer, even though cancer was only found in rats consuming very high doses in lab experiments. Since the mid-1990s most research shows the opposite and that "spinach, celery, beets, lettuce, and root vegetables are responsible for most of the dietary intake" of nitrates and nitrites for adults and do not pose a threat to health.[9]

If cured salami and other cured meat contain synthetic nitrates and nitrites, federal law requires labeling as such. Today, for too many consumers, the words "nitrate" and "nitrite" convey a negative image and message, and they will not buy the meat. For example, Whole Foods and Trader Joe's sell bacon and other cured meats labeled as "uncured" because they do not have "synthetic nitrates or nitrites," meaning manufactured ones. However, many companies use celery salt that contains naturally occurring nitrates or nitrites, for exactly the same rationale as the use of synthetics: safety and color. The label for Trader Joe's "Uncured Apple Smoked Bacon" proclaims in large print "No Nitrates* or Nitrites Added." The asterisk highlights a small flag that states "except those naturally occurring in celery powder." Given that most of us ingest more of these "naturally occurring" chemicals when we eat celery or other vegetables in our tuna salad, the bacon label may reassure consumers, but in my opinion, it misleads.[10]

As a consumer I prefer transparent and truthful labels; nitrates and nitrites are the same whether from a box of synthetic chemicals or from "spinach, celery, beets, lettuce, and root vegetables." Perhaps we can turn down the rhetorical heat and help educate consumers about nitrates and nitrites without frightening them. Now that I think about it, those vegetables would make a great salad with a hot cured or uncured bacon dressing!

Seth and I spent several days on a whirlwind tour of New Orleans restaurants, large and small, all with charcuterie programs. In part because of Hurricane Katrina's disruption of lives and livelihoods, over the past decade established chefs and newcomers reinterpreted the bedrock Cajun and Creole cuisines in both traditional and innovative ways. Boudin, Andouille, and smoked sausage now emerge with new flavors, while reminding us of their roots. Visits to restaurants Ancora, Boucherie, Domenica, Mariza, and Primitivo helped me discover a number of commonalities and connections between chefs, suppliers, and visions about dry-cured meat.

Oh yes, we ate at each of them; my metabolism must have cranked up, because after five days I had not gained an ounce. Maybe we should have eaten more! However, it wasn't until I had an opportunity to digest everything from coppa and information to rillettes and professional relationships did I see how various loops connect and overlap.

One example since Katrina is the presence and ingenuity of Donald Link, whose many restaurants emphasized fine charcuterie, set a high bar of excellence, and attracted young chefs with skills in dry curing. If you are a genealogist, graph the professional connections and overlaps. One beneficiary of Link's interest in charcuterie is New Orleanian Kris Doll, whom I met in 2013 at Cleaver. Kris worked at San Francisco's Perbacco, where he learned how to make traditional Italian salumi with an emphasis on Piedmontese specialties. In 2008 Link persuaded Kris to come home, and he helped launch Cochon Butcher's program.

Doll's next stop was A Mano restaurant, now closed, owned by Panamanian Adolfo Garcia, another leader in the city's food renaissance. Garcia is also a partner in Ancora with Adrien Chelette. Let's add in Nick Martin, who was sous-chef at A Mano, worked with Kris, and now runs Primitivo, another Garcia restaurant! By now you should begin to see a picture of community involvement. Admittedly, a few times it felt as if I just heard the song and more than once the tune picked up again. In 2015 Kris opened his own business, Shank Charcuterie, a full service butchery in the Faubourg Marigny district.[11]

Through multiple dialogues, stretched boundaries, innovations, we're seeing traditional culture constantly in vibrant motion. By themselves these represent clear aspects of any fast-paced food city. For New Orleans, with its unique history and Katrina's aftershocks, the dynamic environment translates into new food ideas and, for us, charcuterie plates.

Mariza

One conversation I had was with Ian Schnoebelen, co-owner of Mariza, the oldest chef and dean of the group we interviewed. A native Hawaiian, Schnoebelen grew up in Southern California, started kitchen work at fifteen, and three years later was a hotel sous-chef. After stops in NOLA, Albuquerque, and England, he returned in 2000 to cook at several New Orleans and Las Vegas places. When Hurricane Katrina hit in 2005, Ian and his partner, Laurie Casebonne, were working at Lilette. They evacuated to Alabama but returned to New Orleans to open Iris in 2006 in the Riverbend district. Iris's subsequent relocation to the French Quarter in 2008 became an opportunity for Nathanial Zimet, who bought the former space and opened Boucherie. The tune returns!

A statement Ian made in 2006 after he and Laurie opened Iris sums up the energy and optimistic vision of so many New Orleanians that ten years later is definitely playing out:

> *New Orleans is like a brand new city in a lot of ways. The community we have now is smaller, it's more intimate and I'm happy to be on the first wave of new things opening here. I think people will be looking for the springtime of New Orleans. We're at the point where new things can crop up.[12]*

In 2013, after an inspiring trip to Italy, Ian and Laurie opened Mariza in Faubourg Marigny, downriver from the French Quarter. Over the past twenty years, Marigny, an area mostly spared from Katrina's destruction, witnessed considerable demographic change and rehabilitation of the area's nineteenth-century homes. Ian buys hogs for Mariza from Home Place Pastures and developed an extensive salumi program to highlight the quality of the farm's hogs. He cures everything in a small cabinet with such Italian items as coppa, speck, lardo, prosciutto, bresaola, and Louisiana-inspired headcheese. He points out that Mariza represents some of the evolution of New Orleans' restaurant resurrection, if not renaissance.

Ancora

Even before Hurricane Katrina, the uptown Freret district had witnessed considerable loss of its population, with many vacant or dilapidated buildings as a consequence. However, post-Katrina the community has undergone a renaissance driven in part by new restaurants and residents. In 2011 Adolfo Garcia and partner Chip Apperson, former classmates in New York, debuted the High Hat Café in a former bakery, abandoned after Katrina. Simultaneously, Garcia, with another partner, Jeffrey Talbot, opened Restaurant Ancora, right next door. These places are in addition to several other Garcia restaurant ventures around the city.

For Ancora, Talbot and Garcia developed a wood-fired pizza menu, ordered a handmade oven from Naples, and agreed to follow the guidelines of the Associazione Verace Pizza Napoletana. The organization seeks to promote and protect "true Neapolitan pizza," whose criteria dictate only four ingredients for dough — flour, water, salt, and yeast — and four basic types of pizza, to which the partners agreed. They also wanted salumi, so Kris Doll moved over from A Mano to set up the curing, and Adrien Chelette became a key figure in production of cured meats.

Adrien grew up in Lake Charles, near the Louisiana-Texas border, and in his midteens was washing dishes at local restaurants. By age twenty Adrien was cooking at the Snake River Grill in Jackson Hole, Wyoming. Returning to NOLA in 2011, he helped open Ancora. Adrien and Kris collaborated on the salumi and soon were buying acorn-fed Berkshire/Duroc crossbred hogs from Chappapeela Farms in Amite City, Louisiana, to make their products. After Jeff Talbot left, Adrien and restaurant manager Bryn Thompson became partners with Garcia.

We sat down in a room dominated by the beautiful domed brick and ceramic pizza oven. Since it was early afternoon, they were just building the hot coals needed for evening dinner. Too bad: When ready, it takes only a few minutes in the 900°F space to bake, cook, and melt the ingredients. As consolation Adrien brought us an Italian-inspired salumi plate with Toscano and other dried salami, coppa, pancetta that we ate raw (outstanding), 'nduja, and sanguinaccio, a five-week-aged Italian-style blood salami (truly outstanding).

While Seth and I were meeting with Adrien, Adolfo Garcia dropped by. You would not fail to recognize Adolfo as someone involved deeply in food and cuisine. With high energy and standards, articulate and interested in what his restaurants do every day, he takes considerable pride in the ongoing challenge of serving great food to customers. From watching different Food Network programs, you might typecast Adolfo as just another chef with an ego, but you would be wrong. Ancora reflects his unwavering commitment to New Orleans and his sense of the possibilities offered him since 2005. Adolfo, together with Kris Doll, Adrien Chelette, Bryn Thompson, and Nick Martin at Primitivo, has impacted and influenced the city and the Freret neighborhood since Katrina. The combination of outstanding pizza and innovative charcuterie might not seem all that important. But in my opinion, these different salumieri show the considerable importance of food and cuisine in a positive, attractive street life and local neighborhood economic viability.

Primitivo

The final stop in Adolfo's restaurant circuit is Primitivo, which opened in 2015 with Nick Martin handling the reins. Nick was born in Memphis and by fifteen was washing dishes for his mother. After a short stint in NOLA, he went to the West Coast to earn a culinary degree. An accidental meeting with Adolfo in 2011 led him to work at A Mano and other Garcia restaurants. In 2015 they opened Primitivo on Oretha Castle Haley Boulevard in what was formerly a well-established African-American community. For decades the community lost businesses and, unlike the Freret district, after Katrina did not see an immediate rebirth. Years of hard work by the Efforts of Grace Inc. and the Ashé Cultural Arts Center, the opening of the New Orleans Jazz Market, and relocation of the Southern Food and Beverage Institute to the boulevard finally brought real attention and financial investment to the area.

During our meeting with Nick, he related how Adolfo and the restaurant investors saw great opportunities along the street. In many ways Primitivo reflects this path — identify places where a great, reasonably priced neighborhood restaurant can attract customers and make a go of it. Garcia pointed out that he saw the potential after a meal at Casa Borrega, a Mexican restaurant across the street from where Primitivo now stands. When Seth and I visited, Primitivo had opened only six months earlier and still had a long way to go to establish itself. But our lunch that day and the recent local reviews certainly point to great food and, let's hope, great success.

One key attraction is watching Nick conduct a symphony over a huge coal-fired hearth, in itself a unique tool rarely seen or used in today's kitchens. He can grill using high heat, slow roast with indirect heat, or smoke meat or vegetables; nearly everything on the menu touches the hearth. One of the co-owners, chef Jared Ralls, adamantly argues that the hearth is a return to a basic cooking platform and techniques. In addition to its distinctive presence, Primitivo uses coal, again highly unusual, an extraordinary heat source. I cannot imagine a day spent working next to the hearth, especially during peak summer heat. In some ways, probably the best way to visualize the hearth and life working around it are from engravings of medieval kitchens.

A lunch of spreadable smoked chicken liver, bone marrow croissant, and porchetta loin and belly served with toast and house-made pickled vegetables was simply delicious. During lunch Nick talked about using Louisiana wild boar. With half a million or more feral hogs in the state, eating them is one small strategy to control the population. The animal has a significant destructive financial and environmental impact on agriculture. Primitivo, like most restaurants and salumi producers using wild boar, buys them from local trappers and farmers. The animals are trapped, held for a week to monitor health, and then slaughtered.

Nick also described how NOLA restaurants now have access to diverse top-notch ingredients from produce to meats. "Coming back to Louisiana at the start of the renaissance of ingredients, it's been great because you can really see the effect it's had on chefs in the city. I think ingredients and accessibility have been huge factors for New Orleans food over the last five years."[13] When we visited in fall 2015, the restaurant's charcuterie was just beginning to get off the ground. Beyond transforming wild boar or locally purchased heritage carcasses into fresh sausage, cured salami, and prosciutto, Nick, Adolfo, and partners contribute to the rebuilding of a neighborhood and its important cultural identity.

Domenica

John Besh, one of New Orleans' most admired and successful restaurateurs, has worked with and nurtured a number of the city's current chefs. Over the years places such as August, Besh Steak, and Lüke established his reputation as a creative chef, entrepreneur, and mentor. For Seth and me the destination was Domenica, Besh's collaboration with executive chef and partner Alon Shaya and home to extraordinary pizza and cured-meat menus. Unfortunately, my trip did not coincide with Alon's schedule, so I interviewed his very capable, articulate chef de cuisine Phil Mariano.

Opened in 2009, Domenica resulted from Shaya's work with Besh, the hurricane, and a year in Italy. Though born in Israel, Alon grew up in Philadelphia, where he learned his grandmother's and mother's kitchen secrets. A Culinary Institute of America (CIA) graduate, he cooked at several places in Las Vegas and St. Louis before arriving in NOLA in 2005 to work at Besh Steak. In 2007 he took a year off with Besh's blessing and went to Italy to study — eat, talk, work in kitchens, eat some more — and learn. And the most important lessons were about himself, cooking, great food, and people. In a 2015 interview Shaya commented about New Orleans:

> *"What I love about this city is its real sense of food community," he continues. "It's going to Willie Mae's for fried chicken, it's eating oysters and crab claws at Curious Oyster, or going to Pascal's Manale or Mosca's. There's no other city in the U.S. that has the present food culture that New Orleans has. I can think of singular dishes from other cities, but I can't think of any city that has a true culture built around food."[14]*

When he returned, Alon and John Besh began plans for Domenica, which opened in 2009. And here we pick up — I'm not kidding; these are facts — Phil Mariano's story. In the 1890s Mariano's great-great-grandparents arrived in New Orleans from Sicily and worked in the sugarcane fields. In late nineteenth- and early twentieth-century Louisiana, Italians often faced considerable discrimination and bigotry. Finding work and a comfortable community was difficult, and many found their way to the city's French Market and its surrounding blocks, which were populated with Italian immigrants. Here in the 1920s Phil's great-grandfather opened a grocery store, and the family lived on the second floor. His grandmother was a local ad agency photographer, and his mother owned and operated several city restaurants, including Back to the Garden; today she cooks at John Besh's Lüke. Talk about apples falling close to the tree!

Food flows through Phil's veins, so much so that one apocryphal story tells how as a three-year-old he used to wrap potatoes in his mom's kitchen while sitting in a cardboard box. As a teenager, when the family moved to Texas, he got a kitchen job and then a culinary degree from CIA in 2008. The following year he spent six months in Florence, Italy, in a self-guided deep immersion into Italian food and cuisine. Returning to NOLA, he started work at Domenica and after quickly showing his skills became chef de cuisine under Alon. The restaurant sent him to Iowa State University to take its short course on cured meats, and from there he managed Domenica's production with Alon's guidance.

Phil explained to me that at August and Lüke, pork fabrication is principally fresh, not cured, sausage with French and German influences and flavors. In 2015 at Domenica Phil was bringing in one Chappapeela Farm Berkshire/Duroc hog every three months, each weighing approximately 180 to 200 pounds. Most of the animal went into Italian salumi: coppa, culatello, guanciale, lardo, lonza, and salami. The initial curing stage of three to five days occurs in a standard walk-in refrigerator, after which each type moves into a fermenting unit. Depending on the type of cured meat, they age from three weeks (generally salami) to a year or more for a special prosciutto. Seth and I sat at the salumi bar facing the display and maturing case, where the final drying stage happens.

I was surprised to learn they make prosciutto only for special occasions and events. Phil explained that since they use a lot of prosciutto every day, it wasn't feasible to produce in-house — approximately eleven pounds or one whole Prosciutto di Parma daily; that is a staggering 3,500 to 4,000 pounds a year! Phil said a sizable portion ends up as toppings on several pizzas. In addition, because the restaurant wants to embrace traditional old-world tastes and flavors, the prosciutto is part of the menu's culinary foundation. The salumi bar contributes to this ambiance and provides the salumiere an opportunity to educate consumers.

The quality of Domenica's salumi is a major attraction of the restaurant. Alon Shaya's vision and Phil Mariano's ability to accomplish consistently distinctive, high-quality cured meats is a wonderful amalgamation of great pork and great talent. In early 2016 I learned Phil became the executive chef at restaurant Josephine Estelle in the newly renovated Ace Hotel in the Warehouse District. The charcuterie program continues at Domenica, as does the purchase of local hogs.

Bourrée at Boucherie

To reach Nathanial Zimet at Boucherie, we drive out St. Charles Avenue, paralleling the streetcar line, past Tulane University, to the Riverbend district. As we approach Carrollton Avenue, Seth points out the levee in the distance; here it rises many feet above the Mississippi River; sadly, not high enough to prevent Katrina's floods that swamped the community. Today the neighborhood is on its way back, with restaurants part of the revival.

Nathanial grew up in North Carolina around plenty of homemade food; in every interview he describes how his mother always had chicken, shrimp, and vegetable stocks in the refrigerator. While at Wake Forest University, he considered law and veterinary medicine, but his experiences working in local restaurants to put himself through school, as well as his family memories, made a culinary career too attractive and compelling. In 2001 he took courses at Le Cordon Bleu in London and Sydney and returned to North Carolina to work at the Fearrington House in Pittsboro. After a series of positions in Durham, he arrived in New Orleans to work at Commander's Palace, Emeril's, and Bank Café, before Katrina shut it down.

He then left for South Florida, where his father lived. One day his dad suggested he build and operate a food truck, a movable barbeque feast, an idea that appealed to him. They secured a loan, a Connecticut company fabricated what became known as the "Que Crawl" or "Purple Truck" for its dramatically painted exterior, and in 2006 he hit the streets of New Orleans. The break came when Tipitina's, one of the city's best-known music clubs, allowed him to sell food in front of its building. But his dream, one he'd envisioned for several years, was to open his own restaurant.

When Laurie Casebonne and Ian Schnoebelen decided to move Iris from Riverbend to the French Quarter, Nathanial and James Denio, his purple truck assistant, moved into the space and opened Boucherie. Their menu combined traditional Louisiana ingredients, flavors, and textures with riffs from Italy and Asia to create unique dishes. Despite the restaurant's small size, it was an immediate success, and scoring a reservation was really difficult. Nathanial, a self-proclaimed porkophile, knows quality and for many years purchased Home Place Pastures hogs for all of the restaurant's fresh and cured pork. He installed a "Cajun microwave" — a meat-smoking box — outside that uses oak and pecan wood to flavor and preserve products.

After Nathanial's Cajun microwave comment, I asked him about the name Boucherie and its connection to South Louisiana. My question immediately sparked a change in his demeanor as he grew serious and reflective. He wants to create an identity different from the city's prevalent cuisines and traditions and yet be deeply respectful of place, culture, and history. He was confident they could take risks, to create not some bastardized fusion but food linked to historical roots, while also moving in new directions.

The Cajun microwave is the ideal utensil of the past, while a curing cabinet opens the door to parallel methods for preservation. Nathanial pointed to 2010, when he became more aware and knowledgeable of the history and cultural significance of the boucherie in South Louisiana. He described his epiphany as both an emotional and a psychological experience and said he wants to contribute to a greater appreciation and understanding of the ritual's value.

Lâche Pas Boucherie et Cuisine

To bring the cured-meat story full circle and learn more about boucherie and Cajun cuisine, Seth and I headed west to Lafayette to meet Toby Rodriguez at Johnson's Boucanière, one of the oldest and best places for boudin. I first heard about Toby several years ago from Alessandra Rellini, a native of Genoa, Italy; Vermont hog farmer; and professor of psychology at the University of Vermont. At the time she was contemplating creating a fresh and cured-meat business using her hogs and thought about inviting him to participate. While a visit didn't materialize, her meat business has soared. I finally met Toby in Denver at the 2015 Slow Meat conference, and we agreed on a visit during my research trip to NOLA and Cajun country.

Perhaps the most outspoken advocate and teacher about boucherie, Toby is a traveling butcher, chef, and educator on Cajun traditions, especially around all things pork. We sat down to a lunch of boudin, ribs, and pulled pork, prepared by Greg Walls, owner of Johnson's. We immediately began a far-ranging conversation about culture, taste, loss of identity, family, traditions and rituals, and the sorry state of how America eats. My notes became covered with grease spots as I attempted to write everything down.

Toby was born in Breaux Bridge, east of Lafayette, where his father was a sugarcane farmer. He points out that a number of Spanish last names show up in the region, many of them connected to sugarcane industry. The family ran a diversified farm and conducted an annual boucherie. He left home at seventeen for a career as an actor, chef, sculptor, furniture designer, and writer. In many ways a true Renaissance man, he is deeply rooted in fundamental connections between how and what we eat and the values and practices lost or often overlooked in today's world. In many ways Toby is a historian, a public advocate for the ways his Cajun roots relate to family, community, rituals, foodways, worship, and respect. Part of what drives him is the region called the Cajun Prairie that includes Evangeline, Acadia, and portions of Jefferson Davis and St. Landry Parishes. Beyond its great music is the unique prairie art of smoked meats, sausages, pulled pork, Tasso, and boudin.

He lives today in Grand Coteau, a small village north of Lafayette. In 2011, after television personality Anthony Bourdain filmed a boucherie, Toby realized he could apply his knowledge to educate people about America's food system and the loss of cultural health. With a group of friends and colleagues, he created Lâche Pas Boucherie, a real-life demonstration of the ancient ritual of communal slaughter. Everything he does during a demonstration articulates what it means to be connected to your food.

In many ways Lâche Pas Boucherie ties closely to the New Orleans and national phenomenon of nose-to-tail butchery and cuisine. Toby feels, however, many of these experiences are too much hype and show, rather than a deeper expression of life and survival. Before they kill a hog, the entire crew prays and gives thanks, a sacrament, an offering to the animal. For Toby such practice is a homage to the animal, place, and family, and a 180-degree turn in the opposite direction from today's commercial slaughter and processing.

He acknowledges our society will not return to boucherie to slaughter and manage winter food supplies. But the attitude, practices, and warped culture of what we do at a commodity level to supply meat could be vastly different. He points out how our language evolved; you start with a hog or pig and arrive at pork; the former is alive, the latter is dead.

Describing the physical, emotional, and psychological aspects of slaughter, Toby portrays the reactions — taking a life; feeling the body temperature warmth; the smell of blood deep in the nostrils, a primal connection. Yes, while theater is part of what he does, Toby wants to touch life in ways the vast majority of us have never experienced. In America and most of the world where our proteins — beef, chicken, fish, and pork, for example — are delivered, not slaughtered or eviscerated in front of us, we need not think about the process. For this very large group of humanity, survival does not depend on hunting, fishing, or farming, and in the space of maybe a hundred to two hundred years, we have forgotten the difficulty of putting food on the table.

Toby and his Lâche Pas Boucherie colleagues teach us something else about food origins. Cured meat was always about survival, ways to ensure we made it through winter or hard times. Life depended on the oral passage of skills from one generation to the next, a communication and transfer of knowledge and culture. For most Americans today survival isn't the issue; we are able to choose what, when, and how we eat. So in addition to the loss of skills, we no longer feel, appreciate, or understand the cultural context. Toby wants to remind us that cultural survival is central to place, family, and community.

In his 2014 book *Charcutería: The Soul of Spain*, Jeffrey Weiss, a self-described hog and pork fanatic, takes readers on a journey to Spain and its centuries-old *matanza del cerdo* (pig slaughter), the annual ritual of slaughter and curing. He describes passionately his participation in the ceremony and how everyone involved expressed reverence, deep cultural connection, and gratitude. Weiss argues in a similar voice to Toby's that to move forward in today's unbalanced food system requires going back to earlier human-animal relations. Like Native Americans who gave thanks to a creator and the game they killed, Weiss described El Maestro, the lead butcher of the matanza del cerdo, who showed respect and admiration for the hogs by the nature of the killing.

Not only does the quality of the slaughter rely on the animal's emotional state in this moment and in the preceding moments of its impeding sacrifice, but a quick death is a matter of respect. Anything less would be disrespectful to the ancient custom, to its modern practice, to the sacrifice of these majestic animals, and to the families that raised the animals over the past years. In fact, even the verb that El Maestro used to describe the action — *sacrificar* — denotes the accepted responsibility and gravity of his work.[15]

Toby Rodriguez and Jeffrey Weiss share an understanding, a reverence, and an appreciation for this concept of sacrifice and know that emotional and spiritual openness changes how we think and act as humans, as well as how we obtain our food. I see these same sentiments in the manner in which New Orleans' chefs and butchers express their connections to Louisiana culture and how their charcuterie and salumi programs reflect traditional methods and contemporary innovations.

More than once during my conversation with Toby, I heard echoes of Slow Food's Carlo Petrini. One of the organization's initial concerns was the loss of regional foods around the world because of fast food and the growth of industrial agriculture and food production. I recall the many times I defined part of the mission as the preservation and celebration of regional foods around the world. It was about how the pleasures of the table, any table anywhere, could draw people together to celebrate, love and commune, argue and debate, teach and learn. Carlo spoke as well about how these traditions, foods, and ideas are legacies or, in his words, the patrimony we contribute and bequeath to future generations. I see Toby and Lâche Pas Boucherie doing exactly that and applaud their efforts.

Johnson's Boucanière

As I write this from cold Vermont, a hot boudin from Johnson's Boucanière in Lafayette would go down really well right now. Greg Walls, owner of Johnson's, joined our conversation and described where boudin sausage fit into the Cajun universe painted by Toby. His father-in-law, Wallace Johnson (Greg called him Mr. Wallace more than once) owned Johnson's Grocery in Eunice, established by his father, Arneastor Johnson, in 1939. Mr. Wallace made boudin only on Saturdays, 1,200 pounds of fresh and smoked sausage that sold out by noontime; in my book that is powerful testimony to a great boudin.

Greg and his wife, Lori, met in college, and he ran an architecture and design firm. But after the Johnson grocery store closed in 2005, she refused to buy any other local sausage. By chance they discovered Mr. Wallace's recipes hidden behind a doorjamb in the old store. So Lori and Greg started to make small quantities to cook on a converted outdoor grill. Soon the word (or was it the aroma?) spread that Greg and Lori were making boudin and Tasso. From a few pounds demand increased weekly to the point at which they were making fifty or more.

After Katrina the Walls sold their house, bought land in Lafayette, and built a new Johnson's Boucanière. Greg's design background helped them craft a building to fit architecturally into its new community. Lori went to work on the old recipes to replicate them and develop new flavors. Today she still mixes the spices and keeps the ratios secret.

Frustrated by the commercial smokers offered for sale, Greg designed one to manage the different types of smoked meats: prairie-style sausage, Tasso, pulled pork, and smoked finger ribs (no bone, from the shoulder). Following Mr. Wallace's practice, he uses oak as the base wood for coals, with green cherry and pecan for smoke. A few practitioners use sugarcane, but Greg feels cane adds too much flavor at the expense of the pork taste. Greg talked about how he developed sensitivity to the weather's effects on smoke. Every morning he faces a different reality around temperature and humidity and must adjust the amount of smoke to achieve optimum flavor and color.

When I asked about breeds, Greg mentioned something called "Blue Butt," a cross between a Yorkshire and a Hampshire that actually has blue spots across its hindquarters. It turns out that a number of local farms raise Blue Butts, and Greg says the flavor and quality of the fat and meat are outstanding. Judging from our empty plates, the Blue Butt hog definitely makes great prairie-smoked meat and boudin.

On the drive back to New Orleans, Seth and I reflected on Toby and Greg's energy and commitment to support and sustain their communities. While pointing to similar characteristics in the city itself, I felt a broad sense of purpose and resolve, at least in the people and places we visited in Louisiana. Food plays a central role in sustaining communities as economic drivers but sometimes most importantly in celebrations of place and people. Of all the places I ventured while researching this book, I hope with great sincerity to understand and reflect a small part of what makes New Orleans and Cajun country unique places in America. Cured meat is a small sliver of how to appreciate and taste part of both the legacy and the future. *Le bon temps roulé* — let the good times roll!

CHAPTER SIX

From Wurst to Szalámi to Салама

*A mighty good sausage stuffer
was spoiled when the man became a poet.*

— EUGENE FIELD

Today, standing at the northeast corner of Eighty-Sixth Street and Second Avenue in Manhattan and looking north, you can just make out several high-rise apartment buildings at Ninetieth Street on the west side of the avenue. They stand on a portion of what was once the Jacob Ruppert Brewery, a complex of thirty-five brick buildings with a labor force of a thousand workers. Next door was George Ehret's Hell Gate Brewery, whose operation in 1877 was the country's largest. The two enormous breweries occupied entire city blocks from Ninetieth to Ninety-Fourth Streets and from Second to Third Avenues.

As symbols of German impact on the United States, these breweries, as well as Yuengling, Schell, Anheuser-Busch, and Pabst, anchored immigrant communities across the country. From the 1830s to the 1870s, fleeing economic hardships and political unrest, nearly one and a half million Germans arrived in the States. In the 1850s more than eight hundred thousand immigrants disembarked in New York City alone, making it at one point the third largest German-speaking city in the world.

Mid-nineteenth-century Germans settled in the city's Lower East Side, built churches, schools, small businesses, and numerous beer halls. For decades the community, known as *Kleindeutschland* (Little Germany), or called Dutchtown by the Irish, was the focus of German culture in the United States. By the late nineteenth century, second-generation German-Americans were moving north to what became known as Yorkville, its heart the intersection of Eighty-Sixth Street, called the "German Broadway," and Second Avenue.

But a disaster in 1904 changed New York's German communities forever. That summer a paddleboat headed upriver from Kleindeutschland, packed with over 1,300 passengers, mostly women and children. The boat, the *General Slocum*, caught fire, a tragedy that resulted in over a thousand casualties. With so many families and friends directly impacted, the entire neighborhood was affected deeply by the loss, and numerous suicides followed. In the aftermath an exodus took place as thousands of German-Americans, unable to bear the neighborhood's pain, moved north to Yorkville.

For the next fifty to sixty years, the blocks surrounding Eighty-Sixth Street and Second Avenue became the heart of German identity in New York; the district boundaries ran west from First to Park Avenue and from Seventy-Ninth to Ninety-Second Street. Yorkville was mostly a German working and middle-class neighborhood, dotted with food stores, restaurants, other small businesses, and civic organizations. Austro-Hungarians, Czechs, and Slovaks lived south of the district, and they too enjoyed businesses and services reflective of old-world culture. Although Yorkville remained the center of German-American life, by 1930 many Germans relocated to Queens, a borough known then for its suburban character.

Schaller & Weber

Again standing on the northeast corner of Eighty-Sixth and Second, if you turn to your left, avoiding the current construction activity, you face the entrance to Schaller & Weber, a German butcher and wurst maker, founded in 1937. Ferdinand Schaller was born in 1904 in Metz, a three-thousand-year-old settled area, and now a city, in Alsace-Lorraine. For hundreds of years the region witnessed constant warfare and conquest, switching back and forth between French and German rule. In 1871, after victory in the Franco-Prussian War, Germany took control, and at the end of World War I, the region reverted back to French governance. In 1918 Ferdinand decided to become a butcher rather than follow the family trade as a plasterer, and he became an apprentice in the city of Neuhausen, Germany, about two hundred miles east of Metz in France. After a five-year training program, he worked in different German cities until 1927, when he found himself in Hamburg, a port city on Germany's north coast.

Schaller became a chef onboard an ocean liner bound for New York, where he disembarked. The city offered him many opportunities, since German and Italian butchers had excellent reputations as meat cutters with the highest standards of cleanliness and quality. Upon his arrival Ferdinand and Fritz Winkler set up a butcher shop at Eighty-Ninth Street and First Avenue. At that time Yorkville extended from First to Park Avenue between Seventy-Ninth and Ninety-Second Streets, so the store on the outskirts of the district did not enjoy the best commercial location. In the mid-1930s Ferdinand met Bavarian-born Anton "Tony" Weber, who had arrived in New York early in the decade. Tony had also trained as a butcher and sausage maker, and he and Ferdinand at some point worked for Stahl-Meyer, another of many German-American cured-meat companies in New York City.

In 1938 Tony Weber contacted his friend Ferdinand about a shop near the center of the community, and the two men, who possessed complementary skills and motivation, moved to Second Avenue, just a few feet from "German Broadway." A key to the company's financial success was the eventual purchase of the building, a decision that reverberates today at a time when rents for small businesses in Manhattan are unaffordable. Within a few years Schaller & Weber established its reputation for excellent fresh meat and numerous German-style cured and smoked wurst and ham. Just like the Espositos in Brooklyn, whom we meet in a subsequent chapter, they obtained excellent pork from New Jersey farms, just across the George Washington Bridge from the city.

The German curing and smoking techniques and practices derive from fundamental differences in climate compared to those of Italy and Spain. In Southern Europe the seasonal changes provide at least one period in which air-drying is possible. In addition, though winters may be very cold, unlike in Northern Europe the risks of frozen meat are small. In Eastern and Northern Europe, however, conditions are both too cold and too damp to ensure safe preservation techniques without additional treatment. For millennia salami and ham were often smoked to further stabilize and protect the meat from spoilage. Germany identifies more than 1,500 types of sausage in three categories: Kochwurst (cooked, 350 types), Brühwurst (scalded, 800 types), and Rohwurst (raw, 60 types), each of which requires different preparations and processing. The extraordinary number reflects regional differences in grind, spicing, degree of smoke, taste and flavor variations, and aging and curing approaches.

Walking into the Schaller & Weber store in the late 1930s, you would see counters and display cases filled with fresh meat and arrays of these cooked, scalded, and raw sausages, all prepared on premises. Ferdinand Schaller debuted the first American-made Black Forest ham. I can imagine walking into the store and being greeted by aromas of smoke, pork, sauerkraut, and mustard, with plenty of rustic breads to accompany the meats. But the outbreak of World War II dramatically changed the company, with the internment of Ferdinand Schaller during the entire war for his pro-German politics. The disruptive effects continued even after the war's end in 1945, and in 1949 Tony Weber sold his share of the business to Ferdinand and moved to Erie, Pennsylvania. There he and his son Magnus purchased the Smith butcher shop and shifted the business from retail meat to commercial manufacture of wieners, sausages, deli meats, bacon, and hams. Today the firm is known as Smith Provision Company, and a third generation of Webers continues to produce outstanding processed meats known throughout western Pennsylvania and the Midwest.

After the war and Tony Weber's departure, Ferdinand was confronted with significant demographic changes in Yorkville as many of the remaining German and eastern European residents left the community. Many German businesses established in the 1920s and 1930s closed or moved. The hog farms just over the bridge disappeared, and Schaller had to go farther to buy pork from farms in western New Jersey and eastern Pennsylvania. The advent of supermarkets in the 1950s, attracting customers who wanted less expensive meat, affected the shop's fresh meat counter. To grow and maintain the business, Ferdinand opened five to six franchise stores in Brooklyn and Queens and in 1959 built a processing factory in Astoria to supply them with products. In 1964 the company expanded and renovated the existing store, and in the 1970s sons Frank and Ralph took over the operation. By introducing vacuum-sealed products, they expanded production and shipped their products nationwide for use in deli and meat cases.

Frank's son, Jeremy Schaller, was born in 1979 and by his eighth birthday was already helping out in the store. He went to Pace University and worked in the store during the summer but then took a different path, choosing initially to work in the fashion business. In the mid- to late 2000s, he returned to the company as brand manager and national sales director and in 2013 took over as owner and full-time operator of Schaller & Weber.

Jeremy was confronted by several problems, both old and new. Perhaps the most immediate problem was the construction of the new Second Avenue Subway and its Eighty-Sixth Street station. The first plans from the Metropolitan Transportation Authority (MTA) called for the demolition of the entire southeast corner and the destruction of Gracie's on 2nd Diner and Schaller & Weber. Although the MTA scrapped this part of the plan, construction beginning in 2010 disrupted business by reducing customer access to the front doors, as well as spreading dust everywhere. Jeremy says the company saw a 20 percent drop in revenue, and while finances ultimately stabilized, until the station's completion in 2016, Schaller & Weber carefully monitored its market and growth.

Another essential ingredient in the store's ability to stay in business was ownership of its buildings, the original store and the expanded space. Jeremy walked me outside and pointed to several first-floor businesses on Second Avenue that pay upward of forty-five thousand dollars a month in rent. Simply avoiding this cost keeps them solvent. Similar situations exist for the next-door Heidelberg Restaurant, where sales dropped 40 percent because of the subway, and Glaser's Bake Shop on First Avenue between Eighty-Sixth and Eighty-Seventh Streets. As with Esposito, Biellese, and Muncan, discussed later, if they did not own their buildings, they might be just memories and for me quite bittersweet ones at that.

While running a food business in a construction site presents obvious difficulties, building consumer interest in German food in a changing community was a different challenge. Newcomers didn't possess the same tastes or food experiences as the existing, aging clientele. When Jeremy Schaller assumed reins of the business in 2013, he needed to update it. "Our clientele was mostly old German ladies. We had to adjust and attract younger customers, new customers, and local customers," he said. But at the same time he didn't want to relinquish the company's heritage as first-rate purveyors of pork and sausage.[1]

Jeremy saw positive shifts in Yorkville's demographics. Many younger professionals and families who could not afford to live in gentrified Brooklyn discovered that less expensive areas, such as Yorkville, actually existed in Manhattan, and they relocated. While not German speakers, these newcomers, familiar with American craft beer, also appreciated great German beer, as well as American artisan cheese and the growing dry-cured meat renaissance. To attract these newcomers to Yorkville, Jeremy renovated the store, modified some salami recipes to accommodate smaller sizes, and added a beer cooler stocked with hard-to-find German beers.

He applied his experience in branding to update the product packaging. Since the company's signature product is double-smoked bacon — cured, cooked, and hardwood smoked — he now buys all of the bacon bellies from duBreton, a certified humane pork supplier in Quebec, founded in 1944. The company also supplies loins, used to make Lachsschinken, a center cut "boneless loin of pork, rolled in a thin layer of fat to assure tenderness and moisture, cured and smoked. Tastes amazingly similar to smoked salmon."[2]

Eastern Pennsylvania farms continue to supply the company with hams to make Black Forest and Westphalian versions. In addition, Schaller & Weber uses trim and variety meat from these farms to make pâtés, spreads such as liverwurst, and cervelat, the German equivalent of salami. In 2016 the company relocated its production facility to Easton, Pennsylvania. Jeremy said he needed to modernize the Astoria plant to meet federal requirements but faced significant capital costs to retrofit the building. In Easton they are only a few minutes away from their supplier farms, and the interstate enables broader national distribution.

In 2015 Jeremy opened Schaller's Stube Sausage Bar, adjacent to the retail store, in the former receiving and cold-storage rooms, complete with overhead rails across the ceiling to move carcasses. The small room, or *stube* in German, offers Berlin-style street food with a handful of seats and a sidewalk counter and serves different sausages cooked to order with various toppings. The small restaurant reflects family heritage, Jeremy's experiences in Germany, and his vision of Yorkville's future. The counter faces Second Avenue and the subway construction. At lunchtime lots of workers emerge from the tunnel to enjoy some fresh air, sun, and a bratwurst, a knackwurst, or a crazy concoction called "The Berlin Wall," with a half-pound kielbasa smothered in a roll. Not sure if eating one of these is the best midday break for a construction worker, but they sell and also attract media attention. Beyond the subway workers, the Schaller's Stube became a hit with local residents, including grandparents from an earlier era of the store and millennials, who stop in for a sandwich and a glass of Austrian or German beer on tap, including Bitburger and Stiegl. In 2016 they opened an outdoor space behind the Stube for lighter fare and good beer.

While the Stube offers great street food, it also introduced a new audience to the flagship Schaller & Weber store next door. With the opening of the new subway extension and the Eighty-Sixth Street station, the store and Stube are accessible from anywhere in New York. One of the few remaining original German wurst producers, Schaller & Weber nurtures an important legacy of northern European charcuterie in America.

Muncan Food Corporation

A map of New York's subway system resembles a jumble of sausages splayed in different directions. For first-time riders the maze of tracks, trains, letters, and numbers is often daunting. And yet, for New Yorkers and visitors alike, the subway entrances and exits are unique gateways to new worlds of buildings, languages and sounds, appearances, smells, and food.

Traveling the subway to Astoria, Queens, you emerge into communities both old and new. In the early seventeenth century, the Dutch settled in the area, followed in the mid-nineteenth century by German farmers and merchants. In the late nineteenth century, the area, named after John Jacob Astor, whose family were butchers in Manhattan, rapidly urbanized and became the home of Italian, Jewish, Czech, Polish, and Slovak immigrants. Today you see vestiges of these settlements mixed together with mid- to late twentieth-century arrivals from Greece, Cyprus, China, India, Korea, Mexico, and Romania. Beyond language, religious practice, and other cultural characteristics, each new arrival introduced food ideas and, very often, desire for products from the old country.

On a beautiful early December day with a temperature more like October's, I climb out of the Forty-Sixth Street subway stop in Astoria to visit Muncan Foods. Turning left on Broadway, I walk northwest; the streetscape is the opposite of Manhattan's tall buildings. The one- to three-story buildings house small Chinese, Indian, and Mexican restaurants; a couple of typical pizza places and delis; and a health food and organic store. A sign above a storefront announces "Adriatic Meat Ćevapi Beef Veal Pork Lamb" — clearly a Balkan store, right next door to Los Manjares (The Delicacies) Mexican restaurant.

I love the juxtaposition of these foods, but what the heck is ćevapi? Turns out it is a delicious fresh, grilled, finger-size sausage made of minced meat, a traditional Balkan food with origins in Persia and Turkey. Like a kofta kebab, ćevapi are handmade from ground beef, lamb, and pork or mixed meats, together with garlic, paprika, and other spices. Depending on whether you are Catholic, Jewish, or Muslim, the butcher's hand is guided differently for the meat in your sausage. For me the ćevapi reflects the ethnic diversity of both the Balkans and Astoria's Broadway.

Across the street from the Adriatic Meat shop, I see "Muncan Foods Corporation" in bold letters above a small green awning proclaiming "Homemade Meat Products." Neither the sign nor the window display prepare me for the olfactory experience as I step through the door. Waves of palatable fragrances engulf me — smoke; meat; spices, especially garlic and paprika; and mushrooms — a nirvana of aromas, a tease of what lies within. The smells communicate a diversity of great cured meats, quality and excellence, the old country, and traditional practices. I'm salivating already in anticipation of tasting and buying some of these extraordinary салама (Serbian for salami). I'm greeted by Marko Stefanovic, third-generation Serbian-American, who manages the Muncan Foods businesses.

Originally farmers from Romania, the Muncan family settled in Vojvodina, Serbia, where they continued to work the soil. The family patriarch, knowing the difficulties faced by farmers, counseled his grandsons, Tima and Jonel, born in the mid-1940s, to find a different occupation. His statement, "Everyone needs to eat forever," directed them into formal training in classical butchery in the late 1950s. Their four-year education, underwritten by the Yugoslav government and similar to traditional apprentice programs, dovetailed closely with the Vojvodina tradition of curing and drying meats.

In 1971 Tima and Jonel Muncan moved to New York City and settled in Astoria. Their butchering skills landed them a variety of jobs, some full- and others part-time, in different traditional European shops and delicatessens. In 1978 the brothers bought Hauser's German Butcher Shop on Broadway, established in 1932, a place where they had worked previously. The brothers converted the shop into a full-service deli with fresh and some cured products. Marko, Tima's grandson, said the community respected German and Italian butchers for their commitment to sell only the best animals while maintaining the highest standards of hygiene and cleanliness. The Muncan brothers also embraced these qualities and soon established themselves as one of the best butcher shops in Queens. Tima and Jonel, knowing how to buy superior quality carcasses, offered patrons the best cuts of meat in their shop.

Initially the company purchased its USDA-inspected meat from vendors at the Hunts Point Cooperative Market distribution center in the Bronx. Marko relates that "the Hunts Point vendors were our earliest suppliers . . . from when we opened until we made other contacts or companies moved out of the coop to other areas around the country. . . . Our vendors . . . for the past 15 years or so are scattered around the Northeast, including a couple still at Hunts Point."[3]

The Muncan family traveled frequently back to Serbia, where Eleonora, Tima's daughter, met Mike Stefanovic, and they decided to marry. Although Mike was a native Serbian, born in the early 1960s, the couple decided not to remain, so in the early 1980s Eleonora and Mike came to the States, and he began working for Tima. While his father-in-law and uncle taught him the trade, Mike understood the basics of handcrafted sausage and cured-meat products from knowledge gathered at home. His family, like many other Serbians, slaughtered hogs and put up meat in the late fall and early winter. The combination of traditional folkways with intense training from the *majstors*, or masters — Tima and Jonel — helped establish Mike's stature. After a few short years in the States, he took over a second Muncan store in Ridgewood, Queens.

While the shops sold mostly fresh meat from the original store's 1978 opening to the mid-1990s, the local community was very enthusiastic about the company's Serbian-, Hungarian-, and Romanian-style cured meats and products. In the 1980s the store produced between twenty and thirty types of cured meats, especially bacons. The other neighborhood European-style butcher shops sold a variety of charcuterie and salami but did not make their own.

The collapse of the Iron Curtain in 1989, coupled with the breakup of Yugoslavia and the subsequent civil war, brought new immigrants to the United States, many of whom settled in Queens. Despite the considerable demographic changes in the borough over the past thirty years, the Muncan businesses thrived because of the community and the company's willingness to adapt to the foodways of new neighbors. Patrons at both stores asked frequently whether Mike could make old-country Serbian, Hungarian, and Romanian products, and he would in turn ask them to bring back examples of cured meats they wanted. His rare ability to intuitively analyze the smell, taste, and texture of each product enabled him to reproduce the old-country favorites, including, for example, Hungarian-style paprika bacon and sausage and *panceta* (pancetta) from the Istria region of Croatia, close to the border with Italy.

By the 1990s the company made forty different eastern European cured meats, and its reputation for outstanding butchering and curing attracted new customers as Astoria changed. But nationwide changes in the distribution of food, especially fresh meat, had a significant impact on the Muncan butcher shop. With new supermarkets offering less expensive meat, customers shifted their buying patterns, and the shop could not compete on price for fresh meat, regardless of its quality.

In 2000 Mike's son, Marko, who helped out in the shop as a child, joined the company after obtaining his MBA. Over the past sixteen years, Mike and Marko have guided the company in new directions to fulfill the needs of a changing community as it evolved and diversified with new immigrants. In 1995 the company sold 95 percent fresh meat and 5 percent cured. Twenty years later the percentages are the opposite and equally remarkable: Almost 100 percent of sales happens in the two shops, where they sell over a thousand pounds of cured meat a week. The company resisted the calls to wholesale its meats, in part because its USDA license permits it only to sell direct to customers. Wholesaling cured meats requires a different level of inspection and regulation; because of that, coupled with a desire to protect the company's reputation, they decided not to expand.

But most important, they like the close interaction with customers; trust and integrity are essential values to them. Without question, while quality products attract customers, Marko talks enthusiastically about the staff's willingness to go the extra mile and how customer devotion pays off. "Our staff makes every effort to learn multiple languages to give our customers a better experience. Much of our staff has English as a second language, but within several months quickly pick up conversational Romanian, Hungarian, [and] Serbo-Croatian, etc." The staff will arrive early if a customer "calls that they wanted to shop, but can't wait until we open" or "stay late . . . to pick up an order after they leave work."[4]

Like similar old-world-style stores in New York and other metropolitan areas, customer loyalty expresses itself in remarkable ways. "Our local customers and those who have moved away, but still make the weekly trip from Jersey or Pennsylvania, are the true heart of our business because without them Muncan Food wouldn't exist."

To attract new customers Marko began to develop additional cured meats made from beef and lamb to attract Muslim residents from the neighborhood. For example, they make a whole dry-cured leg of lamb, prosciuttos from duck and lamb, and beef and lamb salami. Since a large proportion of their workers are Hispanic, Marko developed a chorizo for them.

The company's ability to develop distinctive, consistently high-quality products positioned them well as the renewed interest in locally made charcuterie and salami took off and television and print media sought out cured-meat artisans. The city's food movement literally opened the door to new visitors. Today, while neighborhood and former residents are a mainstay, convenient subway stops welcome customers from other parts of New York.

"I believe that love and care for our customers translates to all areas of our work, from cleanliness to friendly service, and believe our customers notice and appreciate that. This is not due to some company mandate, but genuine interest in customer service and love of the culture of the company. It's a rare thing to have such amazing customers that support us so completely, and we never take that for granted."[5]

CHAPTER SEVEN

The Italian Connection

Life is a combination of magic and pasta.

— FEDERICO FELLINI

A high point of this journey through fermentation and dry-cured meats is a group of New York Italian-American meat and salumi stores that stand out for their excellence and longevity. They represent what once was: defining shops that anchored neighborhoods and gave New York some of its spice, flavor, and cosmopolitan ambiance. That so few remain today reflects also the sad reality of loss.

In my opinion, these businesses are more than a legacy, some precious artifact in a meat museum. They contribute vital economic value, neighborhood identity and attractiveness, cultural relevance, and maybe the schmaltz that helps blend everything together, if I may be allowed a mixed metaphor and ethnic scramble. How do we maintain these legacies without destroying authenticity? I believe support, patronage, and promotion of these artisans and businesses are essential to their futures.

G. Esposito & Sons Jersey Pork Store

From Midtown Manhattan the easiest and fastest way to get to Brooklyn and the G. Esposito Jersey Pork Store is by subway. After several train transfers I arrive at the Carroll Street station, the gateway to the Carroll Gardens community. Walking to the store, I pass Carroll Park, a more than

165-year-old playground that helps anchor the neighborhood. In the 1840s Irish immigrants fleeing the potato famine arrived in New York, and many settled in South Brooklyn, then known as Red Hook. From 1880 through 1925 Italian immigrants from the regions of Campania, Calabria, and Sicily, after disembarking at Ellis Island, often made their way to Red Hook, and the community became heavily Italian. Many Italian men and their sons worked at the Brooklyn Navy Yard and other Red Hook docks.

In 1922 Naples-born Giovanni Esposito opened for business at Court and Union Streets, but the neighborhood was too quiet, so a year later he moved to Columbia and Union Streets in what was a vibrant Italian section of Red Hook. He named it Jersey Pork Store because they bought animals grown just across the Hudson River in New Jersey. The rationale behind the Jersey Pork name was food safety, specifically a fear of trichinosis, a parasite often found in pork; Esposito's New Jersey suppliers guaranteed quality, safe meat. The Italian-American community flocked to the store for Esposito's products as well as imported goods. From its founding the family made Neapolitan-style capicolla and soppressata that tend towards the hot and spicy side, although generally not as hot as the Calabrese versions. Giovanni's grandsons, George and John, started working in the store as children. Today both men, continuing a nearly one-hundred-year-old tradition, use Nonno's original recipes and buy meat from quality farms. Their personalities make the contemporary store unique, as they take great pride in the excellence of their cured meats and mozzarella, or *muzz*, made in-house.

In the 1940s and 1950s, the Red Hook community was sliced in half by the construction of the Brooklyn-Queens Expressway (BQE) to the west and the Gowanus Parkway to the south. Although Carroll Gardens became a distinctive area, the division left the store divorced from its neighborhood. As a result, in 1977 the Espositos moved several blocks east, past the BQE to its present location on Court Street.

The storefront, sandwiched between the F. Monteleone Bakery and Café and the Cusimano fish store, features a large, well-dressed pig out front in white apron and toque to greet patrons and passersby. A screen door and bell rhythmically announce the arrival and departure of customers, the parish priest and nuns, police and firefighters, and friends who just want to say hello. Stepping inside the narrow room, I am embraced by a wealth of aromas: the tang of Calabrese chiles and a slight musky note of delicious salami mold, *muffa*, floating from the hot and sweet soppressata hanging above my head; warm arancini rice balls stuffed with muzz; and a potpourri of sweet, spicy, oily, and herbal smells from the prepared take-out foods or as they make sandwiches to order.

Though arriving after the morning mozzarella ritual, I imagine the sweet milk curd as George and the crew stretch the cheese into several shapes for the day. And oh yes, for all of us who might say, "My mother could do that," there are reasons your mother doesn't make fresh mozzarella. While it looks easy to imitate, to create a delicious ball of muzz requires a willingness to plunge your hands into hot water and patiently stretch the curd until the subtle clues of aroma and texture tell you to stop; ultimately, it's all in the hands!

Likewise, achieving a consistently high-quality sausage or soppressata requires top-notch ingredients. Rather than use leftovers or scraps of pork, George and John make fresh sausage and soppressata from pork shoulder; a simple equation: The best meat makes the best sausage and salami. However, by themselves, the ingredients are just that — raw material. In the experienced hands of the Esposito brothers, the pork is elevated to a different universe. After being ground, seasoned, and stuffed into natural casings, the soppressata rests in the basement, emerging weeks later to hang like so many magic wands from the ceiling racks. I ask George for two small ones, one hot and one sweet; the smallest ones still weigh a pound!

George emphatically celebrates his community, which he acknowledges, while a far different place from fifty years ago, is the principal reason they are still in business. He doesn't mince words when he talks about change and whether the business will survive. In the 1990s young professionals began moving into the community, often precisely because it retained some authentic character and personality of a real neighborhood, with small quality shops selling meat, pastries, bread, fish, and clothing. The irony for the Esposito brothers is that the newcomers no longer had time to shop and cook at home and preferred to visit nearby Whole Foods or Trader Joe's markets. For the present the Jersey Pork Store meets these challenges with an array of prepared foods made on premises and warm personal service to attract older neighborhood residents and, they hope, new families.

While understanding the attractiveness of a Whole Foods, the presence of the Esposito store, the Monteleone bakery, and the Cusimano fish store creates distinctive places, not homogenized sameness. As with farmers' markets, customer interaction with food producers such as the Esposito brothers puts a face on food; you know who grew the vegetable or handcrafted the soppressata. For me the exchange is far more than just a transaction; it acknowledges people, traditional networks and processes, the value of neighbors, and the underlying community. I don't think the issue is how we hold back time but how to maintain the richness of neighborhoods in a world of instant gratification. For the Espositos food and service are the defining elements.

When I first walked in, George wasn't sure what to make of another writer wanting to interview him. Our conversation turned personal and warm when we exchanged stories of our Italian ancestors, George's from Naples, mine from the region of Molise. In addition to the wonderful soppressata in my bag, just before I left George offered me a warm arancini, a rice ball stuffed with muzz and fresh sausage and then fried. *Delizioso*!

Beyond the reality that Carroll Gardens continues to change, the brothers are into their early sixties and must manage physical challenges. Butcher shops, especially those the size of Esposito's, take a heavy toll on owners and employees. The physical work demands lifting heavy loads, hands working constantly with cold meat or in hot curds and whey, and welcoming and serving customers, all of which require standing for twelve hours, six days a week. Doctor Scholl's makes a fortune in places like this. The higher toll for John was having to replace both hips.

Just as with Schaller & Weber in Manhattan, an essential ingredient to the store's longevity is ownership of the building. As the city evolves and neighborhoods change, if you don't own your commercial space or live in a rent-controlled apartment, one day you may be gone. Over the past forty years, such places as SoHo, Manhattan's Meatpacking District, Red Hook, and Carroll Gardens witnessed extraordinary demographic change, with equally astonishing increases in rents and striking changes in land use and population demographics. For the Esposito brothers owning their building makes all the difference.

In a *New York Times* interview, the brothers expressed uncertainty "about the future. 'That's a good question,' said George, 50, whose son, George Jr., 20, works at the store but is not sure he wants to run it. 'We'd hate to give this up.' John Esposito scooped another mass of ground sausage and said, 'Good things sometimes have to die.'"[1]

If making great salumi requires time, patience, attention to detail, and high standards of excellence, the same can be said of Esposito's long tenure on Court Street. Those of us treasuring great products made with respect and care, traditions and history, and the personalities who weave important threads into a community's fabric celebrate Esposito's and look forward to at least another hundred years of gustatory pleasure.

Mike's Deli

A week or two before Christmas, I take the D train to Fordham Road; to say the least, the local takes a long time to finally reach its destination. During the journey, the population of the cars changes a few times; at this station mostly residents and Fordham University students get off. The walk east on Fordham Road to Arthur Avenue feels much longer on a cold, windy morning. Though it's just before the holidays, the avenue is relatively quiet, a great time to enjoy the wonderful Christmas decorations and ambiance. My destination is Mike's Deli, a longtime and well-recognized Italian-American purveyor in the Arthur Avenue Retail Market in the heart of the Bronx's Italian neighborhood.

Walking through the market is, to quote Yogi Berra, "déjà vu, all over again!" But this is the best of déjà vu: food stands with a royal patina of age; shop owners shouting greetings in Italian; the smell of cheese, meat, espresso, and desserts. A small beer garden featuring all New York State brews is new since my last visit ten years ago. I find Mike's toward the back and am drawn by the forest of salami, miniature reddish-brown meat sequoias, suspended over the counter; next is a row of oval, fat prosciutto de Parma hams . . . oh, what a picture of some of the best dry-cured meats in the world. The glass cases are filled with cheese, including the deli's handmade fresh, smoked, and baked mozzarella.

David Greco, proud third-generation Italian-American and owner of Mike's Deli, greets me. David, a tall, handsome man, invites me to sit down for an espresso. Behind me I hear the hiss of steam as a young woman makes our coffees, David proclaiming proudly she is a barista from Italy. As we talk he orders several things, always speaking in fluent Italian; I make out a few words and think, it's only 9:45 in the morning and he's ordering prosciutto, speck, Parmigiano-Reggiano, and Sambuca? They arrive with a bottle of sparking Italian mineral water, toasted bread, and a small dish of flavorful olive oil and balsamic crema. Yes, it's time to break bread, eat, and toast! *Salute!*

We share the meat, always with a bit of cheese dipped in oil and vinegar, and some bread. The Sambuca goes down beautifully, accented by the strong, hot espresso. David describes the prosciutto, twenty-four-month-old gems that he ages for another six months before slicing. The meat is smooth, fatty, and full of pork aromas and flavors, and suddenly it feels like 4 or 5 in the afternoon in Parma, not morning in the Bronx! The feast continues with more plates of wonderful, simple food: unadorned sliced speck, a sixteen-month-old salted and smoked gem from Tyrol, Austria, adjacent to Italy's northern border. Accompanying it comes a different version, fried to crispy texture. So now we have smoke, salt, and crunchy pork! David orders two glasses of Prosecco, and they stimulate different interactions among pork, cheese, and balsamic. *Mamma mia!* To say the least, I highly recommend an occasional midmorning Greco celebration — it's unforgettable.

Although the company does not make cured meats, I include Mike's Deli because of the heart, soul, and integrity of the business and what the family and its history tell us about immigration and success. David has very strong opinions about quality differences between Italian and American charcuterie and salami. David and his father, Mike, celebrate and embody taste memories and perceptions built from decades of eating and selling great Italian cured meats and cheeses, as well as the deli's handmade mozzarella, bread, olives, and so much more. While agreeing domestic cured meats are very good, David regards Parma hams as the world's best and consequently has longstanding commitments with the region's finest prosciutto maestros.

A wonderful book, *Why Italians Love to Talk about Food* by Elena Kostioukovitch, describes and explains the deep cultural connections created over centuries by Italians and Italian-Americans, whether rich or poor. It's in the blood, the heart, and the mind; as David and I share this unexpected culinary celebration, I'm reminded the conversation would be pretty abstract without the presence of this small expression of appreciation and gratitude. As I ask questions about family and food, we find common ground over prosciutto, Parmigiano-Reggiano, Prosecco, and espresso, while David tells stories.

In 1919, after the end of World War I, Maria and Gennaro Cappiello, David's maternal grandparents, arrived from Naples. After settling first in Greenpoint, Brooklyn, they moved to the Bronx because rumor had it that the air was better to the north than in Brooklyn, and it was. In 1922 they opened a grocery store and butcher shop on Arthur Avenue, and the family lived over the store. The first child was born in 1924, followed by several more sons, and daughter Antoinetta.

Late nineteenth- and early twentieth-century New York was an incredibly bustling, noisy, polluted, crowded place. The streets suffered from atherosclerosis, packed day and night with horses, cars, trucks, buses, trolleys, pushcarts; walkways weren't much better, stuffed with vendors and open-air stalls selling everything from food to shoes. In the mid-1930s over fifty thousand pushcarts jockeyed for space. Pedestrians had to maneuver through this frenetic anthill of activity in which you expended lots of energy just to get nowhere, unless on the daily food shopping trip, and then it was a slow excursion into the community's heart.

Market stalls and dozens of pushcart vendors called Arthur Avenue and its tributary streets and sidewalks home. In front of the Cappiello store, a vendors' congregation gathered; in winter Maria Cappiello provided a power cord for a portable heater, but only for one at a time, or the fuses blew!

In 1934 Greenwich Village native Fiorello La Guardia became the ninety-ninth mayor and first Italian-American *sindaco* (mayor) of New York City. During his tenure Mayor La Guardia initiated a number of public works projects, including New York Municipal Airport, later named after him. For most New York neighborhoods, life revolved around the street, and as the city grew larger and more crowded, traffic and pedestrian movement along these thoroughfares became even more challenging. With many households containing just iceboxes, regular food shopping was a necessity. And for many first-generation immigrants, these frequent visits for food also facilitated important cultural interactions with fellow countrymen.

From his work as an interpreter on Ellis Island and as an attorney in East Harlem, La Guardia understood the benefits and demands of street life, especially the presence of outdoor vendors. While committed to removing pushcarts and open-air markets to change the physical street space, he built a number of public markets around the city to provide convenient access to food and maintain cultural identities. Among these were the Fulton Fish

Market; Essex Street on the Lower East Side; La Marqueta in East Harlem; First Avenue Retail; and the Arthur Avenue Retail Market, on land that was formerly a sheep meadow. Opened in 1940, the Arthur Avenue building, like its brethren, housed everything: butchers and sausage makers, cheese emporiums, dry goods and delicatessens, bakers and pasta makers, fishmongers, and florists. In that same year Gennaro passed away, and Maria Cappiello added a second butcher shop in the retail market. But the hustle and bustle of the Arthur Avenue Retail Market was simply too much, and she closed the stall, electing to stay with the original store.

At its high point in the 1940s, the market totaled around a hundred vendors, but after World War II the number declined to thirty to forty businesses. Shops along the avenue experienced similar changes. By the 1970s you could still choose from more than twenty butcher shops and nearly a dozen delis, but in 2010 less than a handful existed.[2]

The second half of David's story involves two young twins, Michele (Mike) and Giuseppe (Joseph) Greco, also from Calabria. Born in 1930, they survived the war with parents Luisa and Luigi Greco because of a pair of horses. During the war they sheltered a family of Jewish tailors whose horses joined the Greco livestock; hiring out the animals to local farmers brought in enough money to keep them alive. After the war the Jewish family gave the Grecos a cart full of tailored suits and the horses in gratitude. The good fortune ended when the horses died mysteriously and Luigi accused Michele of killing them. The result? In 1947 he sent the brothers to America, where the seventeen-year-old men arrived in New York with their father's gift of $100 each and two handmade suits of clothes for both young men.

A willingness to work hard coupled with excellent butcher's skills landed Mike a job at the Cappiellos' Arthur Avenue shop in 1947, where he met Antoinetta, and the couple married a few years later. In 1948 Mike started work for a deli in the retail market, and in the early 1960s he bought the business and renamed it Mike's Deli. Over the next five decades, Mike and then his son David built a reputation for quality products, honesty, humor, and generosity. Throughout his life Mike followed a simple motto: *Cuore, Mente, Palle* (Heart, Brains, Balls)!

To remain a vibrant business over so many years required intelligence, a spirit of giving, and willingness to take risks. As second-generation neighborhood children moved away, the shifting fortunes of Arthur Avenue and the market demanded hard work and attention to detail to stay in business. Although today's market numbers just fifteen shops, Mike's Deli now attracts a local community of diverse heritages: Italian, Hispanic, and eastern European. Part of their continued success rests on Mike's motto but is strengthened by Antonietta's "Five Fs," lovingly related by David: "Faith, Family, Friends, Food, Forever. . . ."

Salumeria Biellese

From Brooklyn to the Bronx, we return to Manhattan and the Chelsea district at Twenty-Ninth Street and Eighth Avenue. If you're taking the subway from either borough, you'll find plenty of convenient lines and stops. Or if you travel by train to Penn Station, a walk down Eighth Avenue to Twenty-Ninth Street is only a few blocks.

But in 1908 Marc Buzzio faced a much longer journey of several thousand miles from a very small village, Curino, in the province of Biella, northwest of Milano. Today a road leads off the Autostrada on the A4 to Torino, up into the hills and then the Alps, toward the French border. The remote Piedmontese mountain location plays several important parts in the story of Salumeria Biellese.

That Marc Buzzio arrived in New York from Curino was somewhat unusual, since most Italian immigrants to the States at that time came from Southern Italy, not the north. He went back to Italy a few years later, got married, and returned to New York, where he and his wife had a son, Ugo. Sadly, Marc died during the Spanish flu pandemic, and Ugo returned with his mother to Curino, where as a young boy he worked for Mario Fiorio, a local butcher and salumiere.

Although the jagged spires of the Alps separate France and Italy, the French House of Savoy ruled the region of Piedmont for centuries. Beyond the cultural legacy and language dialects flavored by France are influences in food, especially chocolate and charcuterie. Mario Fiorio taught Ugo how to make northern Italian salumi, such as prosciutto and bresaola, but also *batsoà*, or boneless fried pigs' feet ("silk stockings," from the French *bas de soie*), as well as French garlic and blood sausages. Ugo returned to New York in 1930 and found a job as a charcutier in a store at Twenty-Eighth

Street and Eighth Avenue, a part of the Chelsea neighborhood with a small French population. Established in 1925, the shop served sandwiches with French and Italian flavors and thrived with Ugo's talents as a charcutier, which gave the business a distinguished reputation.

He bought the business in 1943 and expanded the cured-meat production. After World War II and into the 1950s, business continued to grow. In 1954 Ugo's son Marc was born, and Ugo increasingly felt the need for help. Enter Piero Fiorio, Mario's son, who after lots of cajoling from Ugo arrived and became a partner in 1960. Both men worked long hours and weekends and rarely took a vacation. For them hard work and pride in each day's accomplishments were important rewards.

Marc said he saw his father on weekends and in the summer . . . at the store. The business was strictly retail, with everything done by hand, from sandwiches to cuts of meat and fresh and cured salami, and their reputation as conscientious butchers and innovative salumieri grew. Imagine a first-floor retail grocery, deli, and butcher shop with a narrow staircase leading to the basement, where they handled the fabrication and curing. Meat deliveries, maybe a quarter or half a pig, navigated rickety stairs and low ceilings. The space wasn't the most attractive arrangement, especially for Marc as a teenager in the 1960s. "'My mother would send me in with my father on Saturdays so I'd know what he looked like,' recalls his son. 'They let me make coffee.'"[3] The experience led him to swear he would never become part of the family business.

He stuck by his words and received a bachelor's degree in French literature, a clear indication of how those French and Italian Alps continued to influence the family. By the mid-1970s Marc was teaching school and coaching college football and had started a master's program in French at New York University. "My father called one day and said he was getting ready to retire and was I interested in taking over the business. So I took a year's leave of absence, and I've never looked back."[4]

Ugo retired in 1976, Marc took over, and four years later Paul Valetutti, Piero's son-in-law, joined the business as a partner. The two young men, close observers of the rapidly changing national trends around meat and processing, developed ideas they took to Ugo and Piero to modernize production. One idea of many was to toss traditional hand-knotted salami into history's dustbin and substitute pneumatic stapling. The concepts went over like lead balloons. The older men rolled their eyes and muttered, "My shoes are smarter than you."[5]

In the 1980s, with sixty years of handcrafting salumi and the strong presence of centuries-old Piedmontese traditions, Piero and Ugo knew their products were unique. They saw also a potential loss to America's charcuterie history, an example of which is how they taught both men to hand-tie salami, starting not with a stuffed casing, but a small pine dowel and string. You practiced tying the string around the soft wood and then untied it. If you could see or feel slight indentations in the dowel surface, it was too tight. When you think about the approach, it makes perfect sense. You cannot learn on a real casing with meat, since a mistake dooms it for curing. Working with the dowel and string costs nothing; until you get it right, nothing is wasted. Brilliant in its simplicity!

As Marc and Paul describe vividly, Piero and Ugo indoctrinated them slowly into these traditions. You watch and listen; work the cord around the dowel; handle the meat with care and respect; understand and see the details; appreciate that knowledge comes with time. They learned to smell, recognize the aromas of great fermentation, and immediately grasp when something was off. To an outsider, it appears food artisans have an innate intuition about the weather, a sick cow, and thousands of other factors. But working with milk or cheese takes years of experience to understand nuances the way Ugo, Piero, Marc, and Paul comprehend subtlety. I call it slow knowledge, gained from study, endless practice, patience, and a desire to create the best. Not everyone can do this.

Gradually Salumeria Biellese expanded production to fulfill interest in selling cured products to a handful of New York City restaurants. Some of the styles came from chef requests for particular flavors. For example, a fennel seed finocchiona salami made for Le Cirque or a porcini mushroom salami for Balducci's Market.[6] Biellese products showed up frequently on menus for Thomas Keller, Jean-Georges Vongerichten, and Mario Batali, the latter with his own charcuterie wine bars.

In 1982 they moved the store one block north to Twenty-Eighth Street to provide more space, and opened a restaurant next door named Biricchino (Italian for "naughty little boy"). The business growth required additional competent hands, and in 1992 Fouad Alsharif, Paul's brother-in-law and Piero's son-in-law, joined the company to manage finances and run Biricchino. By the mid-2000s they realized the antiquated equipment, basement setup, difficult delivery arrangements, and inadequate space were hampering business development and growth. And the increasing demand from restaurants, wholesalers, and retailers far exceeded production capacity.

The greatest challenge came in 2002 from the USDA, when new federal regulations to monitor and control food safety in large plants were put in place. There are two paths to choose from when working with meat to make charcuterie. Whole muscle with its sterile interior needs close attention to surfaces; hence, accurate, careful salting is the foundation for safe and delicious coppa, lonza, or prosciutto. Ground meat, however, is an entirely different process, fraught with challenges and dangers.

The best illustration of the risk is the number of instances of food-borne illness attributed to ground beef over many years in the United States. When we mix thousands of pounds of clean beef with even a small amount of contaminated ground meat from one steer, the entire end product is potentially dangerous. Sadly, in our industrial system, these instances happen all too often. In the wrong hands ground beef and pork are dangerous.

The new federal standards required companies to prove products safe and wholesome and free of *Listeria monocytogenes* and *Escherichia coli*. Large companies easily met the requirements because they used one of three different strategies to kill potential pathogens: They could add preservatives, cook the meat, or irradiate the product. Because the latter uses a radioactive source, the consuming public never accepted or endorsed irradiation. Since each approach destroys beneficial microorganisms, most artisan producers of American charcuterie and salami add lactic acid bacteria starter cultures to manage the fermentation cycle and development of components.

To say the least, the USDA had major problems with Salumeria Biellese's method of salami production and shut them down. When Marc described how they make salami, USDA inspectors headed toward the nearest exit to condemn the entire proceeding. Setting aside hundreds of years of similar production in Europe, the idea of allowing meat to ferment and still be wholesome was beyond the accepted USDA framework and understanding of safety. In their most basic steps, Marc, Paul, and their crew grind pork, add sea salt and spices, mix and pack the meat into large bins, and allow the mixture to rest for 35 to 45 days in a curing room at 45° to 55°F. During this phase a naturally active lactobacillus fermentation takes place that raises acid level and contributes to flavor and texture development. In step two the meat warms overnight to allow packing in natural casings that are then tied by hand and hung for a few hours.

Next, a one-day visit to a 70°F fermentation chamber jump-starts development of exterior mold, after which the salami matures in a 55° to 60°F drying room. The curing time depends on the size of the salami; Marc aims for a 50 percent weight loss of water and a well-balanced acid structure. Here the salami develops muffa, its noticeable white mold of different harmless penicillin strains, the ubiquitous *Penicillium nalgiovense* and a recently discovered *P. salamii.*[7]

The partners faced a disastrous situation: The USDA would not back down on its regulations, and Marc, Paul, and Fouad would not change the company's long-established methods of making its salami. The solution came about because of their stubbornness, unshakable belief in their products, and a $100,000 investment. They found a scientist cited in the USDA's literature whom they hired to run tests on the salami. In the wildest experiment imaginable, he injected the salami with pure *Listeria monocytogenes* and *E. coli* and then aged them following the Biellese model. The result, no dangerous bacteria present at all! The USDA accepted the findings, and the partners were back in business.

Marc argues that since most charcuterie and salumi producers, both large and small, use industrial lactic cultures, the end product reflects a certain uniformity. In a similar fashion to artisan cheese, the use of standardized starter cultures removes a key variable in the creation and development of aroma, texture, and flavor. In addition to these standardized cultures, Marc emphasizes that these salami "ferment" at temperatures of 110° to 120°F, a rapid transformation that results in high acid, and therefore safety, but not much flavor. The addition of spices contributes flavors but also masks the lack of slow fermentation.

In 2008 the challenges of working with the USDA and the store's physical difficulties compelled them to relocate production to a new facility in Hackensack, New Jersey. The new building's thousands of square feet, designed and built to fulfill federal regulations, enables them to meet wholesale demand and provide for future expansion. But they encountered a problem similar to other "old school" curing operations — the new building was sterile, especially the aging room where the salami developed its unique aromas and flavors. The room lacked the old store's personality, the terroir, the living galaxy of microflora. The Chelsea basement nurtured and benefited from decades-old yeast, bacteria, and fungus neighborhoods, whose presence and dynamic interaction with the different meats created distinctive Biellese salumi. The symbiotic process over time added layer upon layer of living, natural, safe microscopic salumieri, the spirits of mystical, meaty transformation.

The partners knew their Hackensack products were good but not yet great. Since 2008 they have transported Chelsea cured meat and boards back and forth to the new plant to introduce the Manhattan basement terroir progeny to their new homes. Slowly the dynamic symphony began, building layers of microflora and then aroma and flavor. And finally, a stroke of luck.

In 1946 the Oldani Brothers Sausage Company opened in St. Louis's "The Hill," the heart of the city's Italian-American community. Charles and Leo Oldani knew the Biellese partners, contacted them when they wanted to retire, and sold the business to them in 2014. Maybe the New York–St. Louis connection was beloved Yankees catcher Yogi Berra and former catcher, later broadcaster for the Cardinals and the Yanks, Joe Garagiola, both of whom lived a couple of blocks away from Oldani! Actually, whatever the reasons, baseballs or meatballs, the decision embraced an "old school" philosophy and authenticity of how to play the game and craft great salumi.

Marc and Paul described with great enthusiasm the discovery of decades-old aging rooms, lined with wood boards . . . holy microbes, a storehouse of terroir! The Oldanis' basement was two levels deep underground, opened occasionally to outside humidity and air with potential new mold spores, rather than conditioned air. For the two salumieri the basement was a bit like discovering a Holy Grail, a container of unique microflora. A curing room with seventy years of continuous use just doesn't exist in America.

Salumeria Biellese now makes salumi in the Oldani facility. Equally important, they use material from the Oldani basement to cross-fertilize the Hackensack aging rooms. Over time they anticipate the Hackensack aging room will develop a rich patina of microflora that will enhance and distinguish all of the company's salumi.

The other key ingredients to the company's success are heritage breed hogs and outstanding animal husbandry. In St. Louis they buy Berkshire hogs from Berkwood Farms, a farmers' co-op formerly named Eden Farms. The coalition of forty-seven independent farmers commits to antibiotic-free, all-vegetable-and-grain diets, pasture grazing, and humane slaughter. For the Hackensack plant they buy a variety of hogs — Mangalitsa (for culatello and lardo), Tamworth (for pancetta), and Gloucester Old Spot (for guanciale) — from several New Jersey farms.[8] The majority of the pork is Berkshire, and some of those hogs grow to four hundred pounds! They had to search to find a slaughterhouse large enough to manage the pigs! They also receive wild boar hunted in Texas and beef for bresaola from a Pennsylvania Black Angus farm.

Even with increased production capacity, Salumeria Biellese–cured products are the top of the line, expensive, and difficult to find, especially some of the limited edition salami. Currently, to buy and enjoy their products, you must visit the store or one of the restaurants or specialty food stores listed on their website. They plan for internet sales very soon.

Marc compares the salumi to Rolex watches: "You don't find the watches or the salumi at Macy's." Following through on the analogy, Salumeria Biellese's products are distinctive, sometimes quite rare, timeless, made by craftsmen, and symbols of excellence. And the two companies are separated by just a decade of history. For me, while a Rolex has symbolic value, one watch buys a lifetime of great cured Biellese salumi, depending on how much you eat! *Grazie mille*, Marc, Paul, and Fouad.

CHAPTER EIGHT

New England Italians

During the late nineteenth and early twentieth centuries, southern New England attracted numerous immigrants from the Italian regions of Abruzzo, Calabria, Molise, and Sicily. Cities such as Boston, Hartford, New Haven, Westerly, and Providence witnessed the growth of significant southern Italian communities.

Fortuna's Sausage

One of the first people I interviewed for this book was Patti Fortuna-Stannard, a third-generation Italian-American whose sausage company is based in Vermont. We met on a bright, warm summer day to talk family, Italy, and great salumi. Like so many of us with Italy in our blood, she talked enthusiastically about how soppressata, an ancient cured salami, cherishes history, culture, and family and tastes *delizioso*.

Sometime within the years 1910 to 1912, Patti Fortuna's grandparents emigrated from Calabria to Bridgeport, Connecticut, where a large Calabrese population settled. In 1914 her grandparents opened Joe's Market and made a variety of salami, including soppressata, which became their most popular product. The Calabrese version of soppressata is coarse-ground pork seasoned spicy hot with the region's chiles.

In 1942 Patti's father, Anthony, then fourteen years old, started working in the deli. In the 1950s he opened another store in Westport, and by 1971 the business had expanded into Fairfield. At its peak the family owned seven stores in Connecticut and one in Westerly, Rhode Island, site of a large Calabrese neighborhood. One of the most interesting aspects of her story is that when the Westerly shop opened, the Bridgeport Calabrese were not welcomed with open arms. And from what I surmise, the two Calabrese groups have different preferences for how they like their soppressata.

In 1982 Patti and her husband, Paul Stannard, took over the Westerly deli and four years later began making salami from her grandparents' recipes. By accident Kathie Jenkins, a food writer for the *Los Angeles Times*, stopped in and bought a number of items, including the soppressata that Fortuna named Soupy. After returning home she wrote a glowing review, and the company's fortunes, so to speak, took off. Within a year they went from a hundred pounds a week to thousands. Local and mail-order customers said the food evoked memories of family and culture. One day Paul fielded a phone call from Jay Leno, whom he at first dismissed, not believing who it was. As many people know, Leno has an abiding passion for rare automobiles and loves to ride motorcycles. It turns out that Paul owned a motorcycle business, specializing in trail bikes, and they talked cycles for a long time before Leno placed an order for shipment to the West Coast. Leno subsequently invited Patti and Paul to an appearance on *The Tonight Show*, and the Soupy business boomed.

In 1997 they sold the deli to focus solely on dry-cured salami and opened a manufacturing plant in Greenville, Rhode Island, to increase production. At the same time they reduced the number of items they sold. Patti emphasized that the smaller product line translated into much higher quality. By 2005 and 2006 they had outgrown production and decided to sell the plant and work with copackers. Today producers in New York, Rhode Island, and Vermont make the company's dry-cured salumi.

In 2009 they moved to Sandgate, Vermont, where Patti and Paul had spent vacations. Patti advocates for Fortuna's all-natural approach — no nitrates, humanely raised pigs, spices sourced from Italy and the States; and natural casings from pigs and sheep. The sausages are hand-stuffed and air-dried from eight weeks for pepperoni to twelve to fourteen weeks for the Soupy. They also make a coppa that ages four months or more. Today the company manages all of its shipping and fulfillment from Vermont. I was amazed that mail and internet orders account for approximately 80 percent of sales, while wholesale makes up the remainder.

Patti expresses great pride and accomplishment in Fortuna's being a fourth-generation family business, as her and Paul's children are now involved in the company.

Daniele, Inc.

The Daniele headquarters is in Pascoag, Rhode Island, about twenty miles northwest of Providence. From the access road you don't see much until you round a bend and the huge complex of white buildings comes into view. You must pass through a gate, part of the facility's biosecurity control features; given its size and volume of food products, the company must follow certain federal government food security mandates.

I'm on my way to meet Stefano Dukcevich, who together with his brother Davide is a third-generation salumiere. Their story, family, and business success captures so much of American history and the opportunities for success. My conversation with Stefano starts in mid-twentieth-century Europe and ends in twenty-first-century America, with its contemporary ideas and norms of food and cuisine.

The end of the Second World War in Europe was a time of displacement, migration, and resettlement. Yugoslavia, part of the Balkan Peninsula, fell under the control of Communist ruler Josip Tito, who fought the Germans as a partisan. For many Yugoslavians the war was very costly and deadly, and they feared continued strife and repression under Communist rule.

Stefano and Carolina Dukcevich lived in northeastern Croatia, near its border with Hungary. Stefano was a horse trader, and almost immediately after the war, the Yugoslav Communists confiscated his family's property and belongings. With sons Mario and Vlado, Stefano and Carolina fled across the country to the city of Trieste, by then under Italian and Allied control. They were penniless upon arrival but through several fortunate opportunities found themselves in the meat business. Using recipes dating to the Austro-Hungarian Empire, Carolina made pork frankfurters and smoked sausages, and Stefano sold them to restaurants. As demand grew, Stefano traded in his bicycle for a truck to make deliveries.

The rebuilding of Europe, especially through the Marshall Plan, provided important, timely resources to expand their business, and by the 1950s Carolina and Stefano had created a well-regarded brand in Trieste. With such success they moved to a small production facility, named Salumificio Triestino Dukcevich; added employees; and expanded the product line to include Vienna sausages and smoked Prague hams. In the 1960s Vlado joined the business, and Stefano sent him to Germany and Parma to learn from the prosciutto masters. About the same time Vlado met and married Flavia, a young Trieste woman.

In 1968 Stefano took Vlado on a drive into the hills surrounding Trieste to San Daniele in Friuli (thirty to forty miles northwest) to see a plot of land Stefano wanted to buy. Grandson Stefano said his grandfather told Vlado, "We're going into the prosciutto di San Daniele business." Father and sons — Stefano, Vlado, and Mario — built one of the first dry-curing meat plants and developed a very successful company that produced 100,000 to 150,000 hams annually, some of which they exported for a brief time to the States.

For centuries San Daniele in Friuli benefited from and celebrated the region's unique climatic characteristics. Dry winds sweeping down the Carnic Alps collided with those from the Adriatic Sea; when the seasonal variations blessed San Daniele, the hams were extraordinary. But sometimes weather that was too cold or hot, too damp or dry disrupted the natural curing sequence from one year to the next, and the prosciutti didn't mature properly. Even after World War II, production and curing was at the mercy of weather conditions. Stefano described San Daniele production from 1945 to 1968 as devoid of any climate controls to make prosciutti, and consequently quality varied, just at a time when global interest began to take off. The new dry-curing facility, by eliminating the vagaries of weather, ensured consistently high-quality hams.

The success of the Dukcevich operation encouraged other producers to adopt new techniques and technologies. The region's produttore di prosciutto formed the Consorzio del Prosciutto di San Daniele, an organization created to raise the region's standards, create production protocols, and help brand the name. Today the twenty-seven producer members must adhere to the criteria they helped to establish.

The quality of San Daniele ham was recognized by the Italian government as far back as 1970. The traditional rules according to which it is processed were incorporated into a specific legal provision, making them compulsory by law and introducing penalties for breaches to protect the trademark, the quality, and the typical properties of the product.[1]

But then nature intruded in a devastating manner. In 1967 swine ve-sicular disease was discovered in Italian hogs, and the USDA prohibited the import of many Italian pork products from Friuli and other northern Italian regions. Further restrictions were imposed in 1978 as a result of African swine fever outbreaks, harmless to humans but devastating to hogs.[2] In 1987, after years of work and considerable expense, the USDA amended the ban, and prosciutto from Parma arrived in 1989. The ban on San Daniele prosciutto, again after significant time and money, was lifted in 1996. For both regional brands the USDA demanded the hams age for at least four hundred days (thirteen months in the Consorzio protocols) to meet US standards.

The 1967 and 1978 prohibitions closed a valuable current and poten-tially significant market for the family's hams, and grandfather Stefano needed a new strategy to increase business. According to grandson Stefano, his father, Vlado, at that time in his midthirties, was restless and wanted some adventure. In 1976 grandfather Stefano told Vlado, "You always wanted to go to the States; now you have your chance!" To build a Dukcevich prosciutto business in the States, he sent Vlado to America. Vlado built the first Daniele, Inc., prosciutto plant in Rhode Island because of its environment, clean air, and location between the large Boston and New York Italian-American markets. Stefano's mandate was simple: Just make prosciutto — "a mono-product" — nothing else in the product line.

While its historical roots were in Croatia, the Dukcevich family reflected and embraced northern Italian food traditions, taste, and culture. In Boston, Providence, and New York, Vlado met Italian-Americans whose roots were in the south: Campania, Calabria, Puglia, and Sicily. These southern Italians arrived between 1880 and 1925 and brought with them very differ-ent foodways; prosciutto is far outside their collective food memories. Vlado discovered these communities had no interest in prosciutto: "Distributors would say, 'Prosciutto, what kind of cheese is this?'"[3] But wholesalers and retailers did ask about cured meats, especially soppressata and other salami, associated with southern regions. Realizing his choices were limited, I imagine Vlado most likely saying, "Sure"; otherwise he had nothing to sell.

He built a small curing operation in Pascoag to handle salami and pro-sciutto production, and Stefano, Vlado, and brother Mario owned the busi-ness. In 1977 and 1978 Vlado produced 115,000 hams, but prosciutto sales struggled; fortunately the other cured products helped keep the business solvent. Several factors beyond the initial cultural and culinary differences affected sales. The size of the prosciutto could intimidate both retailer and customer. Most customers only wanted small amounts, and staring at a ten- to fourteen-pound leg propped on a carving stand was overwhelming and a bit exotic. Sometimes a counterman carved slices too thick, and they were therefore too chewy and not very appealing. Other times, impatient customers didn't want to wait for hand-carved thin slices of ham or were put off by the price. Vlado found himself educating distributors, wholesalers, and retailers about the proper handling and carving of a good prosciutto.

Situated in the Northeast, Vlado faced another challenge: the quality of hogs in the region. In the 1970s and 1980s, the country entered the era of "The Other White Meat"; the hogs grew faster, leaner, and with less fat. In contrast, Italian farmers raised specific hogs for prosciutto and matured animals for eight to ten months; they not only got bigger, but the additional time to graze and forage contributed better flavor and intramuscular fat marbling. Vlado succeeded in locating several Iowa hog growers and paid them to raise better quality pigs for additional months beyond the typical American standard.

In the 1980s the Iowa hogs and the advent of new slicing equipment began to change Daniele's business model and fortunes. Now the company could slice and vacuum-pack three-ounce packages of prosciutto, which saved time and money for retailers and attracted consumers. The younger Stefano says the technology made a huge difference in business volume, as they could now ship Daniele prosciutto anywhere in the country.

For many years Vlado ran the company by himself, in part because it wasn't clear if Davide and Stefano would join the business. When he first arrived Vlado expected to build a business, sell it, and return to Trieste and rejoin the family. When clearly that would not happen, he bought his father and brother's interests in the business. What I find so remarkable is that both the Trieste and Rhode Island Dukcevich families' ventures continue to this day and are among the most recognized prosciutto brands in the world. The Trieste family — grandfather Stefano, his son Mario, and later his son Vladimir (Davide and Stefano's cousin) — named the company Principe di San Daniele. Both Mario and Vladimir have served as presidents of the Consorzio del Prosciutto di San Daniele. I am in awe of Carolina, Stefano,

Vlado, and Mario, and how a handful of Austro-Hungarian salumi created two amazing families of cured meat on two different continents.

In contrast, Vlado's sons initially took different career paths. Stefano was attracted to foreign service and international affairs, while Davide was interested in journalism and for a period of time wrote for *Forbes* magazine. But first Stefano and then his brother joined their father and with their energy and skills have contributed to the company's new directions and growth.

By 2004 the company was literally bursting its casings at the seams, and production technologies were years out of date. That year Daniele opened a 150,000-square-foot facility that multiplied capacity several-fold and incorporated a number of new design and technological innovations. One approach integrated production flow to enable faster, more efficient finished items. Over the next ten years, Daniele produced over twenty-three million pounds of cured meat annually and with such an abundant supply was able to develop new markets in the States, the rest of North America, and Asia. The facility produced and cured 250,000 prosciutto hams annually, with most of it sliced into packages. Today with the opening of another facility, the 2004 plant produces only salami.

Stefano and I talked at length about the history of the "salter" in Italy and for a period of time a similar position in Rhode Island. This individual, responsible for salting the hams, was fundamental for quality prosciutto. The salter estimated with great accuracy the weight of each ham and its fat layer. Then he applied precise amounts of salt with just the right pressure to the surface of each prosciutto. Stefano noted that the salters, after they finished patting salt onto each ham, made the sign of the cross in the salt. The ritual speaks to the culture of curing while asking for God's blessing and help to ensure a safe, quality product. When researching Principe di San Daniele, I found photographs from the late 1940s or early 1950s depicting both men and women doing the salting.

In 2012 the company designed and built a 350,000-square-foot manufacturing facility through which they produce ten thousand prosciutti a week. At a cost of more than fifty million dollars, the factory is computer-driven, with robots handling some of the heavy and repetitive tasks. For example, one robot can lift a rack of 216 hams; with each prosciutto weighing nearly 30 pounds, the machine moves approximately 6,500 pounds at a fraction of the time needed by workmen, and a heck of a lot more safely.

Daniele uses high-tech equipment made by Macchine Soncini Alberto, a company located in Parma, Italy. Around the world, producers consider Alberto Soncini the maestro of extraordinary prosciutto equipment. For example, the company makes a massaging and vein-pressing machine that manipulates muscles to soften them for better salt absorption, retains fat and muscle structure, and helps remove blood from large vessels. Daniele uses a Soncini salting machine that lays down precise amounts of salt and pressure, although it's not clear whether the Daniele unit also makes the sign of the cross on the hams.

Daniele prosciutti undergo two salting procedures, each lasting seven days. During the first salting the hams are stacked together. After the first week, the hams are washed, massaged again, and then re-salted and stacked again. At the end of the second week, the hams move into a cold, humid environment, a climate similar to winter conditions in San Daniele, Italy, where they hang from the hock bone.

Daniele prosciutti age from ten to twelve months, sometimes up to eighteen months. The size of the ham dictates the length of curing needed for food safety and a top-quality product. While optimum aging determines top-quality meat, the longer the hams hang, the more expensive they become. The aging process enables wonderful enzymatic transformations of aromas, flavor, and texture and a slow loss of water. Over many months, the hams shrink, thus allowing for concentrated organoleptic characteristics.

Since the interest in American dry-cured meat took off in the early 2000s, so has demand for higher quality hogs raised humanely with proper diets and careful slaughter. The problem for Daniele was how to segment the product line with limited edition prosciutto and at the same time locate the right pigs. Part of the company's strategy was to produce prosciutto made from locally sourced pigs. New England is not known as hog country, so finding local pigs presented real challenges.

For a time they were buying hams from Black River Meats in Vermont but wanted sources closer to Rhode Island. I recall meeting Mike DeCesare, Daniele's director of quality control, several years ago, and listening to him describe the upcoming prosciutto. Mike said the company finally found several southern New England farmers who would raise specific breeds for them.

One Rhode Island supplier is Blackbird Farm, which raises heritage Berkshires for the prosciutto and several other products, including award-winning mortadella and salamis. These hams, named Del Duca Vlado's Riserva in honor of Vlado, are larger and therefore age at least twelve months. "The resulting prosciutto is thick and rich; slightly resistant to the bite, it boasts striations of rich fat through the pink, tender, umami-packed meat. There's something primal about it; you want to tear at it with your teeth."[4]

Daniele slices its best-selling Del Duca prosciutto into three-ounce packages. For most consumers a precut package of exact thin slices makes great sense, offers convenience and affordable prices, and reduces waste. The company supplies Walmart, Costco, and other large supermarket chains. Although not involved with food service, the limited-edition Del Duca Vlado's Riserva prosciutto goes to restaurants.

We discussed how the company positions itself as a large producer of hams. Stefano argues the positive characterizations attributed to small-scale production versus large are predominantly myths. The objective for Daniele is drawing together good food from excellent meat suppliers with stories that resonate with consumers. The company works to build trust with everyone, from farmers to consumers. Though a large producer, Daniele integrates traditional methods of dry curing with current innovations and technologies.

Stefano sees a bright future for better tasting, healthier, and safe foods. He points to the populations of twenty- and thirty-year-olds — sometimes referred to as Millennials — as key drivers in the new food culture. With fast, processed, and bland foods losing market share within this important demographic, the generation is committed to new systems that connect local and organic food, health, celebrity chefs, positive environmental and sustainable change, and social media. While some see these ideas as trendy, the reality is a rapidly changing landscape in which Shake Shack replaces McDonald's and farmers' markets supplant Whole Foods.

CHAPTER NINE

It's a Long Road to Cured Meat!

The restaurant business has a well-earned, sometimes not so attractive reputation for resembling a revolving door. Just when you as a diner become comfortable with a favorite eatery, the chef, maître d', sommelier, or other regarded professional is off to another place via promotion, career shift, or new venture. Depending on the restaurant, the merry-go-round can be a plus or a minus. But many times constant overhaul results in inconsistent food, service, and ambiance.

In 2014 Gramercy Tavern celebrated twenty years in business, an amazing track record in the restaurant world that's even more remarkable in the superheated New York scene. As a result of my charcuterie expedition, I learned how Gramercy's philosophy, execution, and constant evolution are fundamental to its marathon victories. The second restaurant in Danny Meyer's portfolio, the Tavern contributed directly to the education and subsequent success of many food professionals who passed through its kitchen, beverage program, and front of house.

My connection to the Tavern's charcuterie program resulted from a call from Sara Grady, vice president of programs at Glynwood in Cold Spring, New York, about the nonprofit organization's interest in developing a charcuterie program in the Hudson River Valley. During the conversation, Sara mentioned goat prosciutto, or violino di capra, a rare cured meat from Italy's northern Lombardy region. After settling down from my surprise and excitement, I described my 2001 research study in

Italy to learn how to make it. Sara detailed a March 2015 Glynwood charcuterie workshop with master salumiere Francois Vecchio, at which they made a violino di capra. The leg was now resting and curing comfortably with Paul Wetzel, sous-chef and charcutier at Gramercy Tavern. Sara then introduced me to Paul.

I didn't realize how this first step with Paul would educate me about the Tavern's impact on charcuterie and some of the people who developed the program. In the mid-2000s, Gramercy Tavern began to buy whole-animal carcasses, since per-pound costs were less and this made exciting new menu items possible. As in many other restaurants, its chefs no longer worked with just prime cuts — steaks and chops, for example — ordered from wholesalers, but now had to learn how to break down a steer, lamb, or pig. To maximize each animal's value, what today we call "nose-to-tail" cuisine, they used every piece of trimmed muscle, bones, and offal. Along with obvious presentations of fresh cuts and sausages, chefs designed menus around terrines, pâtés, cured whole muscles, and salumi.

In 2007, a year after Michael Anthony assumed the head chef reins from Tom Colicchio, both men very accomplished professionals, Gramercy launched its charcuterie program with Erin Fairbanks, one of the restaurant's line cooks. From my perspective Erin and her successor, Scott Bridi, reflect the company's emphasis on professional development, stewardship, and growth of its employees. The Tavern takes pride in the number of its staff with years of experience and, at the same time, how institutional mentoring leads to new opportunities for many talented individuals.

While not having the opportunity to talk with Fairbanks, I gathered information from other interviews about her journey with meat and food. Fairbanks' work required close relationships with farmers and growers that supplied Gramercy with animals. One of them was Flying Pigs Farm in upstate New York, where in 2009, after departing the Tavern, she directed a farm camp. In 2011 Fairbanks helped start "No Goat Left Behind," a project of Heritage Foods USA. Today she is the executive director of Heritage Radio Network, a nonprofit organization also linked to Heritage Foods.

Scott Bridi started at Gramercy Tavern in 2007, also as a line cook, and soon began collaborating with Fairbanks. After she left, Scott became the charcutier. An Italian-American, Scott grew up in Bensonhurst, Brooklyn, where he still vividly remembers eating sausage and peppers grinders.

Armed with a degree in English, Scott worked for a while in publishing and then at 'inoteca, a small place on the Lower East Side, before joining the Gramercy staff. Everyone at the Tavern was learning about charcuterie, from the basics to flavor and texture development. Part of the challenge was the lack of a dedicated curing room, as everything was aged in the basement wine room, which had uneven temperature and humidity. Scott devised approaches to ensure the salami didn't dry too fast and was responsible for organizing and writing the initial HACCP (Hazard Analysis and Critical Control Points) plans for the restaurant.

In 2009 Scott left Gramercy to become the chef at Brooklyn's Lot 2 restaurant, where he developed its charcuterie programs. A few months later Scott became the charcutier at Brooklyn's Marlowe & Daughters, another valuable experience, and then a year later, in 2010, opened Brooklyn Cured. It may appear contradictory to consider Scott's voyage against my earlier comments about the core values of Gramercy Tavern and longtime employees. Yes, two years is not a long time, but I'm impressed by his standards, adherence to key philosophical principles, and knowledge, which I attribute, in part, to his tenure at Gramercy. While there, he developed strong interests in sustainable meat, whole-animal butchery, and urban food markets, each of which informs his direction today.

Chefs from Gramercy, Union Square Cafe (Meyer's first restaurant), and other Manhattan restaurants are well-known shoppers at nearby Union Square Greenmarket, where they buy and incorporate the day's fresh produce and unique ingredients into an evening menu. Equally important are the daily interactions and in many instances close relationships that chefs and the broader public enjoy with farmers, artisan bakers and cheesemakers, and other small-scale growers and processors.

Union Square Greenmarket resulted from one of the most important twentieth-century "urban renewal" decisions made anywhere in the United States. In 1976 New York City passed various legislation to revitalize the square, previously referred to as "Needle Park," the best place in the city to buy drugs, with its convenient subway stop! It was not, to say the least, a destination touted by the city. Coupled with the city's financial crisis in the mid-1970s, owners of commercial buildings surrounding the square couldn't cope with the negative perception of the area and seemingly couldn't give away lease spaces.

One piece of the city's legislation established the New York Greenmarket organization to provide New Yorkers with access to a bounty of fresh food and regional farmers with direct sales to consumers. Union Square was one of the first designated areas for a farmers' market. Over the intervening forty years, this market, together with adjacent new high-rise apartments, transformed this central area of Manhattan.

In the 1970s and 1980s, an open-air market like Union Square bucked the prevailing trend of bigger and bigger supermarkets with standardized arrays of inexpensive food. But with the city's innovative food community, population density, diverse ethnic and religious communities, and media attention, Union Square and many other city markets became key transforming agents of positive change. The strategic locations of Union Square Cafe and Gramercy Tavern to the square resulted from Danny Meyer's intuition about the strength and value of the Greenmarket.

Public spaces embody millennia-old experiences of bringing people together, from the Greek agora to contemporary pop-up parks. They serve democratic principles as extraordinary places for conversation, sharing, and, in the instance of public markets, the enjoyment of food. In many ways, as with elevators, buses, and subways, you rub shoulders with strangers. For me the key difference, in contrast to these other public interactions, is a gathering around food and dialogue with a farmer, a baker, a cheese maker, and fellow shoppers — those same strangers with whom you probably don't communicate while riding public transportation. Okay, everybody has earbuds today, but this is an opportunity to discover a new vegetable, ask "Just what do you do with kohlrabi?" and then share recipes.

In his book *It's a Long Road to a Tomato*, Keith Stewart relates his experiences as a longtime Union Square farmer and his appreciation of the deep connections he enjoys with customers. Whether it's someone on food stamps, a hipster couple, a Gramercy chef, or a neighborhood resident, all share a common bond, a democratic link around Keith's tomatoes and other fresh produce.

Consequently, it came as no surprise to me to listen to Scott talk passionately about how food professionals can contribute to a more democratic and accessible food system. Scott has a broad view and comprehensive understanding of the overall food system and where charcuterie fits into a sustainable direction for how we eat. He sees changes in our food system as becoming more democratic and accessible.

When Scott opened Brooklyn Cured, his first venture was the former New Amsterdam Market, with a cooler of fresh sausage that sold out the first day. He prized the feedback from customers who returned the following week and are still patrons today. Scott and I reminisced about Robert LaValva, the man behind the efforts to save New Amsterdam. Scott said that without his support and guidance, Brooklyn Cured might not have happened. Years before, Robert and I collaborated on several raw milk cheese projects for Slow Food USA that still have an impact on America's artisan cheese community.

Scott also described the years since opening Brooklyn Cured as a "journey of naïveté," of constant learning and trial and error. The company's product line for three to four years consisted of fresh sausage and then several smoked types. Scott found himself constantly working to balance meat grinds from coarse to fine with different seasonings and then levels of smoke. Each element contributes to aroma, taste, and texture and, in his striving toward authentic styles, required adjustments. For him the evolution spoke deeply to his conviction to move salumi production from preservation to artistry.

The inspiration comes from the traditional types of places that sell great meats, such as Italian-American pork stores, Lower East Side delis, French charcuterie, German beer gardens, wine bars—all of those traditional classic types of establishments that make or serve highly seasoned meats or bacon or sausages or things that people associate with comfort and childhood at some level.[1]

Whether it's a sausage, a bratwurst, an Andouille, or a breakfast link, Scott sees the artistic balance as a delicate dance that ultimately enables the quality of his pork to shine through. He emphasizes the fundamental role of classic practices and techniques in butchery and charcuterie. Likewise, he confronts a similar balancing question to ensure the viability of the business. Scott knew meat suppliers from Gramercy and turned to them for his beef, pork, duck, chicken, and even turkey. Buying more expensive pastured and antibiotic-free pork means a higher-cost item and therefore challenges to how much he can charge for fresh and smoked sausage.

To set up a viable (meaning reasonably profitable) cured-meat business in New York City demanded an innovative strategy. The solution was a collaboration with Piccinini Brothers on Ninth Avenue, a butcher shop established in 1922 and a USDA-certified operation. In exchange for space

Scott set up the company's sausage business, and in turn, they copack his products. He applied all of his restaurant experience and willingness to experiment with different ingredients, such as ginger, pomegranate, and coriander, to create unique flavors.

For several years the partnership with Paul Piccinini met Scott's needs. But to fulfill the steadily increasing demand, he needed to expand volume, which in turn required more space and equipment. In spring 2015 he moved production to the Brooklyn Wholesale Meat Market, where he could make batches in hundreds of pounds, not the twenty back at Gramercy. Now he faced decisions about which sausage recipes could be scaled up without losing integrity. Scott explained that he faced reconciling the chef's desire to create innovative products with the business reality that they might not sell at higher volumes. Ultimately, he felt paring back the product line ensured steady sales without great risk and at the same time allowed him to experiment with new ideas.

For example, in addition to an array of sausage, he incorporated bacon and pastrami, the latter made with honey and coriander, into the menu. In 2014 he created the company's first cured product, a smoked maple bourbon ham: marinated pork in small-batch bourbon, dark brown sugar, and garlic, and then slow cooked and glazed with maple syrup. Look out, Kentucky and Vermont!

Today Scott's products are found in a number of city retail markets, restaurants, and four farmers' markets, where Scott and the staff share the experience of direct interaction with customers. As he said several times during our conversation, creating and running a food business rests on relationships with suppliers, colleagues, staff, and customers. Finally, the other component of his work is teaching, both public classes and the staff, several of whom had never made charcuterie before.[2]

Now let's circle back to Paul Wetzel, whom we left in the Gramercy kitchen holding the violino. Actually, by the time we met in fall 2015, I'd learned that the violino was consumed to rave reviews at a celebratory dinner at Glynwood prior to my visit. For Paul the opportunity to work with Francois Vecchio in March 2015 was a return engagement, since he had previously attended Francois's school in Alaska.

In 2008, after culinary stints in San Francisco's Aqua and New York's Café Grey, Paul joined the Gramercy staff as sous-chef. Among other responsibilities, he oversaw butchery and charcuterie, the latter headed by Scott Bridi, whom Paul described as a genius and a magician.[3] With many New York restaurants now with serious charcuterie menus and especially with a dry-curing focus — for example, Il Buco Alimentari, Otto, and Babbo — the Tavern looked to increase its selection and expertise.

The keys for all of these high-end restaurants are the farms. Throughout all the research and interviews, every charcutier and salumiere with whom I spoke emphasized the same theme: An appropriate diet and great animal husbandry is the foundation upon which you raise great hogs. A couple of individuals even went out on a limb to say that a commodity hog raised on the right diet tastes "pretty good." But Paul wasn't one of them. Gramercy purchases beef from four different farms and pork from three, including Raven & Boar Farm in East Chatham, New York, and Flying Pigs Farm just a bit farther north in Shushan. Both farms raise heritage hogs exclusively — Berkshire, Tamworth, Large Black, Red Wattle, and Gloucestershire Old Spot — and sometimes provide unique diets. Raven & Boar obtains leftover whey from local artisan cheese makers to create a remarkable cornucopia of "whey soaked grains, grass, vegetables, fruits and naturally foraged roots and acorns."[4] The diet and the kindness shown to the animals contribute to truly outstanding meat.

The payoff for Gramercy is whole hog carcasses, from which they utilize every morsel. Paul took me on a tour of the basement; frankly I don't remember whether it was one or two levels down, but every space was a flurry of activity at midmorning in anticipation of lunch and later dinner service. I recall turning a corner and stepping into a cold box, perhaps better described as a cool, slightly damp room. The smell of fresh vegetables and fruit immediately welcomed me. Paul beckoned me into an aisle: "Hey, it's part of the wine storage," where I saw bottles of First Growth Bordeaux and Grand Cru Burgundy . . . and whole-muscle charcuterie hanging at the back end! It's probably the only time in my life when I will see examples of premier wine literally cheek to guanciale in such a setting.

Of course, the arrangement reflects the challenge many restaurants encounter: a lack of space to operate a curing program properly. For Paul and the Tavern's charcuterie, the arrangement is satisfactory. However, sometimes it becomes unsatisfactory in the eyes of inspectors from New York's Department of Health. As we have seen around the country, health regulations differ, and often even within one jurisdiction individual interpretation and understanding may vary. As I learned from several city businesses, given the size of New York and its thousands of food establishments, each visit might be conducted by a new inspector. The result is an ongoing education process and sometimes heated disagreements about individual practices.

From my perspective the variation in the inspection system, whether in Denver, New York, or other cities, does not create incentives for positive change for chefs and restaurants — or for inspectors. Absolutely we must ensure public safety, and yes, some places deserve to be shut down, but the charcutiers and salumieri I spoke with emphasized a desire to cooperate and adjust, if they were met halfway. All of them recognize the critical safety issues and are committed to fulfill their responsibilities to protect the public. Simply put, why run the risk of a food-borne illness that might drive customers away or close the business? Just look at the ongoing issues confronted by Chipotle in 2015 and 2016 to understand the potential consequences of food illness.

Apparently, and I have no direct evidence, a few restaurateurs went "underground" to avoid scrutiny. I am concerned about these practices in the same way I worry about rogue cheese makers who insist on making illegal raw milk cheese. One mistake, one illness, or — heaven forbid — a death from eating rogue-cured meat torpedoes everyone, including those businesses doing the right thing.

For Paul at Gramercy and Scott at Brooklyn Cured, the question is all about quality, distinction, and safe products.

CHAPTER TEN

Pennsylvania

He hath an excellent stomach.

— WILLIAM SHAKESPEARE, *MUCH ADO ABOUT NOTHING*

In 1968 I moved to Philadelphia to attend graduate school at Temple University, thinking I had failed my physical for the draft — that turned out to be wrong. I have vague memories of that fall; the most important ones relate to taking a leave of absence from school when I joined the US Navy instead of being drafted into the Army or Marine Corps. After serving as a meteorologist, I returned to Philadelphia in early 1973 to complete grad school and stayed in Philadelphia until 1995.

Those twenty-two years encompassed graduate studies in the history of cities; tenure as a curator and historian at the Atwater Kent Museum, devoted to the history of Philadelphia; service at the University of Pennsylvania's Morris Arboretum; and then being associate dean at Penn's School of Veterinary Medicine. Looking back, they were unique opportunities to learn, teach, and continue to inform my perspective on food, agriculture, and dried cured meat.

Regardless of where I lived in the city, on most Saturday mornings I left the house to arrive at the Reading Terminal Market just as its doors opened at 8:00. The market was underneath the Reading Terminal, the last nineteenth-century railroad station in downtown Philadelphia. Trains entered from the north along an elevated viaduct and ended their journey at Twelfth and Market Streets, sitting above the Terminal Market. For many years families along the Reading routes north of the city could place a basket containing a shopping list onboard a Philadelphia-bound train. Once at the station, porters picked them up, purchased whatever was on the list, and placed them back on an outgoing train. It was an early twentieth-century version of Amazon.

In the 1970s the market had all sorts of problems, from leaky ceilings and poor lighting to continued loss of merchants and customers, many of whom traced their families' livelihoods back to the Terminal's founding in 1892. On those early morning trips, it sometimes felt as if more rats than people showed up to shop. But you could find unique vendors throughout the market — Harry Ochs's butcher shop; Spataro's for breakfast and lunch; Margerun's for produce; Bassetts Ice Cream; Gottschalk and Halteman for poultry; DiNic's Roast Pork; and on the Arch Street side, Amish and Mennonite stalls and restaurants. Even at its nadir, the market had character, distinctiveness, and foods to delight.

I discovered a fellow named Phil Bush, a Saturday-only vendor, who drove in from Bucks County, north of the city, to sell smoked meat. Over my purchases we discussed meat, double-smoked bacon (the best!), and his small but distinguished cottage industry. When one of the unfortunate ownership changes occurred at the Terminal and rents doubled even for day-trippers, Phil left. Not until several years later, when Siegfried & Son European Gourmet opened, could you again find handmade and imported bacon and wurst.

La Divisa Meats

In the intervening years from 1980 to the present, the Reading Terminal Market experienced enormous changes from additional ownership turnover, arrival of an adjacent convention center, and total rehabilitation of the Reading building. Today the revitalized market has several charcuterie and wurst stalls to visit and enjoy. One of the newest vendors is Nick Macri, owner of La Divisa Meats. Nick grew up in Toronto to Italian-Canadian parents; his family came from Calabria, and his mother was a chef. The extended family made most everything from scratch, including a variety of fresh and cured pork. He remembers the annual ritual of putting up salami, coppa, and soppressata with his uncle and cousins.

Nick arrived in Philadelphia on a soccer scholarship to Drexel University. He enrolled in the university's four-year culinary program, and Chef Alan Segel's class on charcuterie helped him understand the value of his family's interest in curing. After graduation Nick found work in several well-regarded city restaurants, Osteria and FARMiCia, before becoming in 2007 chef de cuisine and charcutier at Southwark Restaurant in the city's Queen Village. At each place, working with locally raised animals, he developed a variety of cooked and cured charcuterie and continued to move toward a dream of his own meat business. In 2013 he moved to the Reading Terminal as manager and butcher of Virginia's Border Springs Farm lamb shop. Border Springs is the same farm that supplies Sam Edwards for his lamb prosciutto.

In 2014, when an opportunity to buy the store came along, Nick jumped in with a partner who provided financial support. Since many essential components were already in place, the initial costs were modest, and he was able to negotiate a five-year lease on the space with the Terminal Market. Wanting a full-service butcher shop, Nick expanded the meat selection to include beef, goat, pork, and veal, together with the store's already well-known lamb. He changed the store's name to La Divisa Meats, a compliment to the location of his grandparents' farm in Calabria.

Most significant to the business, he made a critical decision to purchase pastured and antibiotic- and hormone-free animals from Pennsylvania farms. With this emphasis on local sources, Border Spring's lamb eventually disappeared from the meat case. In fall 2015 when I met Nick, the fresh carcasses came from Country Time Farm (Large Black hogs), Birchrun Hills Farm (veal), Stryker Farm (Kiko goats), and Jamison Farm, one of the country's most renowned lamb producers. Every week he bought two to three hogs, five lambs, and one goat, with 80 percent of the meat sold as cuts, fresh sausages, or cooked items such as cotto salami, pâtés, and terrines.

The remaining 20 percent composes the raw material for Nick's salumi. He uses a basic curing recipe of salt, various spices, and pink salt (sodium nitrate) for the salamis. While sensitive to the debate over sodium nitrate, he argues using it in proper amounts ensures safety without creating any risk to consumers. In a cold box in the basement of the Terminal, the initial fermentation runs twenty-one days, after which the salami ages for eight to ten weeks. Nick flavors several salamis with unusual ingredients: hops, za'atar, or grains of paradise for "Hennepin" coppa. The whole-muscle coppa and prosciutto mature for four to six months, during which they experience a 30 percent weight loss.

Nick celebrates the methods and practices needed to create excellent products. He views his business as a way to blend family traditions, extraordinary locally raised meats, and changes within the city's food community. During his fifteen years in Philadelphia, he has seen greater cooperation among chefs and producers, as well as collaboration with Pennsylvania farmers and growers. Although enjoying a considerable reputation as a chef, he emphasizes that La Divisa is about local, not national, visibility. He wants the store to serve both suppliers and customers, a clear reflection of the Terminal's history. During our conversation customers stopped to buy meat and ask questions about how to cook a particular type of meat or cut. I watched Nick focus visibly and intently to answer the patron in a guiding, respectful manner to help him or her understand and appreciate the steps needed to make a great meal.

I admire Nick's approach to his butchery and salumeria. Its small scale benefits him and customers, in my opinion, because of its intimacy. Shoppers see meat being cut and prepared a few feet away from them. I appreciate as well the connections to the Terminal's long history; it's easy to imagine the value of these small shops as anchors to the attractiveness of the market. Perhaps it's my mental map from years ago, but I think the new businesses offer more than salt and pepper spicing to the contemporary Terminal. Like Phil Bush and Siegfried and Uwe Mauldener, these small enterprises and the people who run them create places with personality.

1732 Meats

Although railroad trains no longer arrive above the Terminal Market, you can walk a block or so to the Market Street subway line and embark on other charcuterie adventures. I take the subway west and transfer to a trolley car that brings me all the way to the city's border with Yeadon, a suburban city in Delaware County, Pennsylvania. The walk from the last stop carries me farther west on Baltimore Pike, past the large Fernwood Cemetery to my right. In the distance stands a white water tower, a good directional landmark for my visit; getting closer, I can read "Rent" in large letters on the water tower.

After locating 1732 Meats in this former light industrial and warehouse complex, Ari Miller greets me at the entrance to his plant. Miller, a stocky, jovial man with a black beard, sports a black porkpie hat . . . thankfully, not a meaty equivalent of a Carmen Miranda assorted fruit chapeau. Ari looks, acts, and speaks like someone in the charcuterie business. His enthusiasm for what he does is infectious and entertaining. He grew up in Berkeley, California, and fondly recalls trips with his father to farmers' markets around the Bay Area. If he made it to the Ferry Plaza market before the building restoration, I understand the roots of some of his later inspiration. At that time you could stand in line at 8:00 a.m. for a fresh grilled, hand-made Bruce Aidells's sausage sandwich.

In Ari's case he moved east in 1998 to marry his fiancée, Elise, and although I don't think the two events were connected, he started to obsess over bacon. Here the story gets really complicated, since he ended up working for Wells Fargo Bank, managing a regional property office. Maybe because in San Francisco one could find both Aidells's maple bacon sausage sandwiches *and* Wells Fargo? Whatever the connection, Ari's interest led to bacon experiments at home. In 2009 when the financial collapse hit, he really shifted gears, left the bank, and went to law school.

Now here's a guy doing bacon recipe tests at home with Elise and their daughters serving as food critics; they described his bacon as awesome. Not until his last semester just before bar exam crunch time did Ari realize that becoming a lawyer didn't compute. Perhaps too many bacon grease stains on his yellow legal pads were pointing him toward the barn, and not the bar.

Now what? One day in 2013, staring across the street from his house at the Lansdowne Farmers Market, he had an epiphany, "Why don't I make some bacon and sell it there?" So one Saturday he showed up with a card table and twenty pounds of bacon and sold out immediately. Next week was the same story, and over the summer production increased to the point at which the Millers' kitchen no longer worked. Production shifted to NoBL Restaurant in Lansdowne and then the Center for Culinary Enterprises in West Philadelphia. By the fall Ari was producing and selling three hundred pounds of bacon a week; that drew attention from consumers beyond one farmers' market. But to continue production at more than three hundred pounds a week for wholesale markets demanded dedicated spaces, new sales outlets, and the required USDA certification.

After looking around Philadelphia at expensive processing facilities, Ari turned to Delaware County Economic Development to locate a building. The solution was a 10,000-square-foot former wholesale fruit and vegetable structure on Baltimore Pike with refrigeration, a loading dock, and other valuable equipment. However, despite all the pluses, bacon and curing production required dedicated areas within the building to meet USDA specifications. In 2014 Ari secured $160,000 to renovate 5,000 square feet for bacon and other cured meats.

Ari, Elise, and their two daughters live in Lansdowne, not far from the business, on a plot of land with links back to William Penn. The original 470-acre estate became the heart of the town, with a manor house built in 1732. Today, on a much smaller piece of land, the Millers celebrate the history of the house and a vision for a meaty future with the name 1732 Meats.

The day I visited, a two-man crew was busy making bacon using one of four dry rubs. One man had previously managed Di Bruno Brothers' charcuterie, and the other was a former chef. The bacon flavors are Spanish Smoked Paprika, Garlic Insanity, Jalapeño, and Black Peppercorn. Ari does not smoke his bacons, to ensure the flavor of the pork shines through. Through D'Artagnan Foods, 1732 buys Berkshire hogs from Iowa Supreme Meats. Supreme maintains a closed Berkshire herd and guarantees antibiotic-free, pastured, and humanely raised and slaughtered animals. In 2015 Ari was making guanciale, pancetta, and lonza from the hogs as well as prosciutto from Latrobe's Jamison Farm lamb. D'Artagnan also supplies Wagyu beef from Strube Ranch in Texas for a bresaola seasoned with sumac.

By 2016 Ari forecasted production to run three thousand pounds every four weeks with an eventual goal of five thousand to six thousand pounds of charcuterie a month. To meet new production levels, he hired really good people who understood food and how to run clean, efficient operations. The two men I met make great bacon and charcuterie and manage costs, inventory control, and interaction with the USDA.

Ari invited me to tag along to a sales meeting with a potential distributor. Despite all my years in Philadelphia, the route we took through Southwest to Washington Avenue in South Philly had me staring out the window more than once. Although I lived in Philadelphia for nearly twenty-five years, the drive was through neighborhoods I rarely visited. Today, especially along Washington Avenue and its former rail lines, you can see the impact of investments along the streets. We stopped at a renovated old warehouse and met his clients, Ari working full steam to cook bacon and offer samples of forthcoming cured meats. They talked about scaling up distribution from Washington and Northern Virginia to New York and Boston. When I reviewed his website in May 2016, it reported a nationwide presence! Not bad for a banker-turned-lawyer who saw a pork light at the end of tunnel.

I finished the tour with Ari at a place called Stargazy, a British-style hole-in-the-wall serving Cornish pasties. Unbelievable: to have started the day with unusual bacon and charcuterie and to finish with a British lunch with damn good tea. This small restaurant on East Passyunk Crossing also represents part of the change in this corner of South Philadelphia.

Le Virtù

Over several centuries areas of South Philadelphia became home to African-Americans, Irish, and then Jews and southern Italians. Into the twentieth century, music was a defining presence in the community, with opera singers Mario Lanza and Marian Anderson, and pop singers Frankie Avalon, Chubby Checker, Fabian, Eddie Fisher, Al Martino, and Bobby Rydell. From its row houses emerged such jazz stars as the Heath Brothers, Pat Martino, and Charlie Ventura; although movie star Sylvester Stallone was born in New York's Hell's Kitchen, his movie *Rocky* brought great visibility to South Philly, the Philadelphia Museum of Art, and the Benjamin Franklin Parkway.

Italian-American restaurants dotted South Philly and popularized versions of southern Italian cuisine with lots of pasta, "red gravy" (tomato sauce), garlic, and fridge-chilled red wine! Places such as Villa di Roma (1963), Ralph's (1900), Dante & Luigi's (1899), and Marra's Cucina Italiana (1927), all still in business, offered residents and visitors great food, laughter, and service. Victor Cafe provided great opera, with such singers as Enrico Caruso, Lanza, Joan Sutherland, and others who stopped by after performing at the Academy of Music. Young opera students from the Curtis Institute of Music, waiting on tables, would break into an aria and bring the place to a standstill; for romance, music, and food, go to Victor's!

Just down the street from the Cornish pasty stand is a restaurant featuring the foods of Abruzzo. When Cathy Lee and Francis Cretarola decided to open Le Virtù on Passyunk Avenue, the response was underwhelming and even a bit critical. "What, no red sauce? Where's the spaghetti and meatballs or the chicken parm?" Their approach was new and very different from the decades-old cultural norm of Italian food in South Philly, and it took some time to change the prevailing food perceptions. But they succeeded.

I visited the restaurant twice in October 2015, once to eat and the other to talk with Cathy, Francis, and Joe Cicala, the chef. Sunday dinner was magnificent; Cathy delivered a salumi plate, brimming with just about everything in stock that day. She said something about my upcoming visit several days later, and that they wanted me to experience the full range of Joe's brilliance. I didn't realize she was one of the owners until the end of the meal.

A profusion of salumi confronted and delighted me. Piled on were such pork royalties as guanciale, capocollo, lonza, *ventricina teramana* (a spreadable salami with orange zest, chile, rosemary, and garlic), *mortadella di Campotosto*, and duck prosciutto. I ate every last morsel . . . my mother always told me to clean my plate, but now I was worried about how much I had ordered for the rest of the meal. Le Virtù makes a variety of fresh pasta and mine, *Spizzichi al coniglio*, a pinched pasta with rabbit ragu, was terrific. Fortunately I asked Cathy to cancel the second course so I could still enjoy dessert!

The story of Le Virtù is one of love, respect, family, place, and culture, all presented and celebrated on every plate. It begins with its name, which in English translates as "the virtues" and seems straightforward and understandable. But the name embodies notions of food and family that are both simple and complex. For one, "le virtù" is the name for a very special soup, a minestrone unlike any other I know: beans, pasta, spices, vegetables and meat, and all the leftovers from the fall and winter pantry; a mixture of seasonal change, happiness, and local ingredients that reflect history, poverty, and community.

The soup originated in Teramo, Abruzzo, a region due east of Rome, backed by the high, sharp, bony Apennine spine and with the Adriatic Sea as its front door. The geography and climate contributed to the isolation of the inland city and surrounding small villages. For most Abruzzesi money was scarce, and everyone put up food for the winter. On May 1, after winter's last vestiges departed, the population turned out to make le virtù, a celebration of seasonal change, survival, and hopes for the coming season.

The soup was made in seven pots and pans, a reflection of how the number seven resonates through Italian Catholicism. The southern Italian *La Vigilia* (The Vigil) celebrated on Christmas Eve, for example, is a seven-course seafood dinner, a reflection of abstinence, of not eating meat on December 24. For le virtù you literally cleaned the larder; everyone's soup was different and contained ingredients in multiples of seven, so thirty-five, forty-two, and even forty-nine ingredients were possible!

Francis's grandfather, Alfonso Cretarola, grew up in Teramo, where le virtù was a part of his life. On one spring visit to Abruzzo, Cathy and Francis realized suddenly they did not have reservations the next day, May 1, to partake in the annual ritual. A generous local baker invited them in, introduced friends and family, and shared le virtù, and then they discovered links to South Philadelphia. To name the restaurant Le Virtù seems serendipitous, destined, poetic, and familial.

As I write this, May 1, 2016, just passed, and the restaurant highlighted this year's amazing blend. To make this year's single giant batch, Joe Cicala didn't place any special orders with suppliers. Instead, he scoured the restaurant pantry. Into a rich stock made from leftover rabbit bones, he tossed all sorts of dried beans. Next into the 25-gallon pot went scraps from assorted salumi (porchetta, guanciale, pancetta, lardo, fennel sausage, and guinea hen sausage), several pastas (ditalini, casarecce, broken-up spaghetti and reginette, chopped fettuccine), and various other ingredients. Last, he added a few fresh vegetables from Green Meadow Farm, such as favas, new potatoes, and spring peas.[1]

Please remind me to make reservations for future May 1 gatherings!

The soup embraces, celebrates, and represents everything about Le Virtù and Cathy and Francis.

Alfonso Cretarola ultimately arrived in Reading, Pennsylvania, a city of hardworking immigrants — Irish, Poles, Czechs, and Italians. To help him fit in, he changed his name to Francis Cratil. Years later his grandson Francis reclaimed Cretarola to arrive at Francis Cratil Cretarola.

Cathy and Francis met in graduate school, where they both received master's degrees in creative writing. A honeymoon to Abruzzo changed their lives, as Francis became aware of deep chords, remembrances of food, music, land, and the panoramas of life communicated lovingly by Alfonso.

"I started to realize that stuff had been implanted in me by my grand-father at a young age — his pride in where he was from, and his sadness for having to leave it due to poverty," says Francis. "I wanted to actually find my family." After three years Francis decided to quit his job at a college reference index and move to Rome. He started studying Italian intensively.[2]

However, illness brought Francis home, and after his full recovery the couple worked at an Italian restaurant in South Philadelphia. They also returned to Abruzzo for several months each year, to learn, taste, appreci-ate, savor, and absorb as much of the region's culture as possible. Listening to them talk, I thought of the expression "to suck out all the marrow of life," to leave nothing to chance and to relish this unique opportunity.

Along the way an idea germinated to open a restaurant, an outpost, a beacon of Abruzzo in South Philadelphia. In many ways this was not a strange idea, since some of the original immigrants to the area came from the region. For example, Danny and Joe Di Bruno of the great Ninth Street store came from a village near Pescara, a coastal city in Abruzzo. Cathy and Francis hired an Abruzzese woman, a great home cook but who had no restaurant experience, and opened Le Virtù in 2007.

Cathy and Francis had a vision of unpretentious but delicious regional foods with ingredients closely matching their Abruzzo counterparts, pre-pared using traditional techniques. The first three years must have been unique; some days everything worked and others not so much. Ultimately, an unhappy chef returned to Abruzzo, and in 2010 they hired Joe Cicala to run the kitchen.

With roots in a Sicilian-American family, Joe grew up outside Washington, DC, and spent a lot of time in the kitchen with his mother, who owned an Italian catering company. When he was older, his interest in family and food motivated him to travel to Italy, where he landed at Al Cenacolo, a Michelin-starred restaurant in Salerno, Campania. After two years working for Pietro Rispoli, he returned to Washington and served in several positions at some of the best Italian places in America. After further stints in New York, Joe's palate and sensibilities were finely tuned to what Cathy and Francis wanted in Le Virtù and their chef.

Once he arrived, Joe immediately began to interpret and develop Le Virtù's unique approach to Abruzzo and *cucina povera*, the food (cuisine) of the poor. Being poor in money does not translate into a poverty of spirit, creativity, or celebration. Simple ingredients in the hands of a maestro, whether at home or in a trattoria, emerge almost like a beautiful butterfly to surprise, please, and reward those who eat. Joe developed numerous pasta styles, different ragu sauces, and a salumi program that mirrored his deep appreciation and understanding of Abruzzo.

Francis and Joe spoke of the irony that creating cucina povera, poor man's food, in Philadelphia is actually rather expensive. When most Abruzzese households farmed or owned small gardens and a hog or two, they grew, harvested, and preserved grains, meats, vegetables, and wild herbs with clear connections to place. One slope might have wild oregano or fennel, while another might see saffron (the area around the city of L'Aquila cultivates some of the world's best saffron). Any attempt on East Passyunk Avenue to replicate cucina povera recipes must use different ingredients and adapt and interpret recipes, not by adulteration or false claims, but through sensitivity and hard work.

Since Le Virtù doesn't have a farm across the street, they developed relationships with growers outside the city who share their passion and vision for outstanding ingredients. The restaurant's philosophy includes using local and international sources:

> We source all we can from the "terra" surrounding Philadelphia: naturally raised pork from Berks County; lamb, chicken and rabbit from Lancaster County; produce from rural New Jersey and Pennsylvania. What we can't find locally, we import from Abruzzo: artisanal honey and cheeses (some of the rarest in America); L'Aquila saffron; extra virgin olive oil for finishing dishes; dried pastas (including a gluten-free option); even the flour we use to make our fresh pasta.[3]

Every week, Joe uses at least two shoulders and two hams, along with racks and bellies for fresh and cured meats. He buys a variety of heritage breed hogs — Large Black, Gloucester Old Spot, and Yorkshire — from Country Time Farms, the same place Nick Macri gets his animals. He transforms this pork bounty into at least thirty different types of salumi, including the ones I devoured during my dinner.

After my meeting I discovered something else about their commitment to the region. For years they conducted culinary and cultural tours, introducing Americans to the land and the people. At some point Francis and Cathy learned about transhumance, *transumanza* in Italian, the ancient seasonal ritual of moving sheep from protected winter common land near villages into the mountains to graze and make cheeses. The paths, called "tratturi," traverse Abruzzo south into Molise and Puglia. With the demise of shepherding, nature slowly returned the tratturi to the land, and we lost eons of cultural and physical history. To focus international attention on the value of the cultural landscape, UNESCO designated the tratturi as the Royal Shepherd's Track. As a celebration and appreciation for the land and people, the couple has contributed money to restore the tratturi.

Listening to Cathy, Francis, and Joe reminds me deeply of Slow Food and its philosophy of how the pleasures of the table teach us about the universe — family, friends, place, history, culture, and life's lessons. So much of daily life and community in Abruzzo and other southern Italian regions centered and revolved around the kitchen, because the poor, the *contadini*, the peasants often lived in one- or two-room dwellings. A kitchen table served many roles, as a place to converse, share, argue, love, grieve, drink, and eat.

Le Virtù serves delicious edible history lessons. Most of us have little knowledge of the several thousand years of war and conquest witnessed across Southern Italy. Each shift in political and military fortunes left aspects, for example, of Greek, Roman, and Arabic food and drink. Grapes, saffron, pasta, tomatoes, almonds, and chiles speak to conquest and assimilation. The influences are real in the land, people, and food; when you partake of Le Virtù salumi, pasta, and sauces, you discover aromas, tastes, and textures, "some vestigial and obscure, some vibrantly alive" that inspire Cathy, Francis, Joe, and hopefully you.[4]

Kensington Quarters

My last train trip was a midmorning jaunt east on the Frankford El to Girard Avenue and the Fishtown community. Twenty-five years ago, when I lived in Philadelphia, Fishtown wasn't a destination unless you lived there. One of the oldest neighborhoods in Philadelphia, Fishtown is the site where William Penn signed a treaty with the Lenni Lenape Indians under a tree in what became known as Penn Treaty Park. Legend says the community got its name from spring shad fishing in the nearby Delaware River. In the nineteenth century the area became populated by Irish, German, and Polish Catholic immigrants.

The neighborhood maintained its working-class character and personality until the late twentieth century, but with a steady loss of jobs, the area deteriorated. Then about ten years ago the availability of inexpensive but well-built housing attracted artists and others looking for affordability as Center City and adjacent communities were rehabilitated. Today Fishtown is considered one of the city's most attractive neighborhoods, and new businesses such as Kensington Quarters are part of the renaissance.

I heard about Heather Thomason from several friends and other butchers in Philadelphia. The concept for Kensington Quarters (KQ) is unusual; as you walk in the door, a long meat case is on your right, with a bar on the left. Between the meat case and an attractive restaurant in the back is a meat storage locker with windows all around. You can see tonight's dinner, tomorrow's ground beef, or ingredients for cooked and cured charcuterie. It reminds me of the first Hong Kong–style restaurants in Philadelphia's Chinatown; as you entered, a huge aquarium-like tank greeted you with dozens of dinner choices — just pick your fish! At KQ fortunately nothing is swimming or making other movements; well, except for the butchers.

Heather is one of a few female head butchers and charcutiers in the United States; cutting meat remains a very male-centered occupation, reflecting hundreds of years of meat cutting as man's work, although historically throughout Europe and America farm women often contributed as much as men to slaughter and butchering. When meat cutting and packing converted into rapid processing, hundreds of women, especially African-Americans, worked for such companies as Armour and Swift. But massive consolidation of the beef, pork, and poultry industries forced women out of many jobs into the industrial processing world we know today — repetitive, mind-numbing work. In post–World War II America, the growth of supermarkets, with their very tight profit margins, welcomed the precut, sanitary packed meats and fired their butchers. For many decades it was nearly impossible to find a real butcher shop anywhere in the country.

At the same time Americans became further divorced from the farms and systems that delivered food to their tables. We thought meat came from a plastic-wrapped package, not from a farm or a real animal. Beginning in the early 2000s, a shift began, in part a result of books by people like Eric

Schlosser and Michael Pollan, who pointed to both the physical and mental distances between food origin, processing, and your plate. Organizations such as Chefs Collaborative, Slow Food International, Livestock Breeds Conservancy, the Humane Society, and Vermont Fresh Network raised consumer awareness about the dynamic connections linking food origin, animal welfare, environmental impact, taste, diet and health, and respect.

Every instance of a food-borne illness linked to ground beef led more consumers to search for new ways to eat. The response to eat differently was correct but, sadly, came about for all the wrong reasons. One of the changes around butchery occurred for a better reason — because of the greater availability of excellent meat. The emergence of quality steers and hogs, a need to maximize the value of these excellent animals, and restaurant and pop-up dining "nose-to-tail" and offal menus all demanded more butchers with much higher skills. By 2004 or 2005 some of the first new butcher shops opened; one of the pioneers was Fleisher's Grass-Fed and Organic Meats (since renamed Fleisher's Craft Butchery) in Kingston, New York, in the Hudson River Valley. Fleisher's, Brooklyn's Marlowe & Daughters, and other new shops across the country spawned the New Carnivore Movement, also known as the "hipster butcher movement"!

Heather, a graphic designer, while working for the Park Slope Food Coop in Brooklyn, saw the challenges to small-scale meat production — slaughter, distribution, and transportation — and wondered what solutions might exist. When a new butcher shop opened nearby, she saw long lines of customers snaking out the door and thought, "Um, something interesting is happening here." After deciding to learn butchery, she banged on a lot of doors and ended up working with Brooks Miller at North Mountain Pastures in Newport, Pennsylvania. Miller and his wife raised pastured animals that sold through a community supported agriculture operation.

The next jump, this time to the West Coast, brought Heather to the Local Butcher Shop in Berkeley, around the corner from Alice Water's Chez Panisse and the Cheese Board; obviously, a nice neighborhood! With Berkeley as her hub, she ventured to San Francisco's Fatted Calf and then Thistle Meats in Petaluma, opened in 2014 by two women, who became her role models. While in California, she partnered with Bryan Mayer, owner of Kensington Quarters, to teach a class on how to prepare porchetta, and he brought her to Philadelphia in 2014.

The philosophy underlying KQ strengthens Heather's commitment to a more efficient and supportive meat system. She works with five to ten farms, principally from New Jersey and Pennsylvania. Three small slaughterhouses, including Smucker's Meats, a third-generation butcher, handle slaughter. In 2006 the Mount Joy firm became a USDA-certified facility after the family saw opportunities to manage slaughter responsibilities for small Pennsylvania farms. A steady decline in the number of slaughter facilities meant long-distance drives for service, not the best situation for farmers or animals. While more expensive, the quality of properly handled animals ensures value to the end user.

The Lancaster Farm Fresh Cooperative, a one-hundred-member farmers' co-op, handles pickup from Smucker's and delivery of carcasses to Kensington Quarters. In 2015 Heather bought one to two steers, two to three pigs, one each of goat and lamb, and anywhere from forty to fifty chickens each week. To ensure the viability of the system, KQ committed to fourteen-day terms for payment to farmers. In much of the restaurant and food world, terms usually start at thirty days or longer, and sometimes the grower must wait even beyond those terms. When we consider the size of these farms, payment within two weeks makes a huge difference to the grower and in the long run benefits KQ; when they need a special favor, excellent financial standing makes all the difference. In my opinion, paying farmers within fourteen days requires extraordinary dedication, especially if the butcher shop and restaurant hit a few weeks of slow sales.

Heather extends her commitment to sustainability by hiring and teaching young men and women with a serious interest in learning butchery skills. I watched them at work handling meat orders and conversing with customers. Currently, about half of KQ's customers are new residents of the Fishtown and Frankford neighborhoods as they continue to gentrify, and the remainder are from South Philly and Mount Airy in northwest Philadelphia. A professional attitude with patrons, teaching them about quality, cuts, and preparation, brings them back regardless of the dollar size of the purchase. Heather has a small curing program; one challenge to KQ is that there's not enough room to hang fresh meat and by extension a lack of appropriate space to cure meat. However, given her interests and the restaurant's success, prospects for more charcuterie look good. With continued demographic changes in surrounding communities, Kensington Quarters should see greater interest and sales for cured products.

In spring 2016 Heather and fellow butcher Cecilie May opened a new company — Primal Supply Meats — to supply restaurants and meat subscriptions to consumers. The women's close relationships with farmers provide further opportunities to grow Philadelphia's market for fresh and cured meats.

Di Bruno Brothers

After completing my shopping at the Reading Terminal Market and drinking at least one double cappuccino, the next stop was the Italian Market on South Ninth Street. Regardless of season or weather, the Saturday routine is ingrained deep in my heart. From the 1970s through the early 1990s, my trek was like a religious pilgrimage. I started at the north end where Christian intersected Ninth Street and made a stop at Fiorella's Sausage, founded in 1892, maybe the oldest Italian-American butcher shop in the country. I crossed Ninth to visit Superior Pasta for great ravioli, manicotti, and pasta, then walked down Ninth. In the winter fifty-five-gallon drums are blazing with fires fueled by empty wooden fruit and vegetable boxes to keep vendors warm; if it was windy the ashes blew everywhere. The market extended into the street, sometimes blocking the old trolleys or buses.

The market developed steadily, changed to suit the times, and hit its full zenith in the 1960s as Philadelphia's Italian Market. It became "Philly's supermarket" and a favorite tourist destination. There were thirty butcher shops and twenty-three fish stores, and the fruit, vegetable, and other stands extended uninterrupted from Wharton to Christian. Jewish people sold clothing, Greeks had spice stores, and Italians had the rest, mostly.

Before refrigeration it was necessary to buy food provisions daily, and the Ninth Street market offered a convenient, centralized location and everything needed to prepare the day's meals, as well as clothing and other household goods.[5]

I stopped at the D'Orazio Cheese store, one of my favorite places for house-made fresh mozzarella and ricotta and the wonderful owners, the three D'Orazio sisters. The journey down Ninth continued to Washington Avenue and a stop at Paul Giordano's for fruits and vegetables, then back up the other side of the street for an occasional visit at Fante's Kitchen Shop. Before and even after the internet, Fante's is one of the great stores for everything; they still sell my same moka pot after many decades.

But before I make my primary visit, let's cross back to the east side of the street and the D'Angelo Brothers, a three-generation family business founded in 1910. Santo D'Angelo Sr. emigrated from Sicily to Downingtown, where, as a teenager, he opened a butcher shop. His style of meat cutting differed from the Pennsylvania German (Dutch), and he relocated to South Philadelphia to start a new shop. Over succeeding decades Signore Santo's son Santo II and then grandson Santo III, "Sonny," took over the store. Sonny D'Angelo created a unique place for charcuterie and salumi. While making prosciutto and some other cured products, he is best known for fresh meat and sausage. The unusual selection covers the globe, from kangaroo and ostrich to alligator, bison, and even African eland. Fresh sausages include a number of pork varieties, as well as veal, venison, and seafood. In my opinion, Sonny's imaginative use of both recognized and, for some consumers, exotic meats created a different level of charcuterie. However, by themselves, unusual animals are just that: different. It takes skill and knowledge to translate any quality meat into great charcuterie and salumi, and Sonny has achieved a level of respect and admiration because of his ability.

I don't remember my first time in Di Bruno's House of Cheese, but even after countless visits over twenty years from the early 1970s to the mid-1990s, my impressions are still very much alive and vivid. You climbed a concrete step painted in the Italian national colors to pull open a glass door, and as you stepped into the narrow shop, a wave of sights, sounds, and smells washed over you. Along the right wall all the way to the back were pasta, olive oil, balsamic vinegar, canned anchovies and sardines, capers, imported Italian tomato paste and authentic San Marzano tomatoes, jars of Nutella, and boxes of amaretti cookies and biscotti!

At the back was a refrigerated case with mozzarella and ricotta, and when you turned to the left was Joe "Bruzz" Abruzzo, a wonderful, sweet Sicilian who ran the back of the store. We're making this loop from front to back along the right-hand wall with a turn left and back toward the front because you rarely walked in without standing in line. It snaked down to the right and back on the left. On Easter and from Thanksgiving through New

Year's, lines would stretch out the door. But around Christmas, especially if it was cold, customers packed in like sardines.

The left side of the counter was the territory of brothers Danny and Joe Di Bruno, who arrived in the States in 1922 as young children, from the Abruzzo village Loreto Aprutino in the province of Pescara. They were processed through Ellis Island; Joe was six, Danny five, and a third brother, Thomas, was two. In the 1930s the young men, neither of whom had much education, worked for a Greek grocer. In 1939 Danny and Joe used their savings and a few loans to open a small store on Ninth Street and established Di Bruno's Grocery Store. Like many other groceries, they carried everything from brooms to soap powder and packaged foods, including some imported products. For the next twenty-five years, they established themselves as smart, dedicated, hardworking, and honest men. They sold bulk pasta, large tins of olive oil, Parmigiano-Reggiano cheese and house-made mozzarella, and lots of salami, including homemade sweet and hot soppressata.

But after twenty-five years the retail world was changing, as automobiles carried former South Philadelphia neighbors to South Jersey and supermarkets gained prominence. In 1965 on a vacation in Switzerland, Danny was introduced to some of Europe's best and finest cheeses. The experience opened an inspired door for Joe and Danny to build a domestic and imported cheese business; they renamed the grocery Di Bruno's House of Cheese. Now they offered "exotic" cheeses such as "Havarti, Jarlsberg, Emmentaler Swiss, Red Wax Gouda, Monterey Jack, smoked gouda, Pepper Jack, and the newly popular, Brie."[6] The cheese selection eventually grew to over four hundred varieties.

Frankly, I didn't realize until recently that my first trip in the early to mid-1970s wasn't long after they refocused the business, since every visit felt as if they had been selling cheese forever. In the mid-1970s when you talked cheese, you talked about European styles, and the two men answered my questions patiently and eagerly offered samples. While you were helping yourself from large drums of Greek and Italian olives, Danny or Joe scooped cheese spreads with flavors like Abruzzese or port-wine into small containers. They concocted these spreads in Danny's kitchen, and today the company sells thousands of containers; sometimes I believe my own past consumption was right up there.

They also made their own wine vinegar with a "mother" starter brought from Italy just before the start of World War II, where every fall Italian families either pressed grapes or bought wine grape juice to make wine in their basements. "Back in the day when things were a little different, Danny and Joe made their own wine. They'd then take a second pressing of the wine and ferment it in 55-gallon whiskey barrels to make homemade red wine vinegar. Four months later, you'd have the perfect salad dressing or marinade to slather on some French fries."[7] Today, working from the same recipe, the company makes 2,800 small-batch bottles a year.

The Di Bruno brothers' simple philosophy to welcome customers with a steady smile and enthusiasm to sell great food established the store as a destination. Chefs and food professionals to movie stars may have been important for visibility, but Danny and Joe built their reputation in the community and with each customer. They offered samples to children; today those six- to ten-year-olds are the backbone of the new generation of Di Bruno's clientele.

Over two decades living in Philadelphia, I witnessed many changes at the Reading Terminal and on Ninth Street. In the late 1970s Vietnamese refugees, arriving in South Philly, clustered at Seventh and Christian and opened numerous restaurants. The Terminal finally saw significant investments and upgrading. Ninth Street also evolved, but Di Bruno's remained an anchor, with Danny, Joe, Joe Bruzz, and young guys Bill, Billy, and Emilio (Em) behind the counter. We went to buy food and got an extra-size helping of generosity, humor, and welcome.

By 1990 Danny and Joe, now into their seventies, with fifty years of service, were ready to retire. Two grandchildren, twenty-one-year-olds Bill Mignucci and his cousin Emilio Mignucci, approached them to buy the business. Bill had just finished college, and Emilio was working as a chef. During a long family meeting, Bill and Em proposed buying the business. The deal satisfied everyone, and in 1990 they became the owners. A short time later Emilio's brother Billy, a financial wizard, became the third partner.

In the intervening twenty-five years, the three grandsons built Di Bruno's into one of the most recognized brands in the United States. With Bill as president and CEO, Billy as the finance guy, and Emilio as VP for culinary pioneering, the company expanded, but always with a clear strategy and direction. The timing for their entrance into the food world was uncanny and serendipitous. Nationwide interest in food was becoming important, and domestic wine and craft beer had firm stakes in the ground. In 1998 they were one of the first companies to take advantage of the internet. By 2000 artisan cheese was tumbling from the vats of hundreds of small producers to accompany handmade bread. To say the least, waves of new products and heightened public interest in food gave the Mignucci cousins a diverse platform to build and eventually expand. New products arrived at the Ninth Street store, and they opened a small shop in Center City.

On the charcuterie front they brought back the Abruzzese salamis using Danny and Joe's original recipes. However, with changes in regulations and the large volume needed to supply the different outlets, Di Bruno's contracted with the Italian company Fratelli Beretta in Hackensack, New Jersey, to produce its salamis. Beretta, founded in 1812, makes a coarse-ground Abruzzese salami and soppressata, both hot and sweet versions, for Di Bruno's. The salamis are among the most requested Di Bruno products.

The biggest change happened in 2005, when they opened a 19,000-square-foot store a few blocks from Rittenhouse Square. The cousins engaged the Wharton School, the business school at the University of Pennsylvania, to help gather, analyze, and interpret data and to help them understand the challenges and opportunities of a significant investment. Today the flagship enterprise anchors a diverse business with wholesale, online mail order, catering, and three additional retail stores, including one in the suburbs. "We introduced the rebranding of 'Culinary Pioneers since 1939' and moved away from the 'House of Cheese,'" explains Bill. "We felt for those who didn't know us, it may have given a limited perception of what we really offer."[8]

More than ten years ago, I reconnected with the Mignucci cousins and since then have enjoyed opportunities to present seminars and workshops at the Chestnut Street store. I am impressed by their willingness to share knowledge and ideas about artisan cheese and charcuterie. Whenever I'm in Philadelphia, I make time to visit one of the stores. The stop is always educational, delicious, fun, and a reminder of how the right people and leadership can nurture a historic business. The pioneering spirit is more than a legacy, it's an open mind to discover, teach by example, see value in staff and customers, and offer us the best of food and people.

Rooster Street

What a difference twenty years makes, even in places where time appears to run at a different, maybe slower, pace. Philadelphia is about an hour from Lancaster County, the heart of Pennsylvania's Amish, Mennonite, and Brethren communities. As America built its first transcontinental roads, one of them, Route 30, passed through Lancaster County. The highway brought millions of tourists to "Pennsylvania Dutch" country, for better or worse.

While living in Philadelphia, I made occasional excursions to Lancaster, always to the city's Central Market and into the surrounding countryside. I vaguely remember one trip to Lititz, a small town north of Lancaster, and stops to visit its antique stores. The landscape between the two settlements was beautiful, with long rows of corn, Holstein cows, and some of the most spectacular barns anywhere in the country.

So when I discovered a new charcuterie shop in Lititz, it caught my attention, and I made plans to visit. My travel companion for the day was Jamie Png, an artisan cheese maker, who worked for New Jersey's Valley Shepherd Creamery at the Reading Terminal and Cherry Grove Farm. We met in 2015 at the American Cheese Society annual meeting in Providence, Rhode Island. Jamie's fermentation interests go way beyond cheese, and her suggestions about charcuterie and salumi were spot on.

We drove to the Lancaster Central Market, grabbed a snack, and then went on to Lititz and the new Rooster Street Butcher. Driving north over the six miles between Lancaster and Lititz, I was struck, if not appalled, by the new housing and strip malls and loss of the former landscape. Gone were my memories, replaced by a physical sameness of so many other American cities and towns. I wondered about the impact of the state's pioneering farmland preservation initiatives from the 1980s and whether efforts to conserve land met with much success. It turns out that it did, although along Lititz Pike the success might be marginal:

> *The program was approved in 1988 and the first easement was purchased in December of 1989. Now, more than 4,700 farms have been approved for easement purchases totaling more than 500,000 acres.*[9]

We arrived in Lititz around noon on a Saturday, and Rooster Street was packed with lunchtime guests, with several lines in front of the meat cases. Jamie and I introduced ourselves to owners Kristina and Tony Page, ordered lunch, and hoped we would not get in the way while they scurried around to fulfill orders and answer customer questions. The building, a former local telephone exchange, is constructed of solid concrete with hardwood floors. The main room contains cheese and meat cases; the whitewashed walls display lots of local antiques, especially roosters and old lard containers.

Behind the displays of fresh, cooked, and cured meats are glass walls that separate the public from the 1,100-square-foot processing area. You can watch meat being cut, fresh sausage production, and the initial steps in the curing process of charcuterie and salumi.

After about twenty minutes Kristina ran over with a beautifully arranged charcuterie plate, all house-made by Tony with far more items than we ordered. They offered us a marvelous culatello, smooth and sweet with a hint of salt; mild saucisson sec; smooth, soft-texture "Keystone cured" prosciutto with an herbal aroma and flavor; mildly smoked speck packed with mushroom aromas and flavors, absolutely terrific; bresaola; "smoke 'n' whiskey" salami, touched with just enough smoke, with a rich, medium-dry texture; a pork and rabbit terrine studded with pistachios; and as a finale a spicy coppa with great balance between heat, sweet, and salt.

What an amazing lunch, over which we talked with Kristina and Tony about themselves and the business. Kristina grew up on a Lancaster County farm and traveled with her parents, who encouraged her interests in food. As a teenager, she worked in local restaurants, then graduated from Kutztown University with a BFA in communication design. After several years in Savannah, she returned to Lancaster, met Tony, went to and left culinary school, and then focused on communication design. If anything, Rooster Street's design reflects her culinary and artistic interests and skills.

Tony is from York, about thirty miles west of Lancaster. At sixteen years old, he started work in his uncle's restaurant and realized his deep passion for cooking and food. After graduating from a local culinary school, he worked at several local and Philadelphia restaurants. In 2009, at the age of twenty-five, he became sous-chef at Emeril Lagasse's first restaurant in the Northeast, at the Sands Casino Resort in Bethlehem, Pennsylvania. The Lagasse kitchen, incorporating a temperature- and humidity-controlled room to age steaks, opened the door to Tony's interest in charcuterie. As he developed recipes he learned the proper curing techniques for a diverse array of cured meats from prosciutto to 'nduja.

A vacation to Paris ignited the couple's interest in exploring the possibilities of opening a butcher shop. Wandering over to Île Saint-Louis for ice cream at Berthillon, they discovered a boucherie, perhaps even the one right across the street from the ice cream shop. Upon returning to Lancaster they began planning for a small shop and in 2012 opened Rooster Street Provisions in Elizabethtown, another small county town. The store sold bacon, fresh and cured sausage, Italian-inspired whole-meat salumi, and headcheese. A year later they leased a stand at the Lancaster Central Market and witnessed increased demand of 10 percent a week for nine months. At one point Tony was butchering four hogs, a thousand pounds a week to meet the home store and market stall needs.

In many ways the growth created challenges that were probably unsustainable — very long hours of strenuous work, providing retail service while managing the business, having insufficient aging capacity, and so forth. They noticed, however, a key detail about Rooster Street Central Market shoppers: The majority of them lived in or immediately around Lititz. Apparently, a number of wealthy families, some old and others newer, live in Lititz and nearby Brownstown. If these individuals drove to Lancaster every Saturday, perhaps they might patronize a full-service store closer than Elizabethtown.

A search for new quarters turned up the present location in Lititz. After nine months' work and a three hundred thousand dollar investment — family, bank loan, and revolving credit — they opened in September 2015. Beyond the 1,100-square-foot butchery and curing area, the building provides nearly 1,800 square feet for the retail store and restaurant and an upstairs apartment for Kristina and Tony. Presently, they are state inspected because Rooster Street sells only direct to customers. I heard people in Philadelphia say how much they would like to have some Rooster Street products to resell. But if Tony started to make salumi for the wholesale market, the entire facility and inspection requirements change, and so do the expenses. At present, they are content to sell direct.

When Jamie and I visited in mid-October, just four weeks after the store's debut, Tony was processing roughly a thousand pounds of pork, one steer, four lambs, and fifty chickens a week. Two-thirds of the pork sold as fresh sausage, with one-third as fresh meat and a smaller amount for cured salami. Ultimately, he aims to cure 25 to 30 percent of the meat.

At present, Rooster Street buys purebred Berkshires from Creek Place Farms in East Earl, about twenty miles away. Tony notes that the best pork comes from the best farmers; you can feed a mediocre diet to and mistreat a valuable purebred hog and end up with nothing. Or as owners Don and Maria Longenecker understand, practice sensitive animal husbandry, offer the best feed possible, and harness contemporary technology to enhance growing techniques, and you grow the best animals possible.

Since opening in Elizabethtown and now in Lititz, Kristina and Tony purchased Berkshires from Creek Place. Tony emphasizes the confidence and trust they share with Maria and Don. Creek Place, recognizing the value of a 100 percent vegetable diet and antibiotic-free regimen, grows its own feed and hay; to say the least, their Berkshires are happy animals. They use only humane techniques to slaughter the hogs, and the practices are reflected in the quality of the pork products made by Tony.

Perhaps the greatest challenge may be if Rooster Street demands outstrip the farm's supply. The manner in which Creek Place raises its hogs doesn't allow for a faster method to grow animals. As soon as speed becomes a variable — greater numbers of faster-growing animals — you change the equation and in doing so alter the hog and the final product.

When Jamie and I started out that October Saturday, we had little idea what to expect and came away impressed and full of great food. Kristina and Tony are consummate professionals, fun to be around, and real artisans. Tony pointed out that since they've opened, at that point four weeks into the new space, demand was double previous experience and initial forecasts.

I asked about collaboration with other producers, and they both looked at each other . . . it was a sensitive topic. In 2012 they contacted several charcutiers and salumieri, who were reluctant at best to discuss any questions. The couple was somewhat bewildered, since they wanted guidance and technical advice, not recipes or proprietary information. Fortunately, three years later, as they embarked on planning the Lititz expansion, more generous help was forthcoming.

The Atlas of American Artisan Cheese contains several profiles of Pennsylvania Dutch cheese makers and my observations about how the national cheese community overlooked the presence and value of Amish and Mennonite producers. That is clearly not the case today for cheese and other Amish and Mennonite farm products. In my opinion, one essential lesson across the state is that these communities are essential to quality animals and meat products. Small-scale butchers and processors want their animals. In turn, the Amish's and Mennonites' centuries-old practices attract new farmers who, while not following the religious tenets, share the values and philosophies. Without this critical community of thoughtful, highly skilled livestock farmers, many of the businesses we visited might not exist. What an extraordinary tribute to some of America's oldest farm families and communities!

CHAPTER ELEVEN

Look for the Hog at the Oak

One of the privileges of volunteering with Slow Food USA and serving on its Ark of Taste and Presidia committee was an annual gathering to review nominations for some of America's great foods. In 2005 we met at Seed Savers Exchange in Decorah, Iowa, and stayed overnight in Lanesboro, Minnesota, about thirty miles north. Our daily commute to Seed Savers took us past beautiful farms in both states, many owned by Amish and Mennonite families who still follow traditional agricultural practices and for the most part shun electricity and gas-powered equipment and vehicles. The roads we traveled in northern Iowa had extra-wide shoulders to accommodate the horse-drawn black buggies.

After leaving Lanesboro in the early morning to arrive at the Seed Savers site, we worked until late afternoon and then enjoyed amazing dinners of locally grown food. Returning one evening, we admired the landscape and stars in the darkness, since whatever light existed came only from farm lanterns and not lightbulbs. About halfway through the trip, a glow appeared on the horizon, a sharp contrast to the surrounding countryside, and we were headed toward it. Cresting a hill, I thought we intruded on a scene from *E.T.* or *Close Encounters of the Third Kind*! Actually, if you have ever traveled the New Jersey Turnpike at night through the cities of Elizabeth and Kearny, past the belching chemical plants lit up as if preparing for a moon launch, that's the scene laid out before us. At any moment, I expected an eruption, a space shuttle takeoff, or at least fireworks. Instead it was a chemical plant to convert local corn into ethanol, a federally mandated gasoline additive. At night it reminded me of those behemoth New Jersey refineries, and in fact, the conversion process resembles refining. Corn goes in one end and ferments into carbon dioxide and alcohol (beer!); the resulting liquid is distilled (refined) into valuable ethanol with a bit of added gasoline so we can't drink it! But Iowa? Why in this beautiful Iowa landscape?

The state possesses some of the world's best soil: deep, dark, fertile tilth; Iowa "black gold," in which a farmer can grow just about any crop, from great squash and tomatoes (some of which we tasted at Seed Savers) to commodity corn (to which we gave a polite "no thanks"). As described earlier, as hog production moved west in the nineteenth century into Indiana and Illinois and then into Iowa, Missouri, and Nebraska, growers moved away from diversified diets for their animals of corn, hay, mast, and nuts to a fundamental reliance on corn, an easily grown, abundant, and subsidized crop. The value of corn as feed over the past 125 years cannot be underestimated, as each surge in hog production was tied closely to available corn supplies. For example, in 1900 Iowa accounted for over 9.7 million hogs, 15 percent of America's total output.[1] In 1936 the state's prominence in raising hogs led to the USDA's establishment of the United States Swine Breeding Laboratory at Iowa State University. In 1950 the state raised 14.3 million pigs, or 21 percent of the national total. In 2014 and 2015 Iowa produced over 21 million hogs, more than 31 percent of the nation's total of 66.9 million.

Although different approaches to raising hogs appeared in the 1930s and 1940s, since the 1970s most pork production has been consolidated into confinement operations, with Iowa, Illinois, North Carolina, and Minnesota as the top four production states nationwide.

As Barry Estabrook describes poignantly in *Pig Tales*, Iowa's industrial hog production relies on corn and soybeans as the foundation for rations that can turn a fifteen-pound piglet into a 250- to 300-pound adult in six months. The actual percentage of corn used directly for feed is rather small, 8 percent of the more than two billion bushels grown in the state. But a by-product of ethanol production is distiller's dried grains with solubles — just like spent grain from breweries — that helps feed the huge hog production facilities and accounts for 15 percent of the state's corn.[2]

But not all of Iowa embraced the rush to industrial hog production; some farmers and food producers looked beyond commodity production and saw a much different world.

How Acorns Grow beyond Hogs: La Quercia

We might entitle this story "the hitchhiker's guide to prosciutto," not because our Iowa hogs embarked on an interstellar journey but because the two protagonists met as a result of a flagged-down ride. In 1974 then twenty-five-year-old Herb Eckhouse was traveling by thumb around the country. Born in Burlington, Iowa, and raised in Chicago by a World War II Jewish refugee, he graduated from Harvard and then hit the road, where he caught a fateful ride to Idaho from a cousin of his future wife, Kathy. Originally from Berkeley, California, she spent time in Europe before crossing paths with Herb. They worked together as ranch hands in Iowa, and in 1979 a job with Wells Fargo took them to San Francisco, where Herb specialized in agricultural finance. Two years later Pioneer Hi-Bred International, a well-regarded seed company, enticed them back to Iowa with a job offer, and in 1985 Herb was reassigned to manage the business's Italian division.

In my opinion, Pioneer had a unique management style, because its international business assignments turned out to be quite prescient and significant. Herb, Kathy, and their family "endured" four delicious years in the city of Parma, located in the northern region of Emilia-Romagna and home to prosciutto di Parma and Parmigiano-Reggiano cheese, as well as great pasta, vino, balsamic vinegar, and other delicacies. And don't forget Ferrari, Lamborghini, Maserati, Ducati, and Bugatti! Gosh, I sure hope they qualified for a hardship allowance from Pioneer!

During their four years in Parma, the Eckhouse family learned to appreciate and embrace a lifestyle, a way of seeing the world, and a commitment to excellence, especially around agriculture, food, and cuisine. It must have been that those countless plates of prosciutto — safe to eat in Italy but not in the States (the USDA ban on importing these hams was still in place) — were very seductive, because an idea germinated, a crazy vision to make a ham in Iowa. In 1989 they returned to Des Moines, where the transformation of the state's hog production from small growers to confinement operations was well on its way. Kathy and Herb envisioned something special; their experience on her aunt's farm, coupled with the deep Parma immersion, argued for a different worldview. They saw Iowa's black gold; appreciated the lessons shared by Italian farmers, growers, and artisans; and believed the state's resources, properly stewarded with the right hog breeds and husbandry, could equal Italy's best, and for the next eleven years, they nurtured this dream.

In 1999 DuPont bought Pioneer Hi-Bred, and a year later Herb decided to leave the company; his experience in agricultural economics pointed to continued consolidation of agricultural businesses with no guarantee of future employment. Perhaps now was the time to consider seriously their dream of creating an American prosciutto.

At the same time that they were witnessing the continued industrialization of American food, Herb and Kathy saw the craftsmanship and success of domestic wine, craft beer, and artisan cheese, all powered by mounting consumer interest in great-tasting, wholesome products. A growing market for new domestic delicatessen and European imported meats contributed to the expansion of specialty food stores and delis. With their knowledge and sophisticated palates, Herb and Kathy saw opportunities to handcraft high-end prosciutto and other cured meats.

In 2001 they made a momentous and delicious decision to create an American prosciutto and returned to Parma to educate themselves and begin the process of building the new business. At a local trattoria they shared several plates of prosciutto and, I imagine, some very good wine and laid the philosophical and emotional foundation for their future. As Herb describes it, "That dinner was when it became clear to me that making something delicious, that caused people to stop and appreciate the eating experience as we and our friends did in Italy, would be the best way to show our appreciation of the beauty and bounty of the land around us, and would enable others to share that feeling of appreciation."[3]

I wonder, did the trattoria charcuterie board include nuts as one of the condiments, most likely chestnuts in place of acorns? Clearly, Kathy and Herb Eckhouse took some real risks to fulfill a dream, but they planted an acorn that over several years grew into their business, named La Quercia; poetically, Italian for "oak," Iowa's state tree! An Italian saying, *Aspetta il porco alla quercia*, translates to "Look for the hog at the oak."

The Death Chamber, 1860. *Courtesy of the Library of Congress.*

The Bachelor of Arts for Xmas '96 shows a chef serving a boar's head. *Courtesy of the Library of Congress.*

Iconic teepee-shaped Edwards smokehouses, ca.1950. *Courtesy of Edwards Virginia Smokehouse.*

Wallace Edwards Jr. (*left*) and S. Wallace Edwards Sr. (*right*) holding country hams. *Courtesy of Edwards Virginia Smokehouse.*

Johnston County Mangalitsa Prosciutto. *Photo by Ron Sloan. Courtesy of Johnston County Hams.*

Nancy Newsom Mahaffey, master Kentucky ham artisan. *Photo by Kate Lacey. Courtesy of Col. Bill Newsom's Aged Kentucky Country Ham.*

Smoking sausages and other meats at Johnson's Boucanière. *Photo by Jeffrey P. Roberts.*

Tony Weber & Ferdinand Schaller. *Courtesy of Schaller & Weber.*

Istrian Usiki Vrat: Istrian-style dried pork neck. *Courtesy of Muncan Food Corp.*

Salumeria pushcart, New York City, ca. 1925. *Courtesy of Mike's Deli.*

Left to right: Salumeria Biellese's Fouad Alsharif, Paul Valetutti, and Marc Buzzio. *Photo by Jason Varney.*

Soupy in drying room.
Courtesy of Fortuna's Sausage.

Label for 1732's Smoked Paprika Bacon. *Courtesy of 1732 Meats.*

1732 Meats charcuterie, including bacon and guanciale. *Courtesy of 1732 Meats.*

Aging salami. *Photo by Kateri Likoudis. Courtesy of Le Virtu.*

House of Cheese. *Courtesy of Di Bruno Brothers.*

Rooster Street's Tony and Kristina Page.
Courtesy of Rooster Street.

La Quercia Prosciutto Americano. *Photo by Adam Albright.*

Heritage Tamworth hog. *Courtesy of Caroline Ford/Wikimedia Commons.*

La Quercia Acorn Edition Whole Leg. *Photo by Adam Albright.*

Melissa Khoury's leg tattoo. *Courtesy of Saucisson Artisan Cured Meats & Sausage.*

Orba spread on board. *Courtesy of 'Nduja Artisans Salumeria.*

Red Table salumi. *Courtesy of Red Table Meat Company.*

Chef and restaurateur Frank Bonanno.
Courtesy of Bonanno Concepts.

Old Salt Marketplace Lebanon bologna.
Courtesy of Old Salt Marketplace.

Greek-style Rigani Loukaniko salami. *Courtesy of Olympia Provisions.*

After returning to the States, they opened a small import business to sell prosciutto from Parma and other regions. From 2001 to 2006 the business helped them learn the details of running a wholesale operation, understand customer preferences and seasonal demand, and "to see if people would buy prosciutto from a guy named Herb."[4] They did!

Moving from a dream to a reality takes guts, hard work, time, energy, money, and wisdom gained through plenty of trial and error. Without experience as food producers, especially in dry-cured meats, Herb and Kathy were beginners, *novellini*! And yet without assumptions, preconceptions, or expectations, by using their intuition and knowledge together with insights from the experts, they could explore and learn from the best and develop everything from facility design to recipes.

The work extended over four years, with Herb making frequent trips to Parma and other Italian cities to consult with prosciutto artisans, as well as investigating and buying equipment. They outfitted La Quercia with Italian-made equipment; Herb said most American companies use the same manufacturers. They received expert advice from many individuals, including Paul Bertolli, former chef at Chez Panisse, who opened Fra' Mani Handcrafted Foods in Berkeley in 2006.

In 2003 Herb and Kathy purchased land in Norwalk, Iowa, a few miles southwest of Des Moines. From the initial facility design to final approvals, they worked with health and meat inspectors to ensure they met all regulatory requirements. Their strategy reflects similar stories from other cured meat producers and artisan cheese makers; by engaging the people responsible to maintain health requirements, producers avoided potential problems, saved money, and built better facilities.

In 2004, with plans in place, they self-financed and constructed the building, known in Italian as a *prosciuttificio*, and in 2005 began production. Herb meanwhile experimented making dry-cured hams, a process fraught with trials and errors, especially since his "curing equipment" consisted of a double refrigerator located in the basement of their house; as Herb described it, "not environmental!" Since the hams required nine to twelve months to cure and develop the right textures and flavors, the experiments overall took several years to reach initial conclusions.

One key element, perhaps the fundamental consideration in the eyes of regulators, is safety. Beyond such requirements as building cleanliness and HACCP plans, inspectors ensure that a salami or ham meets certain functional criteria of water activity, absence of salmonella or other pathogens, and pH levels. After satisfying such standards, you can sell salami or dry-cured ham. As Herb expressed eloquently to me, "*Il maiale morsica piu forte morto che vivo,*" or, "The pig bites harder dead than alive," driving home the point that mishandled pork can be dangerous!

While Herb and Kathy are scrupulous about their products, safety by itself doesn't sell. During their experiments they matched their unique basement efforts against the Parma benchmarks to assess aroma, texture, flavors, and mouthfeel, among many other measurements. To achieve superb prosciutto the Italians emphasize the crucial role of excellent animals; without great meat you have a mediocre product. From the outset of their porcine adventure, Kathy and Herb had no pretensions or illusions about duplicating a Parma or San Daniele prosciutto. Nor did they aspire to a mass-market product. Rather, to create a truly American masterpiece, they wanted heritage-breed hogs from farmers who practice good stewardship of animals and land. For them, just like the Italian artisans, the valuable characteristics of these animals reside in muscle and fat, with their inherent organoleptic qualities, all of which result from excellent genetics and husbandry.

This underlying philosophy resulted in a set of standards and protocols that still guide La Quercia today. Farmers must agree to four stewardship principles to sell hogs to the company; here are two examples:

> All pigs must have access to the out-of-doors, have room to move around and socially congregate, and be able to root in deep bedding. This respects the pigs' social instincts and natural behaviors.
>
> Pigs must not receive non-therapeutic antibiotics, ionophores [feed additives], hormones, or synthetic hormones. Our farmers can treat illnesses, but they do not use hormones or antibiotics to artificially promote growth.[5]

Since the standards apply most directly to farmers and their animals, the La Quercia protocols emulated precedents established in the 1990s by Bill Niman for his former company Niman Ranch. Imagine Iowa in 2005 and that you need to locate four to five hundred hams that fulfill these criteria to get started. With over sixteen million hogs in the state, nearly all confinement raised, you faced a proverbial "hog in a haystack" reality. Fortunately, La Quercia found quality animals grown by Iowa farmer Paul Willis under the Niman Ranch label and Organic Prairie growers.

Consider the Eckhouses' palates after years in Italy and then running a prosciutto import business; to say the least, they developed an acute subjective sense of what they like and qualitative measurements to understand each component of aroma, taste, and flavor. Herb and Kathy love Parma prosciutto, but to achieve these qualities requires large amounts of salt to ensure complete penetration throughout the entire muscle. So part of the basement refrigerator experiment involved contrasting their hams against Italy's best and then figuring out how to accomplish a particular style.

The Eckhouses, together with their friends and colleagues, evaluated the "refrigerator" hams and the Italian prosciutto. The consensus was that they liked a drier ham with less salt to bring out and emphasize the complex heritage pork flavors and textures. To accomplish this task, they departed from traditional Italian methods of butchering and salting hams. In Italy fresh hams are trimmed lightly around the hip joint, while the shank or lower leg, often with the hoof attached, remains. Historically, an oval slit was made above the hoof between the bone and tendon, and it became the loop from which to hang the leg to dry and cure. Next, the salting stage covers the leg with dry salt on the exposed muscles and wet salt on the skin.

La Quercia utilizes a different approach in which they open up the ham and leg by cutting along and separating the major muscles; Herb describes the technique as *sgambato* (flared on the thigh), since they remove the bones and create a cavity between two muscles. Because they can now reach into the cavity with salt, the curing process requires less dry salting to penetrate the meat directly, and therefore, the final prosciutto contains less salt and water. They use only sea salt for curing, in itself a research project to determine the right flakiness of the crystals and the correct mineral content, including a minute percentage of naturally occurring nitrites; the company eschews further addition of nitrates or nitrites.

In Italy traditional hams matured in natural caves, in which nature governs temperature, humidity, and airflow throughout the year. To emulate the four seasons — winter, spring, summer, and fall — to produce its prosciutto, La Quercia built a sophisticated four-chamber structure.

Each room "creates" a separate season; for example, in the "winter" space the cold, salted hams dry; next they move into a warm, moist "spring" where enzymes speed up their magical transformations. The summer and fall chambers complete the curing process. The entire system, designed by the Eckhouses and their Italian consultants, depends upon computers, sensors, and humidifiers or dehumidifiers. Heaters and coolers are closely monitored: While fans must move air gently through each space, too fast and the hams dry too quickly; too slow and they are not dry enough.

Initially, La Quercia reordered Mother Nature by reducing the "curing year" to seven months, the minimum time to satisfy USDA requirements; with experience the aging process now extends to ten months. As Herb described several times during our conversation, each step and adjustment was a matter of "figuring it out yourself." At the end of 2005, the company shipped its first thousand pounds of ham, named Prosciutto Americano, which Herb estimates could offer fifty thousand people a generous slice! In addition to the hams during the first year, the company made a flat pancetta and guanciale.

The Prosciutto Americano arrived on the cured-meat scene with a burst of flavor and texture that immediately grabbed media, restaurant, and consumer interest and demand. The timing coincided with national expansion by restaurants to make in-house charcuterie and new food producers who focused on cured meats. For example, in 2006 Paul Bertolli opened Fra' Mani in Berkeley, and Cristiano Creminelli, an Italian from the region of Piedmont, established his eponymous company in Salt Lake City. Restaurants such as Vermont's Inn at Shelburne Farms, Heartland Restaurant in Saint Paul, Oregon's Higgins Restaurant in Portland, and Gramercy Tavern in New York fashioned charcuterie boards with an array of in-house creations.

The success of Prosciutto Americano provided both resources and greater motivation for Kathy and Herb to strengthen their commitment to heritage animals and best practices, especially around how they were fed. For a couple of years, the company used hams, bellies, cheeks, and jowls from its original suppliers to make prosciutto, pancetta, and guanciale. The next step was, in my eyes, even a greater leap, to move from nonorganic to organic animals. Beyond locating a certified organic farm, the principal challenge is the high cost of organic grains and other feed to raise meat animals and how these expenses affect the final price for cured meat.

It turns out that while Iowa is the center of the commodity corn and soybean universe, the state also leads the nation in production of both organic grains and organic hogs. In 2007 nineteen farms raised nearly 7,000 organic hogs, 41 percent of total national output, while seven years later, fourteen growers raised 5,400 pigs, or a third of US organic hog production.[6]

In 2007 the company launched Green Label Organic Prosciutto, produced from Berkshire/Chester White crosses, grown by Becker Lane Farm, a USDA-certified organic grower in Dyersville, Iowa. Its owner, Jude Becker, feeds his animals 100 percent organic food, and just like the phrase "You are what you eat," it makes the difference. Taste convinced Herb and Kathy! They could easily identify excellent organoleptic differences in organic hogs compared to nonorganic ones. That's not to say the latter ones were not raised according to the company's protocols; they certainly were. It's just that for the Eckhouses to differentiate their product line, taste is everything . . . *Il gusto è tutto!* La Quercia's organic Green Label hams exhibited an astounding depth of flavor with a lingering finish; the organic prosciutto was the first and is still the only one made in America.

Whether raising hogs, turkeys, or rabbits or producing milk, organic feed is expensive. For La Quercia its limited edition, high-end organic products had to attract sufficient numbers of consumers to make it worthwhile. Its decision clearly intersected with the continued growth of national demand for organic products, and despite higher prices, sales of the organic prosciutto are steady.

Beyond the success of organic pork, Kathy and Herb raised the bar even higher and created prosciutto made from acorn-fed animals. American country hams, Italian prosciutto, Portuguese presunto, and Spanish jamón share at least one common historical element: When hogs feed on acorns and other nuts, the curing process transforms muscle and fat into complex aromas and multilayered flavors, as well as exquisite texture. Finding farmers who raise acorn-fed hogs and convincing other growers to collaborate required focus, energy, and persistence. In 2007 they began an acorn edition of cured products. They bought whole carcasses of acorn-fed hogs to make fresh sausage and different cured-meat varieties. The La Quercia Acorn line established a unique niche and contributed to a succession of even more highly defined and refined prosciutto and salami.

Today they work with two acorn-fed heritage hogs, Berkshire and Tamworth, grown by farmers within a hundred-mile radius of Norwalk. B&B Farms in Grinnell, Iowa, specializes in Berkshires, a black-haired, robust hog with beautifully marbled dark red meat, ideal for whole-muscle curing. The hog can grow to six hundred pounds with large hams. Even after aging the Acorn Berkshire Prosciutto for twenty-four to thirty-six months, the resulting cello-shaped ham with the leg and foot still attached may weigh fifteen to thirty pounds. Considering it lost thirty to forty percent of the original weight, those are very large hogs!

Russ Kremer, owner of Ozark Mountain Pork Cooperative and manager of Heritage Foods in Missouri, raises Tamworth hogs for La Quercia. Historically called the "bacon pig," because of its long, lean, muscular body with excellent thick belly fat, the red-haired animals graze on pasture and then enjoy four months to forage in oak and hickory forests. After aging for thirty to thirty-six months, the hams weigh in at fifteen to thirty pounds with a deep mahogany color. And to honor this bacon hog, they also make a Tamworth Smoked Pancetta, a flat version cured with sea salt, rosemary, bay leaf, and black and white pepper and smoked over applewood.

While Prosciutto Americano accounts for half the company's sales, the breakthrough products are the Green Label, Acorn, Berkshire, and Tamworth editions. Their success generates demand backward through the food chain and creates greater opportunities for farmers to raise animals and grow organic grains. Unless consumers are willing to spend more money for a clearly superior product, La Quercia, its farmers, and their suppliers cannot make a living.

I celebrate Kathy and Herb's dinner in 2001; fueled by great food and wine and with a deep belief in themselves, the land, and their vision for how Americans might eat differently in the future, they jumped into the unknown. In my opinion, we are all better for their decision; the company's stewardship is reflected in every bite. *Grazie mille e complimenti!*

CHAPTER TWELVE

Don't We Just Fly over It?

While living in Philadelphia and flying to the West Coast, I carried a set of airline route maps to follow the progress of my trip. I booked a window seat to watch the landscape beneath me and used the maps to identify where we were. If I fell asleep, the challenge upon waking was then to figure out the landmarks and decide where I was. I recall circular corn and crop fields; roads following an overlay of square grids; lakes and rivers cutting their routes; and in the far West the magnificent Rocky, Cascade, and Sierra Nevada mountains. On my first trip to Montana, what a thrill to pick out the Big Snowy Mountains, Square Butte, and the Upper Missouri River, all of which I eventually experienced firsthand.

My view of America was different from the iconic March 29, 1976, Saul Steinberg *New Yorker* cover, "View of the World from 9th Avenue." The cover showed a myopic perception that reached across the Hudson River to New Jersey with the next major feature, the Pacific Ocean, in the distance. In many ways it captured East and West Coast perspectives that the rest of the country wasn't much to look and marvel at. While to some extent the perception still exists, the reality is the exact opposite. Whether we consider its history or contemporary expressions, the regions are diverse, complex, rich, cultural places, and they help feed us.

The cured-meat odyssey takes us from Cleveland to Chicago to Minneapolis and finally Indianapolis. The group of butchers, charcutiers, and salumieri represent some of the region's pioneering artisans and the changes occurring in the heartland.

Saucisson Artisan Cured Meats & Sausage

Cleveland has a long, well-established history of pork and cured meats tied closely to its sizable eastern European populations and neighborhoods, including Croatians, Germans, Hungarians, Poles, Slovenians, Serbians, and Romanians. Several years ago on a trip to Ohio, we visited the Rock and Roll Hall of Fame (outstanding Rolling Stones exhibit) and the city's West Side Market. I stopped at J & J Czuchraj Meats, owned by Jill and Jerry Czuchraj, and Dohar/Lovaszy Meats, now operated by Steve Dohar's daughter, Angela, and son-in-law, Miklos. The market is a microcosm of the city, and I could have spent the entire day talking and eating. After I hauled several pounds of smoked sausage from both stores back home, my suitcase carried the wonderful smoky aromas for several months, long after we ate the sausage. Cleveland is also home to Michael Ruhlman, noted chef and author of *Charcuterie: The Craft of Salting, Smoking and Curing*, one of the first contemporary primers to introduce the science and art of cured meats to the public.

I was very fortunate to connect with Penny Barend and Melissa Khoury, two women blazing new meat trails in Cleveland. Both women have strong, varied culinary backgrounds that they apply to their business, Saucisson. Melissa, who seems to always sport a T-shirt emblazed with "I Heart Swine," was born in Cleveland to a Lebanese-American family. She describes powerful childhood food memories with her mother as they visited local butcher shops, where her treat was a "smoky." After receiving a culinary degree from Johnson & Wales, she headed south to Bacchanalia in Atlanta, where they created house-made charcuterie; she then managed the cured-meat program at Abattoir. Orlando was next, where she worked at Primo in the JW Marriott Hotel and in 2006 met Penny at the same restaurant.

Penny grew up in San Diego, where fresh fish was a frequent, delicious family dinner. She worked for a period of time in British Columbia as a salmon fisher and learned to cook with whatever ingredients she could find. Penny graduated from Northern Arizona University's International Hospitality program, cooked while at school, and then spent time in Florence, Italy. She returned to Flagstaff, worked at the Cottage Place Restaurant for several years, and then returned to Europe. A stint at the Culinary Institute of America, where she worked with master butcher Hans

Sebald, introduced her to traditional European charcuterie. Penny discovered several nearby diversified farms with heritage pigs and related that this was a true farm-to-table experience, similar to what she saw in Europe.

After they worked together in 2006 at Primo, although work paths diverged, the women stayed in contact. Both developed skills in handling meat and charcuterie. Penny went back to the West Coast and then returned to Orlando's Rusty Spoon, owned by another Primo alumna. For Melissa the pull to go back to Cleveland became stronger with each passing year, and she returned home to work at Washington Place Bistro & Inn.

In 2013 Melissa opened Saucisson by renting space in approved commercial kitchen facilities to produce her fresh sausages, pâtés, terrines, smoked meat, and other European-style charcuterie. Sales at farmers' markets and local retail stores quickly took off. Melissa was named Cleveland's "Queen of Pork," which increased business even further, and she called for help. In 2014 Penny arrived and became a partner in the business.

As business continued to grow, the commercial kitchen arrangement limited capacity to expand or develop a dry-cured meat selection. Likewise, while direct sales at farmers' and flea markets generated lots of consumer feedback and profit, they took considerable time to manage. In 2015 they purchased the former Jaworski Meats store in the historical Slavic Village, once the home to the area's largest Polish community. While Jaworski is still in business in a different part of town, the new Saucisson, opened in 2016, is the first butcher shop in the community in many years. It benefits from strong customer interest and support in both the surrounding neighborhood and the city.

Here Melissa and Penny craft the current line of forty handmade, hand-ground products, all nitrate- and nitrite-free, and develop a true dry-cured line with a built-in cabinet. Because the Ohio Department of Agriculture manages inspections, they can increase their wholesale business. Melissa and Penny buy all their pork from New Creation Farm in Chardon, Ohio, where Kristen and Scott Boehnlein raise antibiotic-free, pastured Berkshire/Duroc hogs, as well as Highland steers, lamb, and poultry. They described how the growth of Saucisson works backward to support New Creation Farm. As the new facility and production capacity develop, they see increased opportunities to collaborate with Kristen and Scott to help them build a stronger farm economy.

Melissa and Penny talked passionately about how the business is about more than making a living. They acknowledge the mentors who contributed to their current success and are committed to teaching subsequent generations. The women want to further their knowledge and then educate others, especially women, as chefs and butchers. I am impressed with their drive, willingness to take risks, and focus on goals. The combination of great artisan food, neighborhood revitalization, mutually beneficial links to Ohio farmers, and vision for the future create an attractive recipe for success.

Publican Quality Meats

Chicago has a legendary history around all things meat, from slaughter to processing to great restaurants. With noted shops such as Koenemann's Sausage in Volo, Paulina Meat Market, and West Loop Salumi, the city and surrounding area still make some of the country's best charcuterie. My original plans anticipated a several-day trip to the Windy City for research and great food. Unfortunately, resources dwindled, and with my bum hip, the prospects to visit while writing ended.

Happily, I reached Cosmo Goss, the chef de cuisine at the Publican and Publican Quality Meats (PQM) to learn about his career and the company's dry-cured meat program. Although his grandparents lived in Chicago, he was born in Santa Barbara, California, where his parents, Frank and Tricia, owned Arts and Letters Café and an art gallery next door. As a teenager, Cosmo worked at local restaurants and wanted to become a charter boat fisherman. His path shifted inland to Denver, where he attended Johnson & Wales, and then returned home to work at the Hungry Cat, where he began to learn butchery and how to make salami.

In 2008 a jump to New York (maybe like me, looking down at the Midwestern landscape) landed him at Gramercy Tavern, where he worked with salumiere Scott Bridi (!) and did stages at Le Bernardin. After a year Cosmo went back to California and met Paul Kahan, owner of the Publican, a place he admired and respected. Kahan hired him to work in the restaurant, and a year later Cosmo took over the operation at Publican Quality Meats across the street from the restaurant. Both companies are located northwest of the Loop in the former meatpacking district. In 2013

Goss won Chicago's Cochon555 competition and in 2014 became chef de cuisine at Publican with creative oversight at PQM.

We talked at length about the market's approach to animals, salumi, and sustainability. Cosmo is adamant about diet and lifestyle for raising animals. While PQM works with Berkshire, Duroc, Hampshire, and Old Spot hogs, he argues that proper diets and excellent animal husbandry are the most fundamental elements for the best quality hog and meat cuts. In other words, even with the best pigs, poor diet and exercise does not guarantee a quality animal. PQM buys hogs from Kim Snyder, owner of Faith's Farm in Bonfield, Illinois, southwest of Chicago, as well as Hometown Sausage, Slagel Family Farm, Triple S Farms, and Catalpa Grove.

PQM brings in twenty-four to thirty hogs a month, of which 15 to 20 percent become cured products, with an equal percentage sold fresh. This number attests to excellent farmers and both the restaurant's and butcher shop's success. Cosmo described with great pride and accomplishment the shop's aim for 95 to 100 percent usage of every animal. They render the fat into lard, bones go into the stockpot, and offal is used in sausage mixes as well as restaurant dishes. Nearly all of the salumi is Italian based: coppa, culatello, lardo, lonza, and 'nduja. The company uses no nitrates in the curing, and all of the salami proceed through natural fermentation without any added lactic starter cultures.

They make a unique Piedmontese product called Salam d'la Duja or salami in fat, an essential technique in the provinces of Novara and Vercelli, whose high humidity prevents drying and preservation. The two provinces encompass rice-growing areas of the Po River valley, thus high humidity is a constant. Local valley salumiere allowed fresh salami to dry for a few days, layered them in a clay crock called a *duja*, and covered the sausage with melted leaf lard. The lard kept them fresh and safe for up to a year, and with time they became spicier. The salumiere would remove the sausages, cook them in the lard, and return any remaining fat to the crock.

Listening to Cosmo depict the techniques to make the Salam d'la Duja reminded me of my conversation with Toby Rodriguez about saucisse de graisse and confit. Here again a simple idea crafted from necessity to survive illustrates the ingenuity and knowledge possessed by our forebears. I looked further at the Salam d'la Duja and found its roots are very local; step away from the humidity, and we no longer needed to bury sausage in lard. How far back in history do these ideas extend? Simple and yet so sophisticated a technique — we can protect meat by covering it with lard or duck fat . . . and have an inexpensive, wholesome food to eat months from now that tastes terrific!

Cosmo raised some concerns about the current state of the charcuterie "renaissance." From his perspective the national market looks oversaturated, with just about every American restaurant from the large chains to small bistros and neighborhood joints now offering some salami on the menu. Too often the house-made examples are not very good or they serve commodity products. Cosmo wondered if the drive toward charcuterie and salumi is just a trend. For example, this note about jazzing up a menu:

> *If you want customers to buzz about your restaurant's appetizers, give them charcuterie or ceviche. . . . And no matter what sort of savory dish you offer, it's likely to be talked about more if you add bacon to it.*[1]

I think his caution is well merited, in part because the difference between a fast lactic-acid-fermented commodity salami or semicooked prosciutto compared to natural dry-aged products is like day and night. The differences in price are substantial; regardless of the costs of animals, production, and aging time, many consumers balk at the expense of handmade, carefully dry-cured salumi.

I am reminded about the craft beer and artisan cheese worlds, both of which offer higher priced beverages and food than commodity producers. Both differentiated themselves around craft, real human involvement, attention to resources, and for the most part emphasizing small-scale production. But as Cosmo reflected, we don't know if the next trend will push dry-cured meat off the appetizer plate. For the moment Publican Quality Meats brings excellent fresh cuts and salumi to the Chicago market. As we continue to make strides to change the manner in which America grows and consumes meat, PQM's farmers benefit from the company's success as well.

'Nduja Artisans Salumeria

Every two years Slow Food International stages its Salone del Gusto, a grand celebration of taste, artisan products, and the people who make them. For many years they located the feast at Lingotto Fiere, the former Fiat factory in Torino. You wandered down aisles, called streets, that were bursting with grains, cheese, bread; an olive oil roadway next to one devoted to cured meats. Truly remarkable! A few years ago Slow Food reorganized the food areas by region. Now you could visit Lombardia for violino di capra; Molise for Colonna Olive Oil; Sicily for Pistacchio di Bronte; or 'nduja from Calabria.

Imagine a table with large, deep, bright-red, oddly shaped cylinders; as you approach, an aroma of spicy chili envelops you. The smell drives through you, its warmth enticing. The artisan standing behind the table offers you a taste; he has a hint of a smile as he spoons a small amount. The robust aroma takes off, ricocheting from nose to throat to mouth . . . and then you taste it! Heat, smoke, unidentifiable flavors, more heat and smoke; my eyes water, but what a smile on my face. I have just passed my first red belt 'nduja trial directed by a Calabrese maestro!

'Nduja, a soft, spreadable pork salami made from shoulder, belly, head, and other trimmings, and roasted hot Calabrese chiles, is an example of cucina povera, poor man's food. All it took was fat, neck muscle, or other less desirable hog parts, chiles, and a casing. It was ground all together, sometimes more than once to achieve texture, and then stuffed into casings that ranged in size from six to eight ounces upward to seventy-five pounds. To make larger sizes the salumiere would sew casings together to achieve the giant dimensions. Depending on its dimension, the salami fermented for weeks to months. Despite several centuries of small-scale production, Calabrese 'nduja cannot be exported to the United States because it doesn't meet USDA requirements.

Throughout my research I ran dozens of internet searches looking for artisan cured-meat producers. One of them uncovered a place in Chicago called 'Nduja Artisans Salumeria. The link, through the Di Bruno Brothers' internet store in Philadelphia, fortunately provided some information. I shot off an e-mail and crossed my fingers for a reply. The next morning the phone rang and the caller ID showed an unknown number but the name Agostino Fiasche — the guy who owns the business! Hot stuff, both literally and figuratively. We talked about my book and the tasting I was conducting in Denver in June 2015. He promised to supply us with product and have his son, Antonio (Tony), call me. The Denver tasting of nine cured meats — four prosciutti, three salami, and one bresaola — culminated with

Agostino and Tony's 'nduja. For most of the audience, it was a brand-new food and a tremendous hit.

Several times over the past year, I have talked with Tony about his family, the origins of the business, and how it has evolved. His father, Agostino, came from Coccorino in Calabria, while his mother, Anna, is from Naples. The regions of Calabria and Campania, two of Italy's poorest areas, sent their men and women all over the world to escape their difficult lives. Both parents were in their midteens when they arrived in Chicago with their families.

In 1985 Anna and Agostino opened Ristorante Agostino on Harlem Avenue in the Near West Side of the city. What a wonderful blending of two different food cultures; Anna cooks Neapolitan seafood — zuppa di pesce and pasta with cuttlefish — while Agostino dishes up artichoke and arrabbiata sauces. More than thirty years later, they are still going strong. I can just imagine growing up with two professional chefs spinning out regional dishes.

Tony was born in 1983 and spent almost every summer at his grandparents' home in Coccorino. In 2002 he started work with his parents at the restaurant, sold meat through a local wholesaler, and cooked at Publican Quality Meats. The urge to create an 'nduja salami began about 2010 or 2011. Previously, Agostino had made various salamis at home in the garage for the family's enjoyment. What sparked his creativity was the state of domestic 'nduja, then seeing it begin to show up in restaurants and retail stores. For Agostino the salami was a mere shadow of the original, although he may have said even the shadows didn't rate!

For father and son the critical ingredient was the Calabrese chiles, introduced originally to the area by the Spanish, and then hybridized by regional farmers. Calabria is another example of the value of terroir, in this case volcanic soil, considered some of the best agricultural dirt anywhere in the world. The region's west side around the commune of Spilinga and its nearby hamlet, Coccorino, contain volcanic deposits, and most people point to the area as the historical origin for 'nduja. Growing chiles on this soil added distinctive aroma and flavor dimensions not duplicated anywhere else.

No wonder Agostino was frustrated with the American versions. To solve the problem, he turned to his father to help obtain the chiles, and they began a series of experiments to develop an 'nduja they would be proud of. Through the restaurant and wholesale business, they bought Berkshire hogs from Premier Proteins in Kearney, Missouri. Tony related that his father wanted an absolutely accurate Calabrese style; in other words, packed with chili heat. Tony convinced him to dial back the spice, since the Calabrese prefer it so hot that steam jets from your ears. Americans don't mind a little sweat, but steam, maybe not! They conducted the initial experiments in a small curing cabinet but realized that to have a serious effort went beyond their capacity, and they set up business with a copacker.

In 2013 and 2014 they inaugurated 'Nduja Artisan Salumeria with several sizes, from individual six-ounce vacuum-sealed packages to forty pounders, with a few up to seventy. Tony said the really mammoth ones are showcase items to stimulate business interest. To achieve a spreadable consistency requires 80 percent fat and 20 percent meat. Tony makes an unusual one called the "Orba" that weighs four to eight pounds. The Italian name refers to a hog "middle cap," a large-diameter portion of the pig's intestine. In Italy a salumiere would stuff the Orba with a mixture to create 'nduja, salami la Zia Ferrarese, or soppressata di Calabria. While the small ones age six to eight weeks, the Orba requires four to six months. The really big ones with the sewn casings that Tony compares to patching an old tire will take even longer to mature.

Initially, Tony wasn't sure he wanted to become a salumiere, but since 2014 he has developed a deep appreciation for and an interest in pursuing this path. He discovered how much he likes the process, the creativity to develop new recipes, and the close collaboration with their farmers. In addition to pork from Premier, they buy Wagyu for a beef salami that he developed. Besides Berkshire, they have access to farmers raising Mangalitsa, Ossabaw, and Tamworth hogs. Tony now has twenty different cured products for sale while continuing research and development for new items. One remarkable limited edition style of 'nduja is made with imported fat from the Spanish Ibérico de Bellota acorn-fed hogs. As Tony ramps up his skills and spins his creative genius, I expect to see more amazing salumi emerging from the company.

Red Table Meat Company

You won't believe where Mike Phillips, the co-owner of Red Table Meats, hails from. It took me several attempts with my lousy phonetic spelling to arrive at the correct name, Okoboji, Iowa, a small village located on the lake of the same name. I thought Montpelier was small, but Okoboji is really tiny. Mike grew up as a farm boy, even dated the Clay County Pork Queen, but then moved to the Twin Cities to attend college for music.

Like many of his peers, Mike started cooking while in school and discovered talents for food and music. Clearly, neither of these skills is mutually exclusive; my conversations with Mike led me to write, "He's a poet of salami!" In 1997 he opened the acclaimed Chet's Tavern, a small neighborhood place that emphasized buying direct from farmers throughout the state. Twenty years ago the notion of farm to table was really cutting edge, if chefs and consumers were even aware of the concept, let alone the language. Mike bought whole animals and taught himself and his cooks how to break down a whole carcass. He said working with the entire animal was a creative challenge: "How can we make all of this animal more interesting to ourselves and customers?"

In 1998 he attended one of Francois Vecchio's weeklong salumi semesters and realized the extraordinary potential to create charcuterie in the Twin Cities. Among the many lessons from Francois was the place of integrity and pride in whatever you do. Throughout his culinary journey, Mike adhered to these principles. He described to me the nature of making salumi, how for him they reflect personalities and souls. I hear both Mike and Francois in this musical verse and see how it plays out in the salumi.

After seven years Mike closed Chet's; in hindsight he said the restaurant might have been ahead of its time as a neighborhood place. He moved on to the Craftsman, where he was head chef and deeply involved in the restaurant's charcuterie program. At the time cured-meat production at city restaurants like Craftsman or Heartland received minimal inspection; questions were asked, but significant issues were not raised. For six years he developed and refined the charcuterie program and, with Francois close by in Toronto, had access to his knowledge and expertise.

During his tenure at Craftsman, Mike nurtured an idea to create a full-scale retail and wholesale dry-cured business, and in 2010 he met Kieran Folliard, owner of several Minneapolis Irish pubs. Both men shared the concept; Mike left Craftsman and started to develop a plan to open a meat business called Green Ox. The initial idea evolved into a lengthy, time-consuming, and expensive endeavor that ultimately culminated in Red Table Meats.

Kieran's business acumen also embraced 2 Gingers, a distillery that two years into the project was bought by Jim Beam. His expansive vision for how small-scale food businesses might evolve in Minneapolis led to the purchase and renovation of a 26,000-square-foot building in the northeast corner of the city, now called the Food Building. His idea was to bring three fermentation start-ups together — cured meat, cheese, and bread — with Mike helming Red Table. Second was Rueben Nilsson, owner of Lone Grazer Creamery, a good friend of mine when he worked at the Caves of Faribault. Finally, Steve Horton of Rustica Bakery would run Baker's Field Flour & Bread. Brilliant! What a terrific way to offer small artisans an urban location and opportunity with excellent facilities and the opportunity to collaborate.

But sometimes a great idea hits a speed bump; in Mike's case it was more like a rutted back road in mud season. To accomplish the goal he knew the business needed capital and, since they would sell wholesale nationwide, also needed to secure USDA review and approval of the facility and HACCP plans for each cured meat. He agreed to lease 5,500 square feet and located a partner who brought in $1.2 million for construction, equipment, and, most important, the due diligence to create the salumi and have them approved. Because the other businesses utilize microbes to ferment their products, cross-contamination was a potential problem, so Red Table installed a separate air-handling system.

Part of the delay was lack of knowledge and experience about how naturally fermented salami can be a safe product. Mike, with assistance from Francois, did not want to create fast-fermentation, overly salted, or partially cooked products. Therefore, to fulfill USDA demands, they had to run verification trials for every possible cured meat, and only one University of Minnesota employee was available. Oh, and they had to pay for each test.

The process took months because first Mike had to make every salami and cured whole muscle to meet the desired characteristics and organoleptic qualities he wanted. Then he had to inoculate each sample with pathogens, age them, and then have a laboratory investigate to see if the "bad bugs" were dead. The one fortunate occurrence that helped complete the process was that the university microbiologist, who conducted the verification tests, was a former chef who had previously worked with Mike. Ultimately, the process fulfilled everyone's USDA requirements, quality assurance, and taste expectations, and Red Table opened for business in the fall of 2014.

In every conversation Mike acknowledges farmers as the essential reason for his success. All of the purebred Berkshire, Gloucestershire Old Spot, and Red Wattle hogs processed at Red Table are antibiotic-free; pastured; fed specific diets, often with barley as the basic grain; and finished on nuts to develop unsaturated fats. The company's suppliers include Little Foot Farm, Afton; Hidden Stream Farm, Elgin; Pork and Plants, Altura; and Yker Acres, Wrenshall, in Minnesota; and Moo, Oink, Cluck Farms, in Somerset, Wisconsin.

At a 2015 Denver Slow Meat tasting, we sampled Extra Vecchio, named in Francois's honor, a Felino-style salami. Ground shoulder and belly are mixed with salt, black pepper, garlic, and white wine; stuffed in a pork bung casing; and aged at least two months. Mike sent us two commercial-size Extra Vecchio, three feet long and aromatic, with a tender, moist consistency — another audience favorite. In January 2016 Red Table received three Good Food Awards for Coppa, Big Chet's, and The Royal, a ten- to twelve-pound cured and smoked ham.

Demand for RTM products continues to expand; Mike estimated they would produce 3,500 pounds a week in 2016. I'm not sure whether he pipes music into the curing room as Red Table's special terroir element, but whatever he does, Mike Phillips is winning converts to great salumi.

Smoking Goose and Goose the Market

On a bright October morning, I found my way along East Vermont Street across the railroad tracks, well, under them really, just beyond downtown Indianapolis to the Smoking Goose Meatery on Dorman Street. Directly across is Flat12 Bierwerks and next door is Racer Parts Wholesale. Interesting part of town . . . fast cars, craft beer, and cured meats. The buildings are simple white or gray rectangular boxes that, except for the signs, tell you nothing about what hides within. And within the Meatery, in Indianapolis of all places, are some of America's culinary gems.

The journey involves two travelers, Mollie and Chris Eley, two Hoosier city natives, who made a circuit around the country before returning home. They grew up in Indianapolis and were high school sweethearts. As a teenager Chris worked at Sahm's restaurant in Fishers; he really liked hanging out with the chefs and the kitchen crew, while admitting the food wasn't as important as the camaraderie.

While attending Johnson & Wales University in Providence, Rhode Island, Chris worked at several local restaurants before he and Mollie headed to West Lafayette, Indiana. He received a bachelor's degree from Purdue in hospitality and restaurant management, just the skills needed to work with Rick Tramonto and Gale Gand in Chicago. Chris planned and debuted several of their places: Tru, Tramonto's Steak and Seafood, and Osteria di Tramonto.

Because he was using whole carcasses, his menus required sophisticated butchering skills to maximize the animal's value as fundamental to a restaurant's financial stability. Part of the overall strategy was the development of dry-cured and smoked meat programs at different restaurants, often using the wine rooms as curing cabinets. But for a variety of reasons (perhaps unreliable temperature and humidity controls), the makeshift curing areas did not always result in distinctive products of consistent, high-quality caliber. The curing programs, while well received, required focused attention and better infrastructure to reach the pinnacle of quality.

In 2007, when Mollie and Chris moved back to Indianapolis, Chris made a key decision to focus on doing one thing really well. They decided to build and open Goose the Market in a diverse community northeast of downtown. When she was growing up, Mollie's nickname was Goose, so her moniker helped define the delicatessen. From appearances, the neighborhood is undergoing change, with restoration of early- to mid-twentieth-century houses and several new small businesses. Initially Mollie and Chris were the only employees; today the market has a staff of fifteen. A basement wine room was the foundation for a modest cured-meat program, "a couple of thousand pounds" according to Chris, to supply a few handmade products to the market. Today the small, attractive shop greets visitors with an array of eye-catching cheeses; fresh, cooked, and cured meats; beer and wine; and other items, both local and from beyond. The enthusiastic, knowledgeable staff introduces customers to products and helps them create great tasting pairings.

Because Marion County encompasses the city of Indianapolis, the county's Public Health Department inspectors are responsible for food and consumer safety inspections in the city. Since everything produced at the market was sold on premises, direct to customers, the county inspectors managed the health requirements for the first two years. Chris related that at one point inspectors asked about the cured products, and he was completely prepared with HACCP plans and documentation for each item. He said experience from writing plans while in Chicago prepared him for whatever questions the inspectors might raise. The officials were impressed with the company's comprehensive approach and as a compliment to his thoroughness asked Chris to speak to the county's inspectors about what to look for when reviewing cured-meat production.

Within a year or so of opening, demand for Goose the Market cured products outstripped capacity at the shop, and Mollie and Chris embarked on a significant expansion. In 2011 they opened Smoking Goose in an area east of downtown, the proverbial "other side of the tracks." The original plan considered a "modest" 2,000-square-foot facility, but after working the financial numbers and witnessing growing market demand and consumer interest, they built a 12,000-square-foot enterprise with a plan to sell wholesale and distribute nationwide. We might wonder about a decision to expand in the middle of the Great Recession, as the Eleys were looking at total capital costs of approximately $500,000 to $600,000. But Chris and Mollie were quite clear about financial objectives and control of the business. As he related in an interview, "Like I said, the banks don't want to loan you money, I didn't want to take on partners and I've never been particularly interested in having financial investors, primarily due to the fact they're really just in it for the profit."[2]

Indianapolis's share of recession-driven federal economic stimulus funds created an opportunity for the Eleys to secure a $100,000 grant. With resources in hand, they found banks willing to underwrite the expansion without private investment capital.

Since they wanted to expand beyond direct sale to consumers, the facility and all of its protocols had to pass USDA approval. Chris and his staff invited federal inspectors to review plans and vet each step in the design and construction. The strategy paid off, with federal approval for a structure unique in Indiana. The large building is a basic shell to enclose and protect a smaller "building" inside. The fully contained interior aluminum-clad structure houses the entire operation, from butchering to fresh processing to cured meats. To fulfill health and safety requirements separate, isolated spaces are necessary for each type of production. To work or visit the inside facility means you "suit up" in a white lab coat, hair net even for bald guys (a beard net, too, if you are so blessed), and slip-on booties.

While historically we might have dressed differently to slaughter and process animals, the essential need to maintain product quality and safety demands a clean room and clean workers and visitors to reduce the risk of possible contamination.

Depending on the use, each room or space is equipped with critical temperature and humidity controls. At least initially, most spaces are kept at 38 to 40°F to ensure meat quality and retard bacterial growth. Building on Chris's Chicago experiences, Smoking Goose buys whole carcasses of beef, pork, lamb, and various poultry. The company reduces its input costs with whole animals and also simplifies purchases from farmers and slaughterhouses.

The carcasses arrive first in a cold central butchering area; walking into the room, I initially felt the temperature, but perhaps more important, I smelled clean, meaty aromas, nothing off that might signal a problem. Here, highly skilled, warmly dressed butchers break down the animals, carefully seam cutting the muscles and then, depending on their use, sending the portions in different directions. For example, fresh meats — chops, loins, steaks — are packaged for Goose the Market and distribution to restaurants and other customers.

Other cuts are diverted to a separate processing room, equally cold, to transform them into fresh sausage, cooked and smoked items, and cured salami and whole-muscle meats. Here butchers hand-tie or stuff each piece and season them with a variety of spices. For example, its Saucisson Rouge, a four- to six-week-aged salami made from ground pork fat, heart, and liver, is flavored with red wine, New Mexico Hatch chile, and Espelette chile from the French Basque region.

For smoked products they use simple equipment, burning damp applewood to impart flavor to a variety of meats — lamb and pork bacon; guanciale or pork jowl; hams; duck breast; and Tasso — to name a few.

A salami or whole muscle destined for curing progresses through separate fermentation and aging areas on its path to excellence. The fermentation room maintains a higher temperature and humidity environment to stimulate interior bacteria and external mold development. After the appropriate fermentation time for each item, they are moved into the curing room, another temperature- and humidity-controlled space reserved for only cured meats. In this room, which contains more than twenty thousand pounds of product, we find a succulent treasure trove of salami, pork and lamb hams and prosciuttos, coppa, capocollo, lomo, and more suspended from wood racks as they mature. In contrast to the butchering room, the clean, attractive smell of the aging chamber contains complex and rich aromas that range from mushrooms to spices to sweet pork.

An important but short digression is needed here. In 2001 I led a small research study to the city of Chiavenna in northern Lombardy. We went to investigate the production of violino di capra, or goat prosciutto, a Slow Food Italy Ark of Taste traditional food in danger of disappearing. Fifteen years ago Vermont was one of the leading goat cheese states in the United States. One cheese maker, Laini Fondiller, owner of Lazy Lady Farm, who is anything but lazy, was concerned about how to manage her bucklings, or male kid goats, and the old does when they reached the end of productivity.

Lombardy's northern provinces are well known for goat cheese and violino di capra. Historically, goat cheese makers milked an Orobica goat, a magnificent animal with long, twisted horns and long, gray-white wool. The goats roamed and foraged in the high forests and meadows along the Alpine border with Switzerland. Their milk, varying daily and seasonally, was a rich palette of aromas and flavors from which to create great cheese. The Italian goatherds and cheese makers expressed great pride in the seven-to-nine-year productive life span of their does. For them, after slaughtering an old animal out of necessity, reverence and respect dictated you needed to find a way to use the carcass, not simply bury it.

After many years of the goats traversing mountainsides, the meat was muscular, dense, and tough. But a long curing truly transforms the hind legs, and occasionally the shoulders, into a goat prosciutto, worthy of the same attention and accolades as prosciutto de San Daniele or Parma. We worked with several local salumiere, including Aldo del Curto, the Maestro di Violino di Capra; learned their techniques; and returned to Vermont. Here the project began a series of experiments, culminating eighteen months later with an edible and safe goat prosciutto and appropriate HACCP plans.

But we couldn't get any local slaughterhouses interested in making a commitment for production. In some ways the idea of a goat prosciutto was a bit ahead of the American palate for cured meats. But when I talked with the staff at Smoking Goose in 2015, they expressed interest, so finally, after years of fruitless effort, I sent the protocols off to them, hoping they would follow through.

Stepping into the Smoking Goose aging room, I noticed several hams with a different shape . . . unbelievable: They had an American violino di capra, just a few weeks away from its debut! The goats came from a wonderful, well-regarded dairy, Capriole Goat Cheeses in southern Indiana, owned by Judy Schad, one of the country's pioneering cheese makers. In my opinion, the violino is a tribute to how to better manage and utilize the animals that grace our lives. I just wish it had been ready when I visited.

With such a dynamic facility and vision for the future, moving large quantities of meat for a small business involves both sales and distribution. To attain and manage the company's potential, Chris energized his extensive network of food and culinary contacts, especially in Chicago and the Midwest. These restaurants, chefs, hotels, and other businesses became his first customers outside Indianapolis; today distribution extends to both coasts.

Like other American cured-meat artisans, the company acknowledges and celebrates its farmers. Their suppliers, principally from southern Indiana, Illinois, Kentucky, and Ohio, raise Berkshire, Large Black, Ossabaw, and Red Wattle hogs and perhaps now a few goats. A visit to its website reveals a page entitled "Raw Resources" with a set of fundamental requirements for suppliers, description of the commitments each farm group makes beyond basic prerequisites, list of farms in each group, and inventory of items made with their meats. Chris says:

> *Just because you are buying locally doesn't necessarily mean that you are buying a quality product. We work directly with farmers, and I'm not afraid to work with a farm from Kentucky, Illinois or Michigan just because they aren't local. . . . I mean, we're a huge commodity state for pork, and obviously corn. So, just because something is grown in Indiana doesn't mean that it's great. Ultimately, we're really more concerned with how the animal has been raised, what it's been fed. . . . I'm a huge proponent of pasture raised animals. Organic isn't as big of a deal to me as certified humane. I like stress free animals . . . because I think that humanely raised animals are a better tasting product. We buy from the people we do because they have practices we believe in, they have a good product, that's what it really comes down to.[3]*

For example, the base requirements for all Smoking Goose farms include being a small, family-owned business, not a factory farm; animals must enjoy 100 percent vegetarian feed and receive no antibiotics or growth-promoting drugs; they must be humanely slaughtered; and the use of gestation pens is prohibited. The "Resources" page also shows a "Best by Date Guide" to describe its product labels:

Table 12.1. Key to Date Printed on Smoking Goose Packages

PRODUCT	DATE PRINTED ON PACKAGING
Retail packages sealed on roll pack machine	Packed-on date: based on 365 days in a year
Whole piece items	Packed-on date: white label
Small-format salumi	Packed-on date: stamped with date gun
Frozen fresh sausages	Packed-on date: white label for bulk, stamped with date gun for retail chubs

Source: Smoking Goose, website, accessed November 16, 2015, http://www.smokinggoose .com/resources.

Table 12.2. Shelf Life of Smoking Goose Products

PRODUCT	SHELF LIFE
Smoked sausages	45 days after packed-on date
Fully cooked products	45 days after packed-on date
Sliced, fully cooked products	28 days after packed-on date
Dry-cured/fermented products	180 days after packed-on date
Frozen fresh sausages	14 days after thawing

Note: Freezing can increase the shelf life for some products; however, freezing is not recommended for all products.

Source: Smoking Goose, website, accessed November 16, 2015, http://www.smokinggoose .com/resources.

Smoking Goose works with a small organic slaughterhouse in Terre Haute, Indiana, whose appropriate slaughter techniques are absolutely fundamental to maintain and enhance the quality animals raised by Smoking Goose farmers. Beyond treating animals with respect and compassion, humane slaughter minimizes physical and psychological stress, both of which may compromise quality.

> *So I believe in certification when evaluating new places, but even if they have certification I would still take it one step further to visit, see for myself, see how they slaughter, and see how the animals are raised; I want to see the whole process.*[4]

As of 2015, the Smoking Goose operation employs thirty-five people and its plans to expand and double its capacity will add more skilled workers. Chris said the two companies face some challenges, although not what I anticipated. Although optimistic about the future of cured meat, I expected him to say the market is still an unknown quantity. Quite to the contrary, Chris feels the company can sell everything they produce and, equally important, has a steady, reliable source of hogs and other animals.

His greatest concerns focus on how to maintain high quality standards and the artisan nature of the business. The long and complex continuum from animal genetics and feed to farm environments through slaughter and butchering to final cured products requires significant investments of time, money, and other resources. Because each step is crucial to reach the highest levels of excellence and ensure wholesome and safe products, the company invests in education and training for its farmers, processors, and employees.

For example, staff members visit suppliers to learn about their operations, see animals firsthand, and understand the challenges and benefits of small farms. One objective is to create a sense of pride and ownership in Smoking Goose artisan products. The company's educational program is borne out by the people behind the counter at Goose the Market. Because Smoking Goose uses humanely raised and slaughtered heritage hogs, its costs are higher, and therefore, the dry-cured meats are not inexpensive. The counter staff uses their firsthand knowledge to describe and explain each cured meat and emphasize the careful management of animals, processing, and production as part of the sales approach.

Among other lessons, Smoking Goose and the market represent the best of opportunities and possibilities. First, they show the quality of products coming from Midwestern craftsmen; they are distinctive and in sharp contrast to standardized, industrial foods. Chris's experience as a chef in Chicago positioned them to develop a strong concept and then the steps needed to plan and implement their ideas. Second, Chris, Mollie, and the staff share a vision of great handmade fresh and cured meat, while recognizing the knowledge and skills needed for success and ongoing education to achieve the best.

For those who still fly over the Midwest and Great Plains, allow me to recommend these businesses as representatives of thousands of regional farmers, food producers, white tablecloth restaurants, and diners committed to similar philosophies and practices. If we add craft beer, artisan bread and cheese, and the rich food cultures of immigrants and ethnic groups, the choices are diverse and distinctive. So either drop in by parachute or, more advisedly, plan a visit to experience fine charcuterie and salumi from the region!

CHAPTER THIRTEEN

Mile-High Salumi

O ld railroad stations appeal to me, maybe because my great-grandfather and grandfather worked for the Pennsylvania Railroad in Altoona, Pennsylvania. I can still smell the coal smoke drifting over their house as freight and passenger trains chugged west and hear the engine boilers let off steam as eastbound coal trains waited for the traffic signals to change. Several of the nation's most extraordinary temples of the iron road — New York's Grand Central before and after the restoration; Penn Station, before its tragic demolition; Philadelphia's Thirtieth Street and Reading Terminal; and Washington's Union Station — are part of my railroad memory.

After World War II my father commuted for thirty years into New York from Mount Vernon and later Crugers on the Hudson Line, but ultimately we, like millions of Americans, left our train carriages for cars and planes to get to work or to travel. Most railroads witnessed precipitous declines in ridership, and the stations, the symbols of the country's industrial and economic progress and often a city's most visible declaration of modernity, became abandoned shadows or were torn down.

Fortunately, many survived, resurrected into elegant working landscapes, still handling passengers, and are now destinations to see and experience. Thus, in early June 2015 I walked through downtown Denver to its restored, now vibrant Union Station. Beginning in 1884 Union Station was the grand entrance to the Mile High City. Although not the original building, today's station was opened in 1914 but fell on hard times in the 1960s, as the area around it to the South Platte River gradually became another urban skid row.

By the 1980s Denver had suffered the loss of oil and gas businesses, high levels of pollution, and significant population decline. Strong political leadership and citizen involvement changed the equation with a spectacular airport, major consolidation of rail lines, establishment of historic districts, and public and private investment. Another example of revitalization came in 1988 when the city's first brewpub, Wynkoop Brewing Company, opened downtown; its former owner, John Hickenlooper, is the state's current governor. The 1990s saw a dramatic step forward with the construction of Coors Field, home to the Colorado Rockies baseball team. After the turn of the twenty-first century, Denver witnessed continued growth and innovation. The breakthrough for Union Station came about through recognition of the building's value as a cultural, historic, and aesthetic destination.

Fruition Restaurant
Fruition Farms & Dairy
Mercantile Dining & Provision

Beginning in the 1980s and then accelerating in the 1990s, pioneering restaurateurs opened new places in the city. In 2001 Frank Bonanno's Mizuna restaurant established a new level of sophisticated dining and helped lead to one of the most important contributors to the rebirth of Union Station, Alex Seidel. That evening in June 2015, I headed to Mercantile Dining and Provision, a restaurant and retail market that anchors the entire right-hand ground floor of the station. The creation of Alex Seidel, the operation reflects some of Denver's current best, as well as where the city's contribution to excellent dining, including cured meat, is headed.

Alex Seidel is from Racine, Wisconsin, a city noted for its mix of Germans, Danes, and Czechs and therefore, good wurst and beer. Parenthetically, we should note *seidel* is German for "beer stein," so maybe his good fortune and culinary success are related. In his midteens he worked in kitchens and by twenty became sous-chef at a local Racine restaurant. After obtaining a culinary degree in Portland, Oregon, and then working in several California restaurants, he landed in Vail, Colorado. In 2002 he moved to Denver and became executive chef at Mizuna, where during his tenure Frank Bonanno mentored him on his culinary journey. Among his many innovations, he brought in whole carcasses and had chefs butcher them, with some cuts converted into dry-cured salami, prosciutto, and other delicacies. At the time Bonanno's curing program happened under the radar without inspection, but that's another story.

In 2007 Alex opened a small hole-in-the wall restaurant called Fruition that immediately caught the attention of Denverites and food mavens from afar. While Fruition garnered numerous awards, it was just a first step in an evolving vision around farming and food. Two years later Alex became a farmer and cheese maker when he bought a ten-acre farm, now named Fruition Farms & Dairy, in Larkspur, about halfway between Denver and Colorado Springs. The idea was to grow produce for the restaurant and create Colorado's first sheep dairy to make cheese.

Jimmy Warren, Fruition's sous-chef, changed hats and became part owner and manager of the farm, as well as fruit and vegetable farmer, cheese maker, and hog grower. The farm grows 25 percent of the produce needed for the restaurants. Until 2016 they milked sixty East Friesian sheep to make yogurt and three cheeses: whole milk ricotta; Shepherd's Halo, a soft-ripened bloomy rind wheel; and Cacio Pecora, an aged wheel. But demand for the farm's dairy products exceeded the yearly three thousand to four thousand pounds of cheese produced, and with only ten acres of land limiting the number of sheep, Alex decided to sell most of the flock and bring in sheep milk from Nebraska's Irish Cream Sheep Dairy.

Inspired by the farm work and by former mentor Frank Bonanno, Alex participated successfully in a Cochon555 competition. The event introduced him to several hog farmers, and that in turn led to a decision to buy hogs. Committed to working with heritage breeds, he bought certified Berkshire hogs and a Swabian Hall boar from Carl Blake of Rustik Rooster Farms in Ionia, Iowa. An early nineteenth-century German cross between a Chinese Meishan and wild Russian hogs, the Swabian exhibits extraordinary rich, marbled meat. Seidel also purchased Large Black hogs, another important heritage breed. Because he is raising the pigs sustainably, the animals enjoy a variety of farm-grown produce, with sheep milk whey to wash it down.

Alex described the recent story of Mercantile while we sat at the restaurant's counter. The leaders of the Union Station project approached him with a proposal to become one of the main tenants of the new downtown gateway. He grabbed this extraordinary opportunity and created

Mercantile Dining and Provision, a place for both casual and fine dining, a bar serving cocktails and local craft beer, and a European-style market. The $1.8 million investment came through a loan without any private investors, a successful strategy he had used previously to finance Fruition.

Each component works in concert with the other parts, including the farm. Fruits and vegetables arrive on your plate fresh, cooked, or minimally processed as jarred and pickled items. They make twelve types of pickled vegetables (each with its HACCP plan) and have an on-site pastry bakery. These simple steps allow them to use just about everything from the farm, including slightly bruised or oddly shaped vegetables and fruits that don't make it to your plate. Off in one corner is a small wood and glass cabinet to cure prosciutto and salami.

Alex reflected on the challenges of operating a farm and two very highly regarded restaurants and described farming as far more difficult than he had imagined. "You really have to want to farm, educate yourself, and learn through experience."[1] Despite the hurdles, each venture added to Alex and the staff's repertoire and skills. Many of his employees at Mercantile started with him at Fruition and moved into senior management positions with more opportunities as the business grew. I like the dynamics of the farm as both a source for locally grown and harvested food and a teaching laboratory focused on a wide array of produce, fruit, cheese, and meats. Each endeavor requires skill and sophistication to create and maintain top-notch quality. Alex views curing as inspiration and knowledge. Over time, as interests and experiences broaden, and now with sustainably raised hogs from the farm, he can expand his repertoire to include a variety of cured meats.

In 2016 he realized that the small cabinet, while adding an attractive physical dimension to Mercantile, would never fulfill his vision for a charcuterie program. He decided to open a commissary kitchen with adequate capacity to produce a variety and volume of cured meats. The facility will enable the business to supply distinctive, quality charcuterie for both in-house use and retail sales to customers.

Il Porcellino Salumi

My June evening visit to Mercantile was for dinner with two new entrepreneurs with a dream for a pork shop, or as they call it, Il Porcellino Salumi.

We sat down at an outside patio table on a warm spring night to indulge in great food and the ambiance surrounding Mercantile and Union Station. My dinner companions were Bill Miner and Brian Albano, who were deep into planning and refurbishing a small butcher shop in the city's Berkeley district, northwest of downtown.

We ordered Mercantile's charcuterie board, a mammoth presentation with enough cured meat, pâté, breads, mustard, and preserves to daunt three porkcentric men! It's a presentation proclaiming the best of what Denver and Colorado can do. Throughout the dinner and our many compliments on the food, service, and presentation, Bill and Brian discussed a different and yet complementary vision of charcuterie.

The two forty-something men have accumulated decades of experience working in kitchens, and both received degrees from the culinary school at Denver's Art Institute of Colorado. Bill was executive chef for the well-known Relish Catering Company, during which time Brian worked for him. While there, they experimented with dry-curing whole-muscle meats and, after enthusiastic comments from friends, told themselves in 2012, "This can't be all that hard!"[2] Well, perhaps it was, as they discovered in 2015, when a midsummer opening got pushed back to early fall and finally ended in a successful launch in October.

Bill and Brian draw energy and enthusiasm from a confluence of several key national trends: an improving economy, the farm-to-table movement, an interest in cured meat, and personal philosophies about food and farming that intersect with Denver's renaissance. They talked about the excitement of people moving to Denver to take jobs and nurture the city's economy. Coming from other cities, many young newcomers, attracted to Colorado's craft beer scene and (perhaps) relaxed marijuana laws, quickly embraced other fermented foods and beverages. But rather than a new downtown restaurant, Bill and Brian saw opportunity in the Berkeley neighborhood to establish a small community place for fresh and prepared foods, sandwiches, and small plates, including cured meats. With similar backgrounds, they also set up a small catering operation built around straightforward foods, all of which are made on-site.

Bill and Brian share a deep ethical commitment to local farms, sustainable and humane animal husbandry, and skilled butchery, something for which Denver is now assuming a leadership role. They see the emergence of menus with chef-inspired dry-cured meats and new charcuterie businesses intersecting with consumer demand for these foods. For them the meat renaissance reflects a small but dynamic shift in how we eat. Brian said, "What's old is now new again." Farmers who take the time to grow a grass-fed steer or pastured hog make an investment in animals and their livelihoods. But inhumane slaughter and poor butchering skills compromise the many-months-long effort. Working with whole carcasses demands skill and knowledge of how to make a specific cut or even several different ways to butcher a shoulder or ham, and the partners emphasize their commitment to ensure they waste nothing from each animal.

Il Porcellino Salumi distinguishes itself through its meat program; the company's motto, "Colorado Cured," is a statement both about its Denver location and the state's evolving, diverse food community. During his years at Relish, Bill developed many personal contacts with Colorado farmers, growers, and food producers. Today Il Porcellino Salumi works with more than thirty farms and producers, all within ninety miles of Denver, who supply beef, bison, duck, lamb, and pork to the shop. They buy Berkshire, Red Wattle, and heritage crosses from several producers, including Corner Post Meats, JNP Ranch, Graybill Land & Livestock, and Jack Rupp Hogs.

Beyond offering these meats as fresh and cured, they make lamb prosciutto and salami and bison bresaola and pastrami. They divide their curing approach into seasons and currently offer autumn- and winter-cured products to reflect traditional practices.

Building on their initial success, Bill and Brian became part of the new Union Station Farmers Market in June 2016. The enthusiasm for the Berkeley neighborhood store created opportunities for additional locations around Denver. To meet the growing demand, in 2016 they started plans for a USDA-certified facility for cured meats to sell wholesale and to supply future stores.

Bonanno Concepts

One of Denver's leading restaurateurs and a pioneer in dry-cured meats is New Jerseyite Frank Bonanno. Since opening his first restaurant in 2001, he has contributed to the city's emergence as a culinary destination. Some people might use different words to describe a desire to use old-world techniques and the resulting lengthy squabbles with the city's health department — iconoclast, pain in the ass, and hardheaded, among other polite language. Inventive chef, successful businessman, mentor, and culinary visionary would fit my portrait.

Bonanno grew up in Bergenfield, just north of the George Washington Bridge, which links New Jersey to New York City. Belonging to a family with deep Sicilian roots, he sings the praises of Nonna's pasta and the pleasure of making dishes with his mother from Julia Child's recipes. If you visit a website for one of Frank's restaurants and bars, now ten and counting in 2016, he describes the physical and emotional connections to his youth and food, especially Rudy's Pizza and Vito's Deli for a great grinder sandwich. These powerful memories of mozzarella cheese, thin-sliced coppa, and red sauce that took hours of slow cooking to make continue to shape his career.[3]

Following Horace Greeley's advice to "go west, young man," Frank received a bachelor's degree in financial accounting from the University of Denver, where his cooking interest and skills helped pay for his education. Today, looking at a picture of Bonanno with an intense, serious expression on his face, you celebrate that he decided to become a chef and not a tax auditor. But the business training really underpins his long-term success in the food business, a notoriously difficult way to make a living.

In 1996 he polished his culinary chops with a degree from the Culinary Institute of America in Hyde Park, New York, and then spent several years working in France and Italy. His wife, Jacqueline, a Denverite, brought them back to the city, where in 2001 they opened Mizuna, built on classic French techniques matched with very American ideas and ingredients. Two years later a second restaurant, Luca, named after their first son, directed attention to quality cured meats. While Frank processed some meats, such as mortadella, his father sent "care packages" of Italian prosciutto from Jersey for use in the restaurant. Frank and the Luca chefs experimented with different salami types and styles by using regular salt and sodium nitrate or nitrite curing salts to preserve them. Frank was the designated "king's taster" for these efforts, and if he didn't get sick, they replicated the recipe!

As he explained, for a year or two they made salami, coppa, and prosciutto with only occasional questions from the city's health inspectors. In 2007 they opened Osteria Marco, named after another son, where handmade mozzarella and other Italian-style cheeses, together with house-made cured meats, were the foundations of the food. They spent months perfecting sauces, pasta flavors, and even the pizza crust.[4] To understand Frank's commitment — some might say obsession — to authenticity when he opened Salt & Grinder in 2014, they ran months of experiments with Grateful Bread Company in Golden to replicate the grinder rolls from Frank's childhood.

But as questions gradually increased about appropriate temperatures and humidity at Marco, they installed a curing cabinet in Jacqueline's office above an adjacent restaurant, Bones, legally off-limits to inspectors. They also implemented testing protocols for water activity and pH levels, all of which appeared to fall within the correct parameters. Because of the legal artistry of the curing cabinet location, it was not until 2012 that health inspectors, investigating a possible norovirus food illness problem, discovered the collection of cured meats — several hundred pounds of prosciutto, pancetta, coppa, guanciale, and soppressata. The inspectors destroyed all the meats and Frank's extensive array of house-made cheese.

After months of negotiations, during which all of the Bonanno restaurants remained open because no evidence of norovirus was discovered, everyone moved on. Frank wrote HACCP plans that passed muster with Denver's Department of Environmental Health, with assistance from USDA officials.

> *"Our relationship started changing for the better once we first applied for our HACCP plan. Danica [Lee, a city health inspector] knew that she had to work with us, and she single-handedly made it happen — and, honestly, without her unbelievable cooperation and help, we would have never gotten this approved," he says. "She's eager to learn, she's been amazingly open-minded and forward-thinking, and I can't give her enough credit. It just goes to show you that when we and the health inspectors work together, a lot can be accomplished."[5]*

In the basement of his delicatessen Salt & Grinder, he built an aging room to produce salumi, lonza, prosciutto, and culatello for Luca, Osteria Marco, Russell's Smokehouse, and the deli. To fulfill the needed volume and achieve excellent quality and safety, Frank hired a former baker to become the salumiere. Must be the fermentation genes!

While buying whole Duroc hogs from Colorado's McDonald Family Farm, they purchase additional neck muscle to make coppa, the restaurant's most popular salumi. Frank described putting up two hundred to three hundred pounds of coppa, which after aging for four months weighs 40 to 50 percent less. In addition to dozens of neck muscles, they buy natural casings into which they stuff each coppa; Frank says this is very "old school" and is how he remembers the product.[6] Because the curing room does not incorporate a fermentation chamber, occasionally they must add moisture with a humidifier and warm the air to ensure proper maturation.

Frank is outspoken and honest about the difficult challenges of making distinctive, high-quality, and safe cured meat. Listening to him talk about sanitation reminded me of newly molded artisan cheese makers, who realize shortly after launching a creamery that only a fraction of their time is dedicated to art and science. For most, 75 to 80 percent of a sixteen- to eighteen-hour day is devoted to cleaning, cleaning, and recleaning. To succeed with either fermented food, both salumiere and cheese maker must adhere to scrupulous sanitation standards to maintain excellence and ensure safety. To train and retain a highly skilled salumiere costs money, and Frank invested time and resources to make the best charcuterie possible.

In addition, quality animals are expensive, as they should be, given the current scarcity of heritage hogs and the time and resources needed to grow them with appropriate diets and husbandry. Frank sees the company's charcuterie program as a trade-off financially. In today's market and culinary world, diners expect house-made charcuterie, especially in restaurants with a serious approach to Italian food. But with all of the initial costs, the profit margin is pretty slim.

Since Frank and Jacqueline opened Mizuna in 2001, the restaurant scene in Denver has evolved considerably. In many ways Frank's determination to develop a cured-meat program and his willingness to take significant risks brought considerable notoriety, emotional and financial pain, and maybe even some laughter along the way. Yes, he pushed the boundaries regarding health inspections, but he helped to redefine them to satisfy both restaurateurs and health officials. Perhaps the most interesting and rewarding acknowledgment for Frank was the city's Department of Environmental Health inviting him to consult with them for new curing businesses.

The three Denver businesses drive home points about scale, margins, quality control, safety, and the constantly evolving restaurant world. Their emphasis on local sources bumps up against the realities of available land and facility space, capital investment, profit margin, and consumer expectations. Add in HACCP planning, regulatory scrutiny, and interpretations of food safety requirements, and costs begin to escalate. The challenge for each business is to balance consumer demand and the in-house skills and expertise required to create outstanding products.

CHAPTER FOURTEEN

The Pacific Rim

*The only true voyage of discovery . . . would be not to
visit strange lands but to possess other eyes, to behold
the universe through the eyes of a hundred others.*

— Marcel Proust

The West Coast is a gold mine for great charcuterie and salumi, especially if the mine has the right environmental qualities to age meat. Keeping in mind that I did not interview every company, let's acknowledge several important individuals and firms. Although no longer a small business, Columbus Craft Meats in San Francisco celebrates its one-hundredth anniversary in 2017; *complimenti*! Since 1999 Armandino Batali's Salumi Artisan Cured Meats in Seattle established a new level of excellence and visibility for Italian salumi. San Francisco's Mark Pastore and Chris Cosentino started with Incanto, a remarkable nose-to-heart/liver/sweetbreads and other assorted offal restaurant and then launched Boccalone, devoted exclusively to cured pork. In Napa and San Francisco, we find Fatted Calf Charcuterie, whose porchetta sandwiches-to-go sustained me several times on red-eye flights back east!

More than once I've wished for closer proximity to the array of outstanding charcuterie and salumi from these producers. And yet sometimes the trade-off for a small, local company not going national is all about maintaining its integrity. The same question revolves around artisan cheese and very clearly craft beer. Today, whether living in or traveling to California, Minnesota, Louisiana, or Vermont, we can enjoy local beverages and foods comparable to culinary and cultural experiences found in Europe.

Hunter Angler Gardener Cook

An introduction to and subsequent conversation with Hank Shaw revealed how little I really know about food preservation. Hank, like Sandor Katz, established himself deeply in cured-food communities through writing, practice, sharing knowledge, and how he chooses to live his life. He lives on and off the land as a forager, fisherman, gardener, and hunter; his cooking skills reflect a reverence for nature as he transforms the foods surrounding us into the quality we might find at a white tablecloth restaurant.

Growing up in Westfield, New Jersey, Hank's family relished fishing and foraging for wild foods. His mother learned these skills in Massachusetts during the Depression, when dinner was in the sand or just offshore with a casting line or trap. In addition to teaching the skills for and pleasure of discovering what was in nature's grocery store, his family enjoyed German, Italian, and Jewish cured meats that contributed to his sophisticated palate and pursuit of good food.

In the early 1990s an interest in writing and politics took him to graduate school at the University of Wisconsin in Madison. While in school, he worked as a line cook in a local restaurant, where these new skills became a foundation for his work over the past two decades. After graduation he was a political reporter for newspapers in New York, the Twin Cities, and finally in 2004 in Sacramento, where he was the Capitol bureau chief for Stockton's *Record*. Along the way Hank went fishing, perhaps catching shad in New York, walleye in Minnesota, or salmon and trout in one of California's rivers.

All of these experiences shaped a worldview in sharp contrast with how contemporary America eats, although I imagine Hank might emphatically describe our food system as broken, unhealthy, and detrimental to humans, animals, and nature, among other lowlights. He started to hunt game when a Minnesota colleague encouraged him to try; it was almost a failure, since he had no experience with a shotgun. Until his hunting experience, his attention focused mainly on foods of the coast, beach plants, shell and finfish, and what he grew in a garden. Since 2005 nearly all of his meat, fish, and poultry comes from hunting or fishing or direct from farmers who practice sustainable agriculture and humane practices.

Hank's discovery of and reliance on the diversity and quality of wild foods and produce from his garden contributed more than just sustenance for him and his partner, Holly Heyser. Several times he emphasized how each night, after work as a reporter, cooking dinner brought him back to Earth and kept him sane. After leaving the press corps in 2007, he began writing a blog, *Hunter Angler Gardener Cook*, that combined his multifaceted interests with culinary and writing skills to teach about the natural world.

> *Honest food is what I seek. I am a constant forager, angler, hunter, gardener and fan of farmer's markets. Eating locally and making good food from scratch is what I do. Seasonality rules my diet: In winter, I would rather eat a well-cooked turnip than asparagus from Chile.*[1]

During our conversation, I continued to wonder why people recommended Hank to me. Then talking about hunting venison, duck, even wild boar, he mentioned how he preserved many different foods. Hank makes bacon or sausage fresh, smoked, and cured from what he hunts, often flavored with foraged wild plants. Each of these skills, techniques, and understandings require time, patience (they don't always work), and attention to details. When I asked about his view of the dry-cured renaissance, Hank shifted gears and compared two sides of the changes over the past two decades. First, he believes the initial wave of charcuterie and salumi has crested, in part because many dilettantes jumped on the meat wagon, created mediocre products, realized the costs involved, and fortunately left the scene. In contrast, he celebrates great cured meats from a number of restaurants and small-scale salumi producers; in his opinion, they made the investment of time, education, and money to create excellent products. I literally could not keep up with the names he rattled off, though many of them show up throughout this book.

But perhaps his most telling, eloquent statement about charcuterie came from an earlier interview in 2011:

> *Charcuterie is jazz. In jazz, artists play endlessly with the old standards. There are 1,000 versions of Thelonious Monk's "Around Midnight." Sausage is like that. You have boundaries, rules you need*

to follow. But your ability for expression is limitless within those boundaries. Spices, herbs, ratios of meat to fat, choice of meats, width of a link, length of curing time, temperature and humidity of the cure, etc. etc. The end result is a product that your friends will immediately recognize, but that is intimately bound to your personality.[2]

Reading and absorbing his salami poetry is a powerful reminder of where food comes from and centuries of human innovation to refine, create riffs on a theme, survive, and ultimately celebrate both nature and slow knowledge.

It turns out, through the blog and three books on preparing and cooking wild food, that the culinary community knows Hank and vice versa. Several years ago he received a James Beard award for Best Food Blogger, and subsequent invitations to visit chefs or take a foraging trip into the woods or desert added to his visibility and knowledge.

Throughout our conversation Hank spoke passionately on how the developed world is dislocated from its foods and their origins. He talked as well about his view on generational differences, especially with Millennials who demand closer, meaningful connections to food, farmers, and producers; want to know about humane and sustainable practices; and experiment with different ways of eating. As a hunter and writer about game, he sees the hunting community more involved today with how meats are prepared, including barbeque.

As we talked I was struck by an underlying restlessness, a positive energy about how Hank wants to redefine how we eat. For example, he describes himself as a cook who hunts, not a hunter who cooks. To hunt requires skill, patience, an ability to embrace silence and stillness, and a willingness to accept that you kill a warm-blooded animal. I was reminded of Toby Rodriguez describing a boucherie and the intimate, visceral, emotional reactions to killing and slaughtering a hog. Hank said several times that while hunting is not for everyone, the relationship defines human history and evolution. His recipes for fish and game involve an animal's geographic origin, its surroundings, and what it might eat. For example, he might stew a hare with wild sage and juniper berries.

He is also a man who likes to eat. His blog cheerfully describes his enjoyment drinking Balvenie Scotch, Barolo, and Budweiser . . . although without a disclaimer if he imbibes all at once! In a way his commitment to a closer and deeper appreciation and connection with what he eats is not stated as coming from a purist. Hank knows and embraces good food as a common denominator, and the more we are aware, the better our choices and their implications to us and the world.

Higgins Restaurant

I recall my first trip to Portland in the late 1980s to attend the annual American Veterinary Medical Association convention. Our room faced the Columbia River, and through a sliver of a window we could see Mount Hood. The trip's highlight was a daylong hike up Mount St. Helens, maybe eight or nine years after the eruption. I still remember a look deep into the crater, the presence of smoke and the sulfur smell, and looking north with Mounts Rainier and Baker in the distance, Mounts Hood and Jefferson behind us. Definitely an early bucket-list experience.

While I don't recall the food I ate on that visit, subsequent trips for business always included some pleasure, introducing me to the city's diverse food culture. Great colleagues and friends Peter and Pat de Garmo, Katherine Deumling, and Steve Jones helped guide my way. I remember clearly a 2006 trip to the city's great farmers' market, where I met Joan and Pierre-Louis Monteillet of their eponymous Monteillet Fromagerie and Kathy and Paul Obringer of Ancient Heritage Dairy. Sadly, Kathy passed away several years ago, but Paul and son Hank continue to handcraft great cheese.

Another good Portland friend, writer, *Good Stuff NW* blogger, and all-around great bon vivant, Kathleen Bauer provided a list of companies and people for my research. She put one person at the top of the list: Greg Higgins, chef/owner of the downtown Higgins Restaurant. It's embarrassing to say that despite many Portland trips, including ones where I must have walked by the entrance, I was never there. That will change in the future!

Born in 1958, Greg grew up in the village of Eden, New York, on Lake Erie, southwest of Buffalo. As a teen he worked on dairy and vegetable farms, including in an apprenticeship at Eden's Famous Cheese Factory, where he was introduced to handmade cheese and German-style sausage. He received a BA in art and archaeology from Hartwick College and moonlighted at a local "veal and pasta" place, where he picked up some butchery skills. After graduation he went to Europe and worked with an Alsatian butcher who taught him about charcuterie and wurst.

After stops in Sun Valley, Idaho, and British Columbia, he arrived in Portland in 1984 to help open Heathman Hotel and its restaurant. As Greg describes it, the timing was either impeccable or risky and improbable. At what Greg calls "the height of egg-white omelets," the concept of fresh regional, seasonal food with a constantly changing menu collided with some hotel and Portland diners who wanted steak and no vegetables.

With a background in farming, cheese making, charcuterie, and working with local sources, Greg sought out farmers and food producers around the city. He encouraged farmers to grow certain produce and consider how good husbandry makes for a better animal. It took time, but Greg and his crew added a variety of dry-cured salami and hams made from pork and lamb to the restaurant's focus on vegetables, and as the culinary scene evolved locally and nationally, they were among the leaders in Portland.

In 1994 he and partner Paul Mallory opened Higgins Restaurant and Bar with an emphasis on Alsatian French and German foods with all the ingredients from local sources. For the first ten years, obtaining a consistent, quality animal presented challenges. Greg was not wedded to a particular hog breed; rather, he looked for how the animals were raised and fed and whether they got enough outdoor exercise. Today they buy Berkshire/Duroc crosses from two Oregon ranches—Carman and HangBelly—to make more than seventy seasonal charcuterie products. On Wednesdays Greg breaks down a two-hundred-pound dressed hog and over the next two days converts it into one to two hundred pounds of salami, plus cured hams, pâtés, terrines, and rillettes; these different products become the building blocks for the entire menu.

When Greg and Paul opened, concepts of farm to table and fish to table, vegetarian and vegan, fully organic, and heritage animals and produce were not part of public consciousness or food lexicon. Over the last two decades, all of these, plus artisan cheese, craft beer and spirits, and others became part of the contemporary scene in Portland and nationally. Greg thinks the future of food is exciting and filled with opportunities. Greater travel, more food choices, and diverse healthy ways to eat translate into new directions for restaurateurs and artisan producers.

With nearly thirty years' experience in charcuterie, Greg witnessed the early "seat-of-the-pants" or "do-it-yourself" efforts, followed by maturation of the fermentation community. Restaurants wanted to promote their unique house-made salami, pickles, mustard, bread, and so forth to attract visibility and customers. To accomplish this requires skilled chefs, knowledgeable waitstaff to market products, and excellent ingredients, all of which cost money and have a potential impact on meal prices.

He points to changes echoed by other chefs: that in-house charcuterie, cheese, preserved vegetables, and other fermented foods may no longer headline a menu. Not only are they expensive to make, but each must pass food safety inspections, often including time to write an HACCP plan. As he explained to me, some of the most acclaimed chefs he met in Alsace buy great cheese and sausage from the region's best artisans. The European chefs still bring in whole carcasses but manage the butchery cuts in different ways. They make in-house terrines and pâtés, but since these are cooked, they don't require the same safety documentation. Greg argues that the remedy for American chefs is not to make every fermented food themselves but to engage local farmers and craft producers and showcase them in the same manner we tout the overall farm-to-table connection.

Old Salt Marketplace

My next stop in Portland was with Ben Meyer, who immediately began talking about the history and culture of food, the short life spans of most citizens in ancient civilizations, and the challenges of curing meat when you relied on the weather. Yikes, what a great way to dive into an interview!

Ben took an odd road, maybe the road less traveled, to charcuterie. He grew up in northern Indiana, near Fort Wayne; his Pennsylvania Dutch (German) great-grandmother, Georgia, and his mother expertly preserved their garden produce and the pigs they raised. He helped with the annual slaughter and watched as Georgia put up pork in an old wine barrel. She brined hams, loins, trotters, and bacon in the barrel; the bacon was then slow-smoked for four to five weeks. Among other foods close to his heart were Pennsylvania cottage roll, made from a boneless pork shoulder butt (like a coppa cut) and pickled in a sweet brine. Hearing him describe it took me back to Lancaster County's Pennsylvania Dutch restaurants and finding cottage roll on the menu.

Northeast Indiana is a land of enormous commodity corn and soybean farms and large-scale confinement hog operations. Ben's family was literally surrounded by what he saw as the worst of America's food system. He went to Minnesota to attend St. Olaf College in studio art and philosophy, both of which continue to influence his worldview and aesthetics. In 1995, while at St. Olaf, he decided to become a vegan as a personal statement, to consciously avoid industrial agriculture and its destructive manifestations.

A year later Ben went to Portland in pursuit of music, ended up cooking at several places, owned and sold a small restaurant, and shopped at the city's farmers' market. He then biked around the country for a year working at sixty (!) different farms. In 2004 he went to Vashon Island in Elliott's Bay, between Seattle and Tacoma, where he worked and lived on an organic farm. He met Lauren and Brandon Sheard, butchers and owners of Farmstead Meatsmith, and sharpened his knife skills with them. His experiences on different farms during the bike tour and on Vashon Island changed his view of how food establishments might contribute to a different way of eating.

The first result was his return to Portland to become the chef at Genie's Café. He continued his meat-cutting education and moved to Viande Meats and then to New Seasons Market, at which he handled 120 smoked hams a month. Moving that number of hams every month taught him about production logistics, HACCP plans and documentation, and critical techniques to properly smoke meat. Along the way Ben moved back to being an omnivore, realizing he could eat wholesome local food and serve the same to customers.

In 2009 Ben and partner Jason French opened a restaurant, called Ned Ludd, with a beautiful, large brick pizza oven that remained from the previous owners. This is not in itself unusual; what is unusual is that they looked at the oven and asked what else they could do with it besides pizza. With their connections and knowledge of the local farm community, they brought in lots of produce and at least one pig and lamb a week. The oven, the centerpiece of everything on the menu, challenged and reflected their commitment to Oregon food and perhaps even how different areas of the state expressed their unique terroir. Rather than create strange dishes that pushed the boundaries of "good to eat," they aimed for simplicity and purity of taste.

The name Ned Ludd, a tribute to the famous English anti-industrialist, reflected Jason and Ben's commitment to farmers and ranchers as the bedrock of their enterprise. I encountered a phrase from Ben, "obstructionist cuisine," meaning what came in the door was that evening's menu. Some days you planned; other days you reacted. Each day required flexibility and energy to fulfill their standards of excellence and ensure customers ate well.

We might characterize Ben as a creative and highly energetic or restless man, or both. Just two years after opening Ned Ludd, he started another restaurant. After selling his interest in the former restaurant, Ben with two partners launched Grain & Gristle. It quickly took off, and they found themselves slammed because the kitchen was far too small to meet demand.

So what do you do? If you're Ben, you open another, larger place with room for dry-curing, this one in 2013 called Old Salt Marketplace, a combination delicatessen, butcher shop, informal restaurant and bar, and weekly farmers' market! The guy clearly likes to juggle more than one salami at a time. Here Ben practices all of his skills in butchery and, now with adequate space, does considerable dry curing. The market sells fresh, cooked, and cured meats. In honor of his great-grandmother Georgia, Ben even makes a coarse-ground Lebanon bologna. Every week he buys approximately two steers and four hogs from several of Oregon's grass-fed meat ranchers, including Carman and Hawley ranches and Laney Family and Payne Family farms. All the hogs come from the Payne family, a fourth-generation pork farm established in 1882. They raise Berkshire/Duroc crosses and grow the feed; what makes them really unique are the feed grains, millet and triticale, a wheat/rye cross. They also grind the latter one, so you can have a wonderful pork dinner with a side of triticale pasta.

Ben is a powerful advocate for whole-animal butchery. He utilizes one walk-in to age beef sides, tenderloins, and ribs for sixty to ninety days. In a thirty-by-fifty-foot aging room, he cures a variety of seasonal products, including prosciutto and soppressata. Some are partially cured and smoked: hams, landjäger, Lebanon bologna, and Slovenian-inspired smoked lardo! They also render the skin with some of the fat to make cracklings to further extend its value and potential for meals.

Ben and his two partners look to push back at how many contemporary American places use culinary language without the practice — only the jargon and advertising potential: farm to table; nose to tail; artisan and craftsman; and curated (that one grates on me as well) as examples. Or how they use such practices as false advertising about farm sources or sustainability, or promote the value of consuming truly terrible food, all of which misses the critical reality that the industrial food system has done this for decades. "'What we're doing is just making supper," Meyer says. "I tell the guys, 'Grandma did it every day and no one ever wrote a magazine article about her.'"[3]

The other dimension distinguishing them from many other restaurants across the country derives from the partners' experiences working in kitchens as waiters or dishwashers. Before opening they committed to fair wages, health insurance, and 401(k) retirement plans for all employees. While these benefits clearly affect operating expenses, the restaurant's fresh food and prices are modest, in part because in Old Salt Marketplace, they reduce costs by utilizing everything they buy. In addition, they chose an area of Portland with cheaper rents. The concept challenges how food businesses operate, but as we have seen in Denver and New York, it can work.

The company offers cooking classes, realizing that although many Americans lost the ability to work with good ingredients, today's consumers want to learn. The whole-animal butchery concept translates to home kitchens; buy a whole chicken, and cut it up yourself. Teaching customers how to cook, whether in a classroom or at the meat counter, means they introduce friends to something they prepared and build a committed customer base.

In a 2014 interview Anthony Bourdain spoke about changes in the country's foodways and culture and was described by his interviewer accordingly: "For someone who comes across a bit like a wise ass cynic in his books, someone who might scoff, Bourdain offers what seems like a genuinely idealistic take on it all: the spiritual globalism, you might say, at the heart of the food frenzy culture."[4]

I think he also captured some of what Old Salt Marketplace envisions:

> He has a theory about this I [the interviewer] hadn't considered. That the whole seismic food culture shift isn't American superficiality but the New World learning what the Old World has known for centuries. "We're just catching on," he [Bourdain] says. "We are changing societally, and our values are changing, so that we are becoming more

like Italians and Chinese and Thais and Spaniards, where we actually think about what we're eating, what we ate last night, and what we're considering eating tomorrow. When I grew up in the '60s, we'd go to see a movie, then we would go to a restaurant. And we would talk about the movie we just saw. Now, you go right to dinner and you talk about the dinner you had last week and the dinner you're going to have next week, while you're taking pictures of the dinner you're having now. That's a very Italian thing. A lot of the sort of hypocrisy and silliness and affectation of current American food culture is just fits and starts, awkwardly and foolishly growing into a place where a lot of older cultures have been for quite some time."[5]

I like Bourdain's premise and hope he is right. In our superheated world of instant connection and communication, I wonder how often the message gets lost. Marshall McLuhan's point that the medium is the message is front and center through Facebook, Twitter, Snapchat, and Instagram. These technologies, unknown in 2005, influence dialogue, personal contacts, worldviews, political campaigns, art, and poetry, just to mention a few. Can you imagine the instantaneous report from your restaurant that "so-and-so isn't on their game tonight; go someplace else"? In my view, Ben and his Old Salt partners, Alex Ganum and Marcus Hoover, return us to the past through their emphasis on using everything we receive from nature and farmers. In many ways the philosophy connects its roots to survival; given Ben's decade of veganism as a survival technique in the face of industrial agriculture, Old Salt expresses more about how to navigate in today's culture toward a different outcome.

Olympia Provisions

I urge you to not buy or read Elias Cairo's book entitled *Olympia Provisions*! And if you do, definitely do not open it to "Intermission: Back to Wildhaus" on page 155, or the evening at Aescher on page 184. You are forewarned! Viewing these pages of extraordinary landscapes will motivate you to pack bags immediately for Switzerland and the Alps! I am captivated by the remote, beautiful mountains and Eli's stories of the region's artisans, families, and cultural history of food and cuisine. He helps us understand how an individual, a craftsman, commits to a daily, repetitive performance to make one item; for example, *bündnerfleisch*, a cured beef similar to bresaola.

I first became familiar with Olympia's cured meats several years ago, when rumors of the Portland outfit percolated east and then north to Vermont. Eventually, a salami or two emerged on local store shelves, and treats ensued. I knew an interview with Eli was essential, and through Kathleen Bauer we finally talked.

Here is a man intensely proud of his Greek heritage and the manner in which his family celebrate their relationships, friends, customs, and food. His father was born in the mountains above Sparta, Greece, where the family raised goats, and like everyone else in the village, he was a jack-of-all-trades — butcher, farmer, and distiller — and a master of them all. In his twenties he arrived in Utah and ended up working in a copper mine. To say the least, for a young man accustomed to living on mountains, the idea of digging enormous holes for ore must have felt incongruous at best. He moved to Sandy, Utah, southeast of Salt Lake City, where on less than an acre he grew produce and kept a livestock menagerie, and eventually he owned two restaurants.

Eli and his sister, Michelle, were born in Sandy, and he described weekend family gatherings at which they shared a spit-roasted goat or lamb, garden vegetables, and certainly some or maybe a lot of ouzo! He also enjoyed spending time in the family restaurants, cooking and interacting with guests. Because of the location, Eli learned to downhill ski and snowboard; he was good enough that Burton Snowboards sponsored him to compete internationally.

Tragedy struck in 1997, when Eli and Michelle's father died; Eli was nineteen. He gave up the sponsorship and through a series of fortunate connections ended up at Alpenrose Hotel in Wildhaus in northeastern Switzerland. The Swiss and German culinary world has a different approach to training people than attending culinary school or starting as a dishwasher. Though you might wash dishes, restaurants and hotels participate in rigorous apprenticeship programs. These generally last four years, after which a job awaits you. The idea has similar characteristics to teaching other highly skilled professional trades; the process conveys fundamental ideas, techniques, and practices, and you either make it or you don't. Actually, the selection process is very vigorous, so most apprentices do well enough to continue on their career paths. Reading "Intermission:

Back to Wildhaus," you understand Eli's deep affection and appreciation for the time spent in the Alps and how the apprenticeship shaped his future.

At Alpenrose they made everything, and the source for much of the food was just outside the door — game, wild herbs, flowers, mushrooms — or dropped off by local artisans. Because of its remote location, deliveries were not as convenient as they are in the States, so you made do. Eli makes the connection between his father and Greek ancestors and how we see today's culinary world, in which "do it yourself" for them was just "life."[6]

When Eli returned in 2004, he moved to Portland, where Michelle lived. He shared the same initial experiences as Greg Higgins and Ben Meyer: There was plenty of great regional food, but it was not yet an innovative culinary scene. In 2005 he went to work for Monique Sui at Castagna, one of the city's culinary leaders, and over the next four years hatched an idea for a cured-meat business.

The idea coalesced around several other people who became partners in Olympia: chefs Nate Tilden and Tyler Gaston and mentor Marty Schwartz were the original crew. The business was twofold, a restaurant in the front and a butchery/curing facility in the rear. The location was in Southeast Portland in the former Olympic Cereal Mill building, now on the National Register of Historic Places; the mill also lived on in the name Olympic Provisions. On a tight budget they built a 900-square-foot setup, using wine coolers and re-purposed metal racks. They opened for business in 2009 with the intention of supplying the restaurant and a few farmers' markets. For Eli and his partners, these venues were vital to development and refinement of their charcuterie.

Fate intervened again when the company received four Good Food Awards in 2009 and the phones started to burn up. A key retailer, Sam Mogannam, owner of San Francisco's Bi-Rite Market, was one of the first to call and place an order. Demand quickly outstripped supply, and in 2011 they opened a second restaurant with adjacent production space, and Michelle Cairo came in as CEO and new partner. Now with two facilities they had 4,000 square feet dedicated to production to supply both restaurants and more farmers' markets. Olympia buys Berkshire/Duroc crossbred hogs from Carlton Farms, founded in 1956 in Carlton, Oregon. Carlton sources its animals from local and national growers and provides Olympia with quartered portions.

And it still wasn't enough production. In early 2014 they inaugurated a third facility with 34,000 square feet of capacity. Then one day in 2014 they received a "cease and desist" notice from the International Olympic Committee; their use of "Olympic" was in violation because of the word's connection to the Olympic Games. Changing the name to Olympia, Eli realized, was just as good, if not better — a clear expression of Michelle's and his heritage.

Although interviewing Eli by phone, I could hear him shake his head: two restaurants and sausage markets; 40,000 square feet of capacity that produces six thousand pounds of sausage and cured meats a week; seventeen farmers' markets; and at least 120 employees. He hinted that some days Aescher and the Alps look very appealing!

Eli ventured some ideas about the future and his own goals. Amazed with the company's growth, he and his partners are very aware of its economic impact in Portland and beyond. The addition of each facility required greater knowledge, more sophisticated monitoring and quality control, and simply far greater involvement of all five owners. They see challenges in controlling the product line, especially to deliver salami when it's ready to eat.

Earlier, I described bündnerfleisch. One man named Jörg Brügger and his assistant make thirty thousand pieces annually, all by hand, meticulously crafted from local beef with a constant eye on the vagaries of weather to ensure it matures properly — and all of it sells. Today Mr. Brügger is the only person who makes bündnerfleisch, and his children will not follow in his steps. I sense in my conversation with Eli and in reading his book that tension between the small-scale, sometimes sole proprietor, and craftsmen with whom he worked and the scale of Olympia Provisions today. Eli works in sausage production every week, but it requires a different set of skills to manage six thousand pounds of salami.

I celebrate the company's success and impact in the city and for the partners. They created an extraordinary company with compelling products and a commitment to build a strong Portland food and farming community. And by the way, reward yourself — read Eli's book. But don't go to the Alps until I get there!

Fra' Mani Handcrafted Foods

During this journey of the place of meat in our diets of wonderful controlled fermentation and the balance of art and science, I'm struck by the many chefs and food artisans who started with a totally different pursuit. Perhaps cross-fertilization or the intersection of different disciplines provided Proust's new eyes that open to the possibilities of discovery.

So how about we add in Italian-American Paul Bertolli, trained as a classical pianist, who today produces some of the country's best salumi. As we conversed about family and his early life before he entered the professional culinary world, I imagined him as a Giacomo Puccini or Claudio Abbado. But though he chose a different path, I hear and see a precision, working with his hands, muscle and sensory memory, of attention to details that create distinguished music and, in Paul's instance, great salumi.

His maternal grandparents from Verona met on a boat to America. They settled in Chicago's South Side, where his grandfather owned a butcher shop and cured meat, while his grandmother ran a clothing store. Paul grew up in an Italian neighborhood in San Rafael, California, one of seven children. Their house was surrounded by orchards, and he talks passionately about ripening fruit, his sense of smell, and annual packages of underwear and socks lovingly wrapped around a huge soppressata. In a 2004 interview he described his ability to smell and the parallel to music:

I think of it that way because I studied music. Some people are gifted with the ability to hear notes in their head and be able to identify them as absolute pitches. I can do that with scent. I can remember, I can bring to my mind the smell of something.[7]

At fourteen he started work at Maison Gourmet, part of San Francisco's Petrini's Markets, and enjoyed the store's diverse array of Czech, Italian, and German cured meats. By sixteen he was a journeyman butcher with a union card. From 1972 to 1977 he attended the University of California, Berkeley, and continued to work in local food businesses. After receiving his music degree — he played guitar, lute, and piano — Paul went to New York's Manhattan School of Music for piano. While in New York he made a fateful decision to leave music because he recognized the challenges of a music career.

Paul went to Italy and realized the great foods he had appreciated as a child, although wonderful, were Italian-American versions of extraordinary, complex regional cuisines, most of which had foundations of cucina povera, poor man's food. He returned to San Francisco and helped Mark Miller open Fourth Street Grill, where one of his kitchen colleagues opened a door for him to work at a restaurant near Florence. He left for eighteen months; cooked at several trattoria; experienced the land, people, culture, and food; and enhanced his already keen sense of smell. However, it was the work of a norcino, a traveling butcher, that truly touched him. The norcino had an intuitive ability, a craft built from years of work, to cut meat and make salumi. Paul knew he had to learn how to do this.

He worked for a decade at Chez Panisse, collaborating closely with Alice Waters, writing menus, and making salumi. Paul learned about the science of food and credits Chez Panisse with the opportunity to build his skills and further develop his own voice. In 1993 he began work at Oliveto, where he stayed for twelve years. Paul contributed to two of the most important restaurants battling for a different way for Americans to grow, process, and eat food. Beginning in the 1970s there followed decades of meat consolidation, the drive for the lowest cost, and creation of a common denominator hog. The skills to butcher meat disappeared with the people. Supermarkets didn't need butchers; the meat arrived precut and prepackaged. Since no one asked for meat to cut to order, butchers disappeared even if they had a union card.

For both Chez Panisse and Oliveto, Paul purchased hogs from Paul Willis, a key Iowa hog farmer and one of the first to partner with Niman Ranch. Bill Niman's ranch in Bolinas was very well known in the Bay Area, and in the mid-1990s the best restaurants bought from him. Sadly, after a series of sales, the company is owned today by Perdue Farms, and Bill is no longer associated with the company that bears his name.

While Paul made salumi at both Chez Panisse and Oliveto, he dreamed of something different. He wanted to support farmers committed to better hogs, sustainable agriculture, and humane husbandry and slaughter by exploring the world of salumi. In 2005 he left Oliveto and opened Fra' Mani in Berkeley. He works with several Midwestern hog growers, including Heritage Acres Farm, American Homestead's Hampshire hogs, and Paul Willis's Farmers' Hybrid pigs. The company's core business is salumi and includes capicollo, salami, fresh and cooked hams, and sausage. Paul is adamant about rebuilding a respect for animals with both producers and consumers. In addition to the standards of raising and slaughtering the hogs, he feels an obligation to use every animal thoughtfully and with reverence, exactly the attitude and philosophy of the norcino.

Part of his attitude emerges from years of working in kitchens, where the process is very ephemeral and after time felt uncomfortable:

> *The hard thing about being in the restaurant is when you are doing fine food like that, is it's so perishable. I got tired of the perishability of the art form. That you make it and it's in some sewer three hours later. So I wanted to do something that had more of a long arc to it — more of a beginning, middle and end that took place over time, and kind of ride that continuum rather than create it, destroy it, create and destroy it, every night.*[8]

To achieve his goals at Fra' Mani, Paul asked a very basic question: "What is it going to take for you to stay in business?" Part of the answer rested on his pork farmers; to ensure he did not encounter supply issues, he made guarantees for payment. Working with them, he collaborated on protocols for the animals' feed, pasture access, bedding, diet, and slaughter. Second, Paul transforms all of the trim from primal and subprimal muscles — hams, loins, and shoulders — into salami. Third, to achieve certain efficiencies he bought German and Italian equipment. Paul argues that using mechanized processing tools does not compromise product integrity. He designed a meat chopper to emulate the motions of hand cutting and dicing; it's faster, safer, and cleaner, and he still has the right-size dice for each style of salami.

He uses nitrate and nitrite in his salami recipes together with a bit of dextrose (sugar) and starter cultures and a wide variety of spices and seasonings. For the salami he aims for a 20 percent fat to 80 percent meat ratio. They use collar and plate fat rather than leg because their firmness holds up during processing; leg fat is too soft, it smears, and it may spoil. His mortadella, finely ground from leg, shoulder, and belly, contains diced jowl fat; the dry-roasted product has no more than 26 percent fat. As they make salami, the mixtures are placed in a stuffing machine, from which they pull out tubes of different diameters and lengths and then tie each salami by hand. Paul described the tying process:

I was fascinated by the hand work in playing and the mechanics of the keys. . . . The mind can know certain things, but teaching the body is hard. Learning to play Chopin takes practice. After several tries in Italy, I learned how to make the pirouette twist in the knot which ties casings to salami. I teach this to our employees. Manual dexterity in a chef or sausage maker is critical.[9]

Can you imagine the handwork, trial and error, and time commitment to get it right? It reminds me clearly of how Marc Buzzio and Paul Valetutti as youngsters learned to tie salami at Salumeria Biellese.

Twenty-six distributors move Fra' Mani products nationwide to retailers and food service. Paul does not sell via the internet because the scale to manage sales and the costs of shipping are far too expensive. However, a number of online retailers carry and ship his products.

During our two conversations Paul drew together many issues about the global future of food. Today Americans have access to a wide variety of commercially made salumi, much of it produced from commodity hogs in large industrial processing plants. I think the four West Coast charcuteries and salumieri pose fundamental questions about how we eat. They are not alone; if anything, most artisans of dry-cured meat have similar philosophies and strategies. To encourage Americans to recapture long-lost senses, especially of smell, requires constant vigilance and hard work.

I want to return to the piano . . . and snowboards, art, archaeology, journalism, and more music. While none of these pursuits is a direct path to dry-cured meats, the sensibilities expressed by these West Coast salumieri are rooted in craft and knowledge beyond curing. In my opinion, their liberal and fine arts foundations provided the new eyes to see and understand the world and where wandering paths led to cured meat. Compare playing the piano with snowboarding: Each requires discipline, commitment of time, endless practice, sometimes enduring pain, and exquisite shaping and educating of muscles to create physical memory. Such skills built over time are the foundations upon which the pursuit of culinary excellence emerges. These four West Coast experts represent similar journeys for many food entrepreneurs across America.

Epilogue

Charcuterie is jazz. In jazz, artists play endlessly with the old standards.
There are 1,000 versions of Thelonious Monk's "Around Midnight."
Sausage is like that.

— HANK SHAW, *HUNTER ANGLER GARDENER COOK*

In 2014 Slow Food USA organized a Slow Meat conference in Denver to help elevate our collective awareness and knowledge of America's approach to meat production and consumption. The meeting included visits to local producers, a bison-butchering demonstration, numerous workshops, and amazing food. I offered a tasting seminar on dry-cured meats, artisan cheese, and craft beer. To avoid our inherent biases about who makes the best, participants tasted all of the meats "blind" with no information about the producer, the breed, or other identifying characteristics. I wanted to challenge the group to taste the foods on their merits of color, texture, aroma, and flavor. To further conceal origin I told the group we might have a European import on the menu. The tasting was a lively discussion of quality and differences in style, and while it turned out no import existed, a number of people chose one of the cured hams as an Italian-made prosciutto that clearly said something about the quality of American dry-cured products!

The workshop success led to a subsequent invitation to organize another program in 2015. That seminar featured nine American cured meats, highlighted by four aged hams, with the same ground rules. We sampled four hams, three salamis, a bresaola, and an 'nduja, from nine producers, paired with terrific Colorado artisan cheese and craft beer. After tasting all of the meats and enjoying and comparing the many aroma, taste, flavor, and texture combinations, we reviewed each cured item. To start our discussion about cured hams, I asked the audience what is the difference between a traditional American country ham and prosciutto. With several cured-meat producers in attendance, one answer was, "No difference; they are all cured and therefore safe." A few people pointed out that most country hams are smoked at some point in the process, but this practice does not hold for prosciutto.

After I asked, "What about cooking these hams?" several chefs described how a country ham would be soaked, baked, or boiled, perhaps served as a ham steak with red-eye gravy or biscuits with small slices as a sandwich. For most aficionados of prosciutto, this would be a sacrilege! Paper-thin slices of prosciutto di Parma or San Daniele with melon, on a salumi plate, perhaps part of a ravioli mixture or a pizza topping — these are ways we celebrate prosciutto. For me one unanswered question was why do Italians thinly slice ham at all? Was it to stretch a product in the same way espresso made with small amounts of finely ground coffee makes possible great taste *and* frugality?

Many conversations continued after the tasting, including one with Illtud "Bob" Dunsford, a Welsh butcher, who described similar cookery practices and history in Wales and England. Our conversation highlighted some contemporary assumptions about traditional practices viewed from the twenty-first century and whether such perspectives are accurate. After returning home, Illtud sent me a long message about curing and cooking in Britain:

> *Salting of a pork leg with a mixture of salt, saltpetre and occasionally sugar, the salting was often done in a carved slate tray with a hole allowing water/blood to drain. Salting would take on average 30–45 days depending on the size of the pork leg. There are two general methods — one is to submerge the ham in salt which creates a "crust of salt," the other is to re-apply salt over the 30–45 day period. Traditionally, pigs for ham production would be heavy pigs and once bred gilts or sows were commonly used weighing in excess of 150 kg/330 lbs. Once salted the hams would be cleaned and hung to air dry in a shaded area with good airflow — this could be in the farmhouse kitchen, in a large chimney, under the eaves of an outbuilding etc. In some cases hams would be wrapped in muslin cloth or in stockinette.*

Smoking is rare, but the practice of hanging in a farmhouse kitchen would provide some degree of smoking from the open fires for cooking. This form of salting was a preservation method — the maturing period would depend largely on the amount of pork eaten by the family. A young ham would be around 3 months of age, but in our family we would often keep them for over 9 months (they were after all a way of providing meat through the spring/summer when animal slaughter wasn't commonly an option). The older the ham the better the flavour as the moisture loss over [a] longer period would provide a concentrated pork flavour. Cooking was in two forms: leg steaks were cut and pan-fried, or whole hams or joints of ham were boiled and/or baked to make a cooked ham. If the hams were overly salty they would be soaked in water to reduce the level of salt prior to cooking.[1]

Illtud's message reinforced my opinion that seventeenth- and eighteenth-century English immigrants brought well-established traditional practices of salt and smoke to North America. These methods and cultural experiences mirror Illtud's description and those of today's Kentucky, North Carolina, Tennessee, and Virginia country ham artisans. The discovery of Nancy Newsom Mahaffey's fifteenth-century Lancashire ancestors and references to meat smoking drew quite an exclamation from me! While Americans can certainly link many foodways to historical antecedents, seeing a direct family line over six hundred years seems truly remarkable.

Digging deeper into the history and culture of cured meat, I found links to a Roman Catholic Egyptian patron saint of butchers, comparisons of racing cars to feral hogs, and numerous linguistic relationships. Each of them helps me understand the critical place of pigs in human history and how wide a spectrum of attitudes exists about them. The most unusual was Sant'Antonio Abate (Saint Anthony the Abbott), born in the second century CE in Egypt, the founder of Christian monasticism. He was "particularly important throughout southern Italy and is the patron saint of butchers, domestic animals, basketmakers, and gravediggers; he also protects against skin diseases, especially shingles known as 'Fuoco di Sant'Antonio' (Fire of Saint Anthony) in Italy."[2] To treat skin diseases, doctors used pork fat as salve, and since Saint Anthony cared for people with these conditions, artwork often depicted him "accompanied by a pig. People who saw the artwork, but did not have it explained, thought there was a direct connection between Anthony and pigs — and people who worked with swine took him as their patron."[3]

In some ways Saint Anthony reminds me of the role patron saints played when survival occupied daily life for most people. While today we may speak of a 1 percent advantaged class, for most of human history a similar proportion existed, and the remaining 99 percent faced a constant threat of famine. From a twenty-first-century vantage point, food preservation seems distant and not part of our contemporary lives. Why worry when supermarkets, corner stores, or farmers' markets are close by and accessible? If anything, the Great Recession taught far too many Americans how quickly our relationship to abundance and hunger can change. Whether for peasants or urban dwellers, for thousands of years starvation was a constant companion, and winter through early spring months could challenge everyone's survival. Saint Anthony, together with other food saints, blessed the next growing season or offered solace to parishioners when supplies ran low and bellies ached. Most important, we recognized that survival depended on our ability to preserve food, whether for our own use or to help someone else.

Preserving food reminds me of Aesop's fable of the grasshopper and the ant. The industrious ant worked all summer storing food, while the grasshopper spent his day playing music and singing songs (certainly in the Walt Disney version!). With winter's arrival the grasshopper implored the ant for food and shelter but to no avail. While we may laugh at the grasshopper's travail, food shortages were no laughing matter, so skills, patience, and foresight could help us survive until the spring, when we might celebrate with the Abruzzo le virtù soup.

In America today the issue for most people isn't a question of putting up food to survive but rather will the skills, knowledge, patience, and culture of dry-cured preservation survive? Nearly every charcutier and salumiere spoke to this point, a deep concern for the future of their craft and its cultural antecedents. While linking salami and innovation to Thelonious Monk, Hank Shaw would argue that you have to understand and master the basics. Monk's ability to create new forms of jazz rested on mastery of the piano.

Part of the problem today is the extent to which we elevate artisans and chefs to pedestals and rock star status; survival food grows into white tablecloth cuisine; the latest hot trend becomes passé very quickly; and the essential techniques and underlying culture may be lost. If companies such as Edwards, Newsom, Biellese, and Esposito disappear, we lose more than just a great-tasting ham or salami. We lose the slow knowledge gained over decades and the history and culture surrounding these foods as well.

While significant challenges exist, I see valuable trends exemplified by the stories of people like John Besh, Frank Bonanno, Scott Bridi, Smith Broadbent III, Chris Eley, Greg Higgins, Nick Macri, Danny Meyer, and Alice Waters. They understand the value of mentoring colleagues, the next generation of practitioners, to create wonderful cured meat and nurture and preserve the cultural antecedents. The experiences of Eli Cairo in Switzerland, Jeremy Schaller in Germany, and Alon Shaya and Phil Mariano in Italy, reflect their businesses' commitment to craft and tradition. Their European journeys illustrate one clue to possible future training programs modeled on German and Swiss apprenticeships.

One key figure who helped draw attention to the culture and practice of charcuterie is Francois Vecchio. Over many years he introduced and trained such farmers and artisans as Bill Niman, Mike Phillips, and Paul Wetzel; consulted for Columbus Salame Company; and contributed to Glynwood and Slow Food USA. I recall meeting Francois in 2014 at the Denver Slow Meat conference, when he spoke eloquently about the sad state of America's meat production and processing. He brings a European craft perspective to cured meat, contending that traditional Swiss and French concepts of training and practice still have great value. He reminded me of Jacques Pépin's arguments about the fundamental place of technique: Until you master the simplest practice, like tying a salami, you're not ready to innovate.

Throughout the research I was struck by the breadth and diversity of backgrounds and pursuits, especially in the creative and liberal arts, for so many of these individuals: fashion, economic and political reporting and writing, foreign service, French literature, classical music, graphic design, philosophy, furniture making, and agribusiness. While coming from different places and traveling on unique paths, they share similar attitudes and philosophies about their craft. In my opinion, these artisans embody a strong statement about the benefits of a liberal arts education, an ability to think and solve problems. If we are to solve the myriad issues confronting America's system of producing meat, we need practitioners who understand the challenges and have an ability to articulate choices, often by serving great food.

Francois Vecchio mirrors the discipline expressed by charcutiers and salumieri throughout the country. I celebrate the stories of Marc Buzzio and Paul Valetutti, Paul Bertolli, Francis Cratil Cretarola and Catherine Lee, Nancy Newsom Mahaffey, and Toby Rodriguez, for example, because they teach the value of vision and hard work, of a discipline hard won through constant practice, to create and constantly improve what they make.

In contemporary America we can identify at least four generations of artisan charcutiers and salumieri that stretch back centuries. The first generation is the country ham producers, Sam Edwards III, Nancy Newsom Mahaffey, Smith Broadbent III, and Beth and Ronny Drennan with Rufus Brown and Allen Benton as their brethren. The second generation, generally pre–World War II immigrant businesses, includes Patti and Paul Fortuna-Stannard, Marc Buzzio and Paul Valetutti, George and John Esposito, the Di Bruno Brothers, and Jeremy Schaller. The postwar group, the third generation, incorporates the Dukcevich and Muncan/Stefanovic families.

The three generations represent what's left of the earlier diverse American cured-meat community. They are the survivors, the ones who weathered the storm, confronting changes in hog production, more than a hundred years of changing food regulations, demographic and geographic shifts, and revolutions in diet and nutrition. In some ways, by their reminding us of our past, we may capture lessons and attitudes from them to apply in the future.

The fourth generation is by far the largest group of artisans — not surprising, given the renaissance of fermented beverages and foods that began in the 1970s and exploded after 2000. A handful of chef pioneers set the stage for the rapid changes that began right after the turn of the twenty-first century, among them Paul Bertolli, Frank Bonanno, and Greg Higgins. Many of today's charcutiers and salumieri began careers in kitchens in the 1990s as great American craft beer and artisan cheese began to appear. A few explorers looked at the growing chef-farmer movement that has since morphed into today's farm-to-table presence and began butchering whole carcasses. Chefs such as Aaron Josinsky (Vermont's Misery Loves

Company), Nathan Anda (Washington, DC's Red Apron Butcher and Partisan), Craig Diehl (Cypress and Artisan Meat Share, Charleston, South Carolina), Chris Eley, Nick Macri, Ben Meyer, and Tony Page developed professional skills in places full of fertile new ideas and exploration.

The contemporary generation of artisan cured-meat producers know one another; share information; articulate strong opinions about sustainability, animal welfare, and fair labor practices; educate consumers about food choices; and practice what they preach. At the same time, many have learned through the heat in the kitchen that they may not accomplish all of their ideals. I see a movement away from "I have to do it all" to a more balanced approach to emphasize what an individual does well, especially in the professional food community. For example, Matt Jennings in Boston and Rick Gencarelli in Portland buy excellent salumi from nearby producers. They argue that "local" doesn't mean that a chef or restaurant must make everything from scratch. Why not buy from an outstanding artisan whose product might be better than yours, is less expensive in time and money, and supports a local economy as well?

A countervailing tendency, however, is the expansion of some small companies into one with national distribution and recognition. To fulfill America's huge market requires very different strategies, including more mechanized production and sometimes the use of lactic starter cultures to speed up the fermentation process. Many producers argue that scaling up and the use of these "shortcuts" compromise product integrity and excellence. Perhaps this is true, but in a market the size of the United States, comprising many segments at different price points, an array of business approaches makes sense on the one hand but may also undermine public understanding and appreciation of the best charcuterie and salumi.

Chris Eley's concerns about adequate training and how to maintain a standard of excellence highlighted the phenomenon for me. The choice of scale challenges every craft brewer, artisan cheese maker, or charcutier. I recall programs for aspiring cheese makers sponsored by the former Vermont Institute for Artisan Cheese (VIAC), at which we posed a challenge or question: "What is most important to you? Selling every ounce you make or appearing on a New York City or San Francisco restaurant cheese cart?" The answer sets the foundation for an entire "hazard analysis critical control point" plan, not for sanitation and safety, but rather a business concept and execution. Where are your "hazards and critical points" to success? To meet production demand for national distribution, do you feed a commodity hog a better diet and remove it from confinement? Will you still have a faster-growing but less expensive pig that meets your criteria for charcuterie, country ham, and salami?

The challenge of growing bigger carries a risk of losing touch and connection to the physical, emotional, and sometimes visceral experience of making food. Toby Rodriguez and Jeffrey Weiss, while concerned about the loss of a human physical relation to animal slaughter, are realists. I view their work as powerful, a way to remind us of the past and how we can still give respect and reverence to killing an animal so we may eat.

I think a tension exists around how to create balance between fulfilling consumer demand for great charcuterie and salumi and an artisan's philosophy and respect for craft. As more quality hogs are produced, will consumers enjoy better quality and less expensive fresh and cured pork?

Most of the individuals described here are committed to distinctive, high-quality products that taste good, are healthy and nutritious, and contribute to local economies. Especially when they deal directly with growers, cured-meat artisans look to make positive contributions to animal welfare, soil and water resources, and overall environmental health.

In 2006, while researching and writing *The Atlas of American Artisan Cheese*, with its 345 profiles of small-scale cheese makers, I was reminded constantly of the rapidly expanding universe of dry-cured charcuterie, country ham, and salami. In my opinion, producers of cheese and cured meat are authentic geniuses who practice both art and science, in this case microbiology, to offer us foods deeply reflective of history and culture. Their artistry and passion, combined with good microbes, sculpt simple ingredients into charcuterie, country hams, and salami whose aromas, flavors, and textures are immediately perceived and enjoyed, while connecting us deeply to our ancestors.

> *The actual lines of a pig (I mean a really fat pig) are among the loveliest and most luxuriant in nature; the pig has the same great curves, swift and yet heavy, which we see in rushing water or in a rolling cloud.*[4]

INTERVIEWEES

I thank the following individuals for taking time to share their enthusiasm, insights, knowledge, and perspectives on American charcuterie, country ham, and salumi. Whether in person or by phone, they helped educate me, and I sincerely hope I learned a lesson or two. In addition to inspiring conversations, many times we shared their creative genius on a plate!

1. Brian Albano and Bill Miner. Il Porcellino Salumi, Denver, CO. June 2, 2015
2. Nathan Anda. Red Apron Butcher, Washington, DC. April 4, 2016
3. Penny Barend and Melissa Khoury. Saucisson, Cleveland, OH. March 28, 2016
4. Paul Bertolli. Fra' Mani, Berkeley, CA. March 9, 2016
5. Frank Bonanno. Bonanno Concepts, Denver, CO. April 20, 2015
6. Scott Bridi. Brooklyn Cured, Brooklyn, NY. December 14, 2015; May 3, 2016
7. Rufus Brown. Johnston County Hams, Smithfield, NC. March 3, 2016
8. Sean Buchanan. Black River Produce and Meats, Springfield, VT. April 13, 2015
9. Marc Buzzio and Paul Valetutti. Salumeria Biellese, New York, NY. April 26, 2015
10. Elias Cairo. Olympia Provisions, Portland, OR. March 21, 2016
11. Adrien Chelette. Ancora Pizzeria & Salumeria, New Orleans, LA. December 7, 2015
12. Francis Cratil Cretarola, Catherine Lee, and Joe Cicala. Le Virtù, Philadelphia, PA. October 27, 2015
13. Robert Del Grosso. Drexel University, Philadelphia, PA. April 29, 2016

14. Mark DeNittis. Sysco Denver, Product Specialist, Denver, CO. June 3, 2015

15. Craig Diehl. Cypress and Artisan Meat Share, Charleston, SC. March 16, 2016

16. Beth and Ronny Drennan. Broadbent's Hams, Kuttawa, KY. March 15, 2016

17. Stefano Dukcevich. Daniele, Inc., Pascoag, RI. July 28, 2015

18. Herb Eckhouse. La Quercia, Norwalk, IA. February 16, 2016

19. Samuel Edwards III. S. Wallace Edwards & Sons, Surry, VA. March 11, 2016

20. Chris Eley. Smoking Goose and Goose the Market, Indianapolis, IN. October 15, 2015

21. George Esposito. G. Esposito & Sons Jersey Pork Store, Brooklyn, NY. November 2, 2015

22. Anthony Fiasche. 'Nduja Artisans Salumeria, Chicago, IL. May 3, 2016

23. Jacob Finsen. Artisan Meats of Vermont, Waitsfield, VT. October 15, 2015

24. Patricia (Patti) Fortuna-Stannard. Fortuna's Sausage Company, Sandgate, VT, and Charlestown, RI. June 25, 2015

25. Adolfo Garcia. Ancora and Primitivo, New Orleans, LA. December 4, 2015

26. Rick Gencarelli. Lardo Restaurant, Portland, OR. March 1, 2016

27. Josh Gibbs. Mad River Food Hub, Waitsfield, VT. October 15, 2015

28. Cosmo Goss. Publican Quality Meats, Chicago, IL. April 21, 2016

29. David Greco. Mike's Deli, Bronx, NY. November 20; December 15, 2015

30. Seth Hamstead. Continental Provisions, New Orleans, LA. December 3, 2015

31. Greg Higgins. Higgins Restaurant, Portland, OR. March 12, 2016

32. Matthew Jennings. Townsman, Boston, MA. April 22, 2016

33. Aaron Josinsky. Misery Loves Company, Winooski, VT. January 21, 2016

34. Nick Macri. La Divisa Meats, Philadelphia, PA. October 26, 2015

35. Nancy Newsom Mahaffey. Newsom's Country Ham, Princeton, KY. March 18, 2016

36. Phillip Mariano. Domenica, New Orleans, LA. December 7, 2015
37. Nick Martin. Primitivo, New Orleans, LA. December 4, 2015
38. Ben Meyer. Old Salt Marketplace, Portland, OR. March 12, 2016
39. Emilio Mignucci. Di Bruno Brothers, Philadelphia, PA. October 26, 2015; March 10, 2016
40. Ari Miller. 1732 Meats, Yeadon, PA. October 27, 2015
41. Becky Mumaw. Cleaver & Co., New Orleans, LA. December 3, 2015
42. Kristina and Tony Page. Rooster Street Butcher, Lititz, PA. October 24, 2015
43. Bob Perry. University of Kentucky, Lexington, KY. June 3, 2015; March 9, 2016
44. Mike Phillips. Red Table Meat Company, Minneapolis, MN. March 14, 2016
45. Jamie Png. Artisan cheesemaker, Philadelphia, PA. October 24, 2015
46. Toby Rodriguez. Lâche Pas Boucherie et Cuisine, Grand Coteau, LA. December 5, 2015
47. Mike Satzow. North Country Smokehouse, Claremont, NH. April 13, 2015
48. Jeremy Schaller. Schaller & Weber, New York, NY. November 4, 2015
49. Ian Schnoebelen. Mariza, New Orleans, LA. December 4, 2015
50. Alex Seidel. Fruition; Fruition Farms & Dairy; and Mercantile Dining and Provision. Denver, CO. June 3, 2015.
51. Hank Shaw. *Hunter Angler Gardener Cook* (blog), Sacramento, CA. March 2, 2016
52. Marko Stefanovic. Muncan Food Corporation, Queens, NY. November 10; December 15, 2015
53. Heather Thomason. Kensington Quarters, Philadelphia, PA. October 27, 2015
54. Christopher Thompson. Coda Di Volpe, Chicago, IL. June 3, 2015
55. Greg Walls. Johnson's Boucanière, Lafayette, LA. December 5, 2015
56. Paul Wetzel. Gramercy Tavern, New York, NY. November 3, 2015
57. Nathanial Zimet. Boucherie and Borrée, New Orleans, LA. December 4, 2015

PRODUCERS AND RESTAURANTS

CHAPTER THREE

S. Wallace Edwards & Sons, Inc.
Sam Edward, III, owner
11381 Rolfe Highway
Surry, VA 23883
(800) 222-4267
www.edwardsvaham.com
At this writing, the retail location is closed
indefinitely because of a fire.

Johnston County Hams
Rufus Brown, owner
204 N. Brightleaf Boulevard
Smithfield, NC 27577
(800) 543-HAMS (4267)
Retail store and internet sales
www.countrycuredhams.com

The Pig
Sam Suchoff, owner
630 Weaver Dairy Road
Chapel Hill, NC 27514
(919) 942-1133
Restaurant and retail store

R. M. Felts Packing Co.
Robert M. Felts, Jr.
35497 General Mahone Boulevard
Ivor, VA 23866
(757) 859-6131
Retail store only

Darden's Country Store
DeeDee and Tommy Darden, owners
16249 Bowling Green Road
Smithfield, VA 23431
(757) 357-6791
Retail store only
DardensCountryStore@gmail.com
dardenscountrystore.com

CHAPTER FOUR

Col. Bill Newsom's Aged Kentucky Country Ham
Nancy Newsom Mahaffey, owner
Newsom's Old Mill Store
208 East Main Street
Princeton, KY 42445
(270) 365-2482
Retail store, mail order and
internet sales
newsomsham@yahoo.com
www.newsomscountryham.com

Broadbent's B&B Foods
Beth and Ronny Drennan, owners
257 Mary Blue Road
Kuttawa, KY 42055
(800) 841-2202
Retail store and internet sales
order@broadbenthams.com
www.broadbenthams.com

Benton's Smoky Mountain Country Hams

Allan Benton, owner
2603 Highway 411 North
Madisonville, TN 37354
(423) 442-5003
Retail store and internet sales
bentonscountryhams2.com

Olli Salumeria

Oliviero Colmignoli and Charles Vosmik, owners
8505 Bell Creek Road, Suite H
Mechanicsville, VA 23116
(877) OLLI-YES (655-4937)
Wholesale with national distribution
info@olli.com
www.olli.com

CHAPTER FIVE

Cleaver & Co.

Nathaniel Wallace and
Daniel Sinclair, owners
3917 Baronne Street
New Orleans, LA 70115
(504) 227-3830
Retail store only
info@cleaverand.com
cleaverand.co

Home Place Pastures

Marshall and Jemison Bartlett,
president and vice president
1513 Home Place Road
Como, MS 38619
(662) 292-5808
info@homeplacepastures.com
homeplacepastures.com
Business on hiatus as of 2016.

Mariza

Laurie Casebonne and
Ian Schnoebelen, owners

2900 Chartres Street
New Orleans, LA 70117
(504) 598-5700
Restaurant
marizaneworleans.com

Ancora

Adrien Chelette, Bryn Thompson,
and Adolfo Garcia, owners
4508 Freret Street
New Orleans, LA 70115
(504) 324-1636
Restaurant
ancoranola@gmail.com
www.ancorapizza.com

Primitivo

Nick Martin and Adolpho Garcia, owners
1800 Oretha Castle Haley Boulevard
New Orleans, LA 70113
(504) 881-1775
Restaurant
primitivonola@gmail.com
www.primitivonola.com

Domenica

John Besh and Alon Shaya, owners
123 Baronne Street
(historic Roosevelt Hotel)
New Orleans, LA 70112
(504) 648-6020
Restaurant
info@domenicarestaurant.com
www.domenicarestaurant.com

Boucherie and Bourrée

Nathanial Zimet and James Denio, owners
1506 S. Carrollton Avenue
New Orleans, LA 70118
(504) 862-5514
Restaurant and retail store
info@boucherie-nola.com
www.boucherie-nola.com

Lâche Pas Boucherie et Cuisine
Toby Rodriguez, owner
Grand Coteau, LA
(337) 680-9620
Traveling butcher and chef
contact@lachepasboucherie.com
www.lachepasboucherie.com

Johnson's Boucanière
Lori and Greg Walls, owners
1111 St. John Street
Lafayette, LA 70501
(337) 269-8878
Restaurant and retail store
johnsonsboucaniere.com

CHAPTER SIX
Schaller & Weber
Jeremy Schaller, owner
1654 Second Avenue
New York, NY 10028
(212) 879-3047
Retail, wholesale, and internet sales
and sidewalk stand
store@schallerweber.com
www.schallerweber.com

Muncan Food Corporation
Tima Muncan, Mike and Marko
Stefanovic, owners
Retail store and mail order
but no internet sales
www.muncanfoodcorp.com
Astoria store:
4309 Broadway
Long Island City, NY 11103
(718) 278-8847
Ridgewood store:
60–86 Myrtle Avenue
Ridgewood, NY 11385
(718) 417-5095

CHAPTER SEVEN
**G. Esposito & Sons
Jersey Pork Store**
George and John Esposito, owners
357 Court Street
Brooklyn, NY 11231
(718) 875-6863
Retail store only

Mike's Deli
Mike and David Greco, owners
Arthur Avenue Retail Market
2344 Arthur Avenue
Bronx, NY 10458
(718) 295-5033
Retail store, mail order, and internet sales
www.arthuravenue.com

Salumeria Biellese
Marc Buzzio, Paul Valetutti, and
Fouad Alsharif, owners
378 8th Avenue
New York, NY 10001
(212) 736-7376
Retail store and wholesale
with national distribution
info@salumerianyc.com
www.salumeriabiellese.com

Calabria Pork Store
Peter Parotta, owner
2338 Arthur Avenue
Bronx, NY 10458
(718) 367-5145
Retail store only

Charlito's Cocina
Charles Wekselbaum
21–09 Borden Avenue
Long Island City, NY 11101
(718) 482-7890
Wholesale and internet sales
info@charlitoscocina.com
www.charlitoscocina.com

Faicco's Italian Specialties
260 Bleecker Street
New York, NY 10014
(212) 243-1974
Retail store only

CHAPTER EIGHT
Fortuna's Sausage
Paul and Patti Fortuna-Stannard, owners
723 Stannard Road
Sandgate, VT 05250
(802) 375-0200
Wholesale and internet sales
office@fortunasausage.com
www.fortunasausage.com

Daniele, Inc.
Vlado, Stefano, and
Davide Dukcevich, owners
105 Davis Drive
Pascoag, RI 02859
(401) 568-6228
Wholesale with national distribution
www.danielefoods.com

**Moody's Delicatessen &
Provisions and New England
Charcuterie**
Joshua Smith, owner
468 Moody Street
Waltham, MA 02453
(781) 216-8732
Retail store and restaurant
info@moodyswaltham.com
www.moodyswaltham.com

Smith's Log Smoke House
Andrew Smith, owner
PO Box 817
Monroe, ME 04951
(207) 525-7735
Retail store and internet sales
libbysmithsmokehouse@gmail.com
www.logsmokehouse.net

CHAPTER NINE
Gramercy Tavern
Danny Meyer, owner;
Michael Anthony, executive chef;
Paul Wetzel, charcutier
42 East 20th Street
New York, NY 10003
(212) 477-0777
Restaurant
www.gramercytavern.com

Brooklyn Cured
Scott Bridi, owner
326 22nd Street
Brooklyn, NY 11215
(917) 282-2221
Wholesale to retail outlets
and farmers' markets
info@brooklyncured.com
www.brooklyncured.com

CHAPTER TEN
La Divisa Meats
Nick Macri, owner
Reading Terminal Market
51 North 12th Street
Philadelphia, PA 19107
(215) 627-2100
Retail store only
info@ladivisameats.com
www.ladivisameats.com

1732 Meats
Elise and Ariyeh (Ari) Miller, owners
6250 Baltimore Pike
Yeadon, PA 19050
(267) 879-7214
Wholesale only with regional
distributed
www.1732meats.com

Le Virtù
Catherine Lee & Francis Cratil Cretarola,
owners; Joe Cicala, chef.
1927 E. Passyunk Avenue
Philadelphia, PA 19148
(215) 271-5626
Restaurant
www.levirtu.com

Kensington Quarters
Michael Pasquarello, owner
1310 Frankford Avenue
Philadelphia, PA 19125
(267) 314-5086
Restaurant and retail butcher shop
info@kensingtonquarters.com
www.kensingtonquarters.com

Di Bruno Brothers
Billy Mignucci, Emilio Mignucci, and
Bill Mignucci, owners
Italian Market:
930 South 9th Street
Philadelphia, PA 19147
(215) 922-2876
Rittenhouse Square:
1730 Chestnut Street
Philadelphia, PA 19103
(215) 665-9220
Retail store, wholesale, and internet sales
info@dibruno.com
www.dibruno.com

Rooster Street Butcher
Kristina and Anthony Page, owners
11 South Cedar Street
Lititz, PA 17543
(717) 625-0405
Restaurant, retail store, and
Lancaster Central Market stall
roosterstreetbutcher@gmail.com
www.roosterst.com

Wursthaus Schmitz
Douglas Hager, owner
Reading Terminal Market
51 North 12th Street
Philadelphia, PA 19107
(215) 922-4287
Retail store only
www.brauhausschmitz.com/wursthaus

CHAPTER ELEVEN
La Quercia
Kathy and Herb Eckhouse, owners
400 Hakes Drive
Norwalk, IA 50211
(515) 981-1625
No direct sales; mail orders handled by
Zingerman's and Murray's Cheese
prosciutto@laquercia.us
www.laquercia.us

CHAPTER TWELVE
**Saucisson Artisan
Cured Meats & Sausage**
Penny Barend and Melissa Khoury, owners
5324 Fleet Avenue
Cleveland, OH 44105
(330) 242-9839
Farmers' market and wholesale
iheartswine@saucissoncleveland.com
www.saucissoncleveland.com

Publican Quality Meats
Paul Kahan, owner;
Cosmo Goss, chef de cuisine
825 W. Fulton Market Street
Chicago, IL 60607
(312) 445-8977
Retail store and regional distribution
info@publicanqualitymeats.com
www.publicanqualitymeats.com

'Nduja Artisans Salumeria

Agostino and Antonio "Tony" Fiasche,
owners
2817 N. Harlem Avenue
Chicago, IL 60707
(312) 550-6991
Wholesale with national distribution
info@ndujaartisans.com
www.ndujaartisans.com

Red Table Meat Company

Mike Phillips, owner
1401 Marshall Street NE #100
Minneapolis, MN 55413
(612) 545-5555
Minneapolis farmers' markets and
wholesale with national distribution
contact@redtablemeatco.com
www.redtablemeatco.com

Smoking Goose

Mollie and Chris Eley, owners
407 Dorman Street
Indianapolis, IN 46202
(317) 638-MEAT (6328)
Retail store, nationwide distribution,
and internet sales
info@smokinggoose.com
www.smokinggoose.com

Goose the Market

Mollie and Chris Eley, owners
2503 North Delaware Street
Indianapolis, IN 46205
(317) 924-4944
www.goosethemarket.com

J & J Czuchraj Meats

Jill and Jerry Chucray, owners
West Side Market, Stand B10
1979 W. 25th Street
Cleveland, OH 44113

(216) 696-7083
Retail store and internet sales
smokedmeats@jandjmeats.com
www.jandjmeats.com

Dohar/Lovaszy Meats

Angela and Miklos Szucs, owners
West Side Market, Stand F1–F2
1979 W. 25th Street
Cleveland, OH 44113
(216) 241-4197
Retail store
westsidemarket.org/vendor
/dohar-lovaszy-meats

West Loop Salumi

Greg Laketek, owner
1111 W. Randolph Street
Chicago, IL 60607
(312) 255-7004
Retail store, wholesale, and internet sales
info@westloopsalumi.com
www.westloopsalumi.com

Salume Beddu

Mark Sanfilippo, owner
3467 Hampton Avenue
St. Louis, MO 63139
(314) 353-3100
Restaurant, retail store, and
internet sales
info@salumebeddu.com
www.salumebeddu.com

Salt & Time

Ben Runkle, owner
1912 E. 7th Street
Austin, TX 78702
(512) 524-1383
Restaurant and retail store
info@saltandtime.com
www.saltandtime.com

Underground Meats

931 E. Main Street #18
Madison, WI 53703
(608) 467-2850
Wholesale with national distribution
and internet sales
meats@undergroundfoodcollective.org
www.undergroundmeats.com

CHAPTER THIRTEEN
Mercantile Dining & Provision

Alex Seidel, owner
1701 Wynkoop Street #155
Denver, CO 80202
(720) 460-3733
Restaurant and retail store
mercantiledenver.com

Il Porcellino Salumi

Bill Miner and Brian Albano, owners
4324 W. 41st Avenue
Denver, CO 80212
(303) 477-3206
Delicatessen and retail store
info@coloradocured.com
www.ilporcellinodenver.com

Bonanno Concepts

Frank Bonanno, owner
701 East 7th Avenue
Denver, CO 80218
(303) 832-4778
Restaurants and deli
www.bonannoconcepts.com

Creminelli Fine Meats

Cristiano Creminelli, owner
310 Wright Brothers Drive
Salt Lake City, UT 84116
(801) 428-1820
Wholesale with national distribution
and internet sales
info@creminelli.com
www.creminelli.com

CHAPTER FOURTEEN
Hunter Angler Gardener Cook

Hank Shaw, owner
Blog, podcast, and books
Email: scrbblr@hotmail.com
Web: www.honest-food.net

Higgins Restaurant and Bar

Greg Higgins and Paul Mallory, owners
1239 SW Broadway
Portland, OR 97205
(503) 222-9070
Restaurant
higginsrestaurant@comcast.net
www.higginsportland.com

Old Salt Marketplace

Alex Ganum, Ben Meyer, and Marcus
Hoover, owners
5027 NE 42nd Avenue
Portland, OR 97218
(971) 255-0167
Retail store and restaurant
core@oldsaltpdx.com
www.oldsaltpdx.com

Olympia Provisions

Elias and Michelle Cairo, Nate Tilden,
Tyler Gaston, and Marty Schwartz,
owners
Northwest:
1632 NW Thurman Street
Portland, OR 97209
(503) 894-8136
Southeast:
107 SE Washington Street
Portland, OR 97214
(503) 954-3663
Restaurants, retail store, farmers' markets,
and national distribution
info@olympiaprovisions.com
www.olympiaprovisions.com

Fra' Mani Handcrafted Foods 2006

Paul Bertolli, owner
1311 Eighth Street
Berkeley, CA 94710
(510) 526-7000
Wholesale with national distribution
info@framani.com
www.framani.com

Salumi Artisan Cured Meats

Gina and Brian Batali, owners
309 Third Avenue South
Seattle, WA 98104
(206) 621-8772
Restaurant, retail store, and email sales
orders@salumicuredmeats.com
www.salumicuredmeats.com

Boccalone Salumeria

Chris Cosentino and Mark Pastore, founders
Ferry Building Marketplace, Shop 21
San Francisco, CA 94111
(415) 433-6500
Retail store and internet sales
salumisociety@boccalone.com
www.boccalone.com

Fabrique Délices

Antonio Pinheiro and Marc Poisignon, owners
1610 Delta Court Unit #1
Hayward, CA 94544
(510) 441-9500
Wholesale with national distribution
info@fabriquedelices.com
www.fabriquedelices.com

Fatted Calf Charcuterie

Taylor Boetticher and
Toponia Miller, owners

Napa:
644 C First Street
Napa, CA 94559
(707) 256-3684
San Francisco:
320 Fell Street
San Francisco, CA 94102
(415) 400-5614
Retail only at both stores
www.fattedcalf.com

Meat Men

Albert Juarez, owner
8280 Clairemont Mesa Boulevard, Suite 110
San Diego, CA 9211
(619) 708-9849
Farmers' markets and other
regional retail stores
www.meatmenstore.com

EPILOGUE
Misery Loves Company

Aaron Josinsky, owner
46 Main Street
Winooski, VT 05404
(802) 497-3989
Restaurant
info@miserylovescovt.com
www.miserylovescovt.com

Red Apron Butcher and Partisan

Nathan Anda, chef
Union Market:
1309 5th Street NE
Washington, DC 20002
(202) 524-6807
The Partisan:
709 D Street NW
Washington, DC 20004
(202) 524-5322
Market and restaurants
www.redapronbutchery.com;
thepartisandc.com

Cypress
Craig Deihl, executive chef
167 E. Bay Street
Charleston, SC 29401
(843) 727-0111
Restaurant
reservations@hmgi.net
www.cypresscharleston.com

Artisan Meat Share
Craig Deihl, executive chef
33 Spring Street,
Charleston, SC 29403
(843) 641-7299
Delicatessen and retail store
artisanmeatshare@hmgi.net
www.artisanmeatsharecharleston.com

NOTES

INTRODUCTION

1. Cheryl Day, "8 Things to Consider in Your 2016 Hog Marketing Plan," *National Hog Farmer*, February 2, 2016, http://nationalhogfarmer.com/marketing/8-things -consider-your-2016-hog-marketing-plan.
2. Marian Burros, *Cooking for Comfort* (New York: Simon & Schuster, 2003).
3. R. W. Apple Jr., "The Smoky Trail to a Great Bacon," *New York Times*, February 16, 2000, http://www.nytimes.com/2000/02/16/style/the-smoky-trail-to-a-great-bacon.html.
4. Steve Reddicliffe, "No More 'Banging on the Shutters,'" *New York Times*, June 7, 2014, http://www.nytimes.com/2014/06/08/nyregion/walters-in-mamaroneck-reopens -its-hot-dog-stand.html.

CHAPTER ONE: FROM THE SILK ROAD TO THE FORUM SUARIUM

1. Mark Essig, *Lesser Beasts: A Snout-to-Tail History of the Humble Pig* (New York: Basic Books, 2015), 28–29.
2. E. F. Binkerd and O. E. Kolari, "The History and Use of Nitrate and Nitrite in the Curing of Meat," *Food and Cosmetics Toxicology* 13, no. 6 (1975): 655–661, doi:10.1016 /0015-6264(75)90157-1.
3. Juling He, "Cured Meat, a Southern Specialty," *The World of Chinese*, February 2, 2012, http://www.theworldofchinese.com/2012/02/cured-meat-a-southern-specialty.
4. Ibid.
5. Essig, *Lesser Beasts*, 10.
6. Ibid., 69.
7. Ibid., 75.
8. Mirco Marconi, personal interview with the author, September 9, 2015.
9. M. Jean Svoronos, "The Origins of Coinage," *American Journal of Numismatics* 44, no. 1 (January 1910): 16, https://www.jstor.org/stable/43583557.
10. "Yorkshire," National Swine Registry, accessed March 22, 2016, http://nationalswine. com/about/about_breeds/Yorkshire.php.
11. "Breeds of Livestock — Danish Landrace Swine," Oklahoma State University Division of Agricultural Sciences and Natural Resources, accessed March 29, 2016, http:// www.ansi.okstate.edu/breeds/swine/danishlandrace.
12. "Breeds of Livestock — Italian Landrace Swine," Oklahoma State University Division of Agricultural Sciences and Natural Resources, accessed March 29, 2016, http:// www.ansi.okstate.edu/breeds/swine/italianlandrace.
13. "Duroc," National Swine Registry, accessed March 22, 2016, http://nationalswine.com /about/about_breeds/duroc.php.

14. Essig, *Lesser Beasts*, 79–81.

15. Alan Davidson, *The Oxford Companion to Food* (Oxford: Oxford University Press, 1999), 368.

CHAPTER TWO: FROM THE OLD WORLD TO THE AMERICAS

1. "Ossabaw Island Hog," The Livestock Conservancy, accessed April 12, 2016, https://livestockconservancy.org/index.php/heritage/internal/Ossabaw.

2. Stephanie Shapiro, "A Slice of History," *Baltimore Sun*, November 9, 2005, http://articles.baltimoresun.com/2005-11-09/news/0511080137_1_lebanon-bologna-lebanon-county-weaver.

3. Charles W. Towne and Edward N. Wentworth, *Pigs from Cave to Corn Belt* (Norman: University of Oklahoma Press, 1950), 86.

4. Ibid., 87–97.

5. Shapiro, "A Slice of History."

6. Ibid.

7. "Pennsylvania Dutch Meat," Welcome to Lancaster County, accessed April 4, 2016, http://www.welcome-to-lancaster-county.com/pennsylvania-dutch-meat.html.

8. "Our History," Seltzer's Lebanon Bologna, accessed April 4, 2016, http://www.seltzerslebanon.com/about-us.

9. Matthew Allen, "National Sausage Loses Its Skin," Swissinfo.ch, June 13, 2007, http://www.swissinfo.ch/eng/national-sausage-loses-its-skin/52396.

10. William Hedgepeth, *The Hog Book* (Garden City, NY: Doubleday Books, 1978), 42.

11. Towne and Wentworth, *Pigs from Cave to Corn Belt*, 111.

12. Sam Bowers Hilliard, *Hog Meat and Hoecake: Food Supply in the Old South, 1840–1860* (Athens: University of Georgia Press, 2014), 196.

13. Liz Gray, "Porkopolis: Cincinnati's Pork-Producing Past," Great American Country, accessed October 13, 2015, http://www.greatamericancountry.com/places/local-life/porkopolis-cincinnatis-pork-producing-past.

14. Bob Perry, personal interview with the author, June 3, 2015.

15. Gray, "Porkopolis."

16. Ibid.

17. Isabella L. Bishop, *The Englishwomen in America* (London: John Murray, 1856), 125–126.

18. Hilliard, *Hog Meat and Hoecake*, 219–220.

19. Roger Horowitz, *Putting Meat on the American Table: Taste, Technology, Transformation* (Baltimore: Johns Hopkins University Press, 2006), 54.

20. Matthew Jennings, personal interview with the author, April 22, 2016.

21. Rick Gencarelli, personal interview with the author, March 1, 2016.

CHAPTER THREE: A TALE OF THREE SMITHFIELDS

1. Helen C. Rountree, "Uses of Domesticated Animals by Early Virginia Indians," *Encyclopedia Virginia*, May 30, 2014, http://www.encyclopediavirginia.org/Domesticated_Animals_During_the_Pre-Colonial_Era.

2. John Noble Wilford, "First Settlers Domesticated Pigs before Crops," *New York Times*, May 31, 1994, http://www.nytimes.com/1994/05/31/science/first -settlers-domesticated-pigs-before-crops.html.

3. Mark Kurlansky, *Salt: A World History* (New York: Walker & Co., 2002), 148.

4. "Todd Family of Smithfield, Virginia," Ancestry.com, accessed March 22, 2016, http:// freepages.genealogy.rootsweb.ancestry.com/~jganis/toddfamily.html.

5. Janet Larsen, "Meat Consumption in China Now Double That in the United States," Earth Policy Institute, April 24, 2012, http://www.earth-policy.org/plan_b_updates /2012/update102.

6. Charlie LeDuff, "At a Slaughterhouse, Some Things Never Die; Who Kills, Who Cuts, Who Bosses Can Depend on Race," *New York Times*, June 16, 2000, http://www .nytimes.com/2000/06/16/us/slaughterhouse-some-things-never-die-who-kills-who -cuts-who-bosses-can-depend.html.

7. Evelyn Baker, "Grove Priory," in *Medieval Archaeology: An Encyclopedia*, ed. Pamela Crabtree (New York: Garland Press, 2001), 147–148.

8. Michael Olmert, "Smokehouses," *Colonial Williamsburg*, Winter 2004–2005, https:// www.history.org/Foundation/journal/Winter04-05/smoke.cfm.

9. Ibid.

10. Diane Ackerman, "Smell," chap. 1 in *A Natural History of the Senses* (New York: Vintage Books, 1990).

11. Craig Rogers, "Lamb Ham," Lowcountry Rice Culture Project, Facebook post, January 15, 2015.

CHAPTER FOUR: HAMS OF MANY GENERATIONS

1. "Descendants of William Newsom," accessed April 1, 2016, http://www.edebby.com /genealogy/newsom1.htm.

2. Ibid.

3. Olmert, "Smokehouses."

4. Ibid.

5. Deborah Lake, "NEWSOM-L Archives," Roots Web, May 4, 1998, http://archiver .rootsweb.ancestry.com/th/read/NEWSOM/1998-04/0893464524.

6. Nancy Newsom Mahaffey, personal interview with the author, March 18, 2016.

7. Steve Coomes, *Country Ham: A Southern Tradition of Hogs, Salt & Smoke* (Charleston, SC: The History Press, 2014).

8. Rick McDaniel, *An Irresistible History of Southern Food: Four Centuries of Black-Eyed Peas, Collard Greens and Whole Hog Barbecue* (Charleston, SC: The History Press, 2011), 89.

9. Frederick K. Ray, "Meat Curing," Oklahoma Cooperative Extension Service, accessed April 4, 2016, http://pods.dasnr.okstate.edu/docushare/dsweb/Get/Document-2055 /ANSI-3994web.pdf.

10. Amy Evans, "Ronny and Beth Drennan — Broadbent Country Hams," Southern Foodways Alliance, August 22, 2005, http://www.southernfoodways.org/interview /ronny-and-beth-drennan-broadbent-country-hams.

11. Sandra Myers, "Trigg Ham Takes Prize," *Kentucky New Era*, August 25, 2000, http://www.kentuckynewera.com/article_dca6007c-2418-5826-8910-1e333ae78e73.html.

12. Coomes, *Country Ham*, 71.

13. Evans, "Ronny and Beth Drennan."

14. Jeff DeYoung, "Iowans Held Key Roles in Genetics History," *Missouri Farmer Today*, November 6, 2008, http://www.missourifarmertoday.com/news/iowans-held-key-roles-in-genetics-history/article_120203c5-f5c4-5cfe-8b2f-5ce3624c12e8.html.

15. Robert Perry, "Heritage Hog Carcass Yields," University of Kentucky, https://dhn-hes.ca.uky.edu/content/heritage-hog-carcass-yields.

CHAPTER FIVE: LE BON TEMPS ROULÉ

1. Calvin Trillin, "Missing Links," *New Yorker*, January 28, 2002.

2. Robert Carriker, "Southern Boudin Trail," Southern Foodways Alliance, accessed May 9, 2016, https://www.southernfoodways.org/oral-history/southern-boudin-trail.

3. Ian Brown, "Historic Importance of Salt," in *The Role of Salt in Eastern North American Prehistory* (Baton Rouge: Louisiana Archaeological Survey and Antiquities Commission, 1981).

4. Robert Carriker, *Boudin: A Guide to Louisiana's Extraordinary Link* (Lafayette: University of Louisiana Press, 2012).

5. George Graham, "The German Cajuns of Roberts Cove," *Acadiana Table*, September 28, 2015.

6. "History," Jacob's World Famous Andouille and Sausage, accessed November 30, 2015, http://www.cajunsausage.com/history.htm.

7. "Cold," *How We Got to Now*, television miniseries, hosted by Steven Johnson, 2014, PBS.

8. "Our Principles," Home Place Pastures, http://www.homeplacepastures.com/our-principles.

9. "Nitrate and Nitrite: Health Information Summary," New Hampshire Department of Environmental Services, accessed May 11, 2016, http://des.nh.gov/organization/commissioner/pip/factsheets/ard/documents/ard-ehp-16.pdf.

10. Joe Schwarcz, "Is Celery Juice a Viable Alternative to Nitrites in Cured Meats?" McGill University, April 4, 2013, http://blogs.mcgill.ca/oss/2013/04/04/is-celery-juice-a-viable-alternative-to-nitrites-in-cured-meats.

11. "Chef Kristopher Doll — Biography," *StarChefs*, March 2012, https://www.starchefs.com/cook/chefs/bio/kris-doll.

12. Ian McNulty, "Clean Slate," *Gambit*, January 24, 2006, http://www.bestofneworleans.com/gambit/clean-slate/Content?oid=1245179.

13. Amanda Wicks, "Q&A with Chef Nick Martin," *Bone & Seed by Dinner Lab*, May 13, 2016.

14. Martine Boyer, "What No One Told You about Alon Shaya," GoNOLA, July 20, 2015, http://gonola.com/2015/07/20/what-no-one-told-you-about-alon-shaya.html.

15. Jeffrey Weiss, *Charcutería: The Soul of Spain* (Chicago: Agate Surrey, 2014), 43.

CHAPTER SIX: FROM WURST TO SZALÁMI TO САЛАМА

1. Gary Stern, "How One Old-Fashioned Pork Store Survived and Thrives," *New York Business Journal*, December 7, 2015, http://www.bizjournals.com/newyork /news/2015/12/07/schaller-weber-new-york-city-pork-store.html.
2. "Lachsschinken," Schaller & Weber, accessed April 11, 2016, http://www.schaller weber.com/product/lachsschinken.
3. Marko Stefanovic, email to the author, November 13, 2015.
4. Marko Stefanovic, interview with the author, November 10, 2015.
5. Ibid.

CHAPTER SEVEN: THE ITALIAN CONNECTION

1. Patrick Egan, "A Meat Store Grandmother Would Love," City Room, *New York Times*, November 18, 2010, http://cityroom.blogs.nytimes.com/2010/11/18/a-meat-store -grandmother-would-love.
2. Salvatore Cappiello, *My Life on Arthur Avenue* (Denver: Outskirts Press, 2011), 60.
3. Mary Ann Castronovo Fusco, "Miracle Cure," Jersey Living, *New Jersey Monthly*, January 16, 2012, https://njmonthly.com/articles/jersey-living/miracle-cure.
4. Ed Levine, "Sausage Making as Art, as Craft, as Family Tradition," *New York Times*, October 7, 1992, http://www.nytimes.com/1992/10/07/garden/sausage-making -as-art-as-craft-as-family-tradition.html.
5. Marc Buzzio and Paul Valetutti, personal interview with the author, April 26, 2015.
6. Fusco, "Miracle Cure."
7. Benjamin Wolfe, "A New Mold Species Discovered on Salami," Microbial Foods, January 17, 2015, http://microbialfoods.org/science-digested-new-penicillium -species-discovered-salami.
8. Fusco, "Miracle Cure."

CHAPTER EIGHT: NEW ENGLAND ITALIANS

1. "Production Specifications," Prosciutto di San Daniele, accessed May 17, 2016, http:// www.prosciuttosandaniele.it/en/the-ham/strict-specifications-to-ensure-quality.
2. Toni H. Lydecker, "Prosciutto — The Pick of the Pork Products," *Washington Post*, July 28, 1982, https://www.washingtonpost.com/archive/lifestyle/food/1982/07/28 /prosciutto-the-pick-of-the-pork-products/33707414-d236-4b52-aa0e-3cc56712b684.
3. Charlotte Wilder, "How an Italian Family Built a Prosciutto Empire in Rhode Island," *Cook's Illustrated*, May 29, 2014, https://www.cooksillustrated.com/articles /225-how-an-italian-family-built-a-prosciutto-empire-in-rhode-island.
4. Ibid.

CHAPTER NINE: IT'S A LONG ROAD TO CURED MEAT!

1. "Artisan Profile: Scott Bridi of Brooklyn Cured," Nona Brooklyn, December 23, 2010, http://nonabrooklyn.com/artisan-profile-scott-bridi-of-brooklyn-cured.
2. Scott Bridi, personal interview with the author, December 14, 2015.
3. Paul Wetzel, personal interview with the author, November 3, 2015.

4. "Raven & Boar Farm," Raven & Boar Farm, accessed April 26, 2016, http://ravenand boar.com/about.

CHAPTER TEN: PENNSYLVANIA

1. Danya Henninger, "This Weekend Only: South Philly's Le Virtù Serves a 49-Ingredient Minestrone," *BillyPenn*, April 30, 2016, http://billypenn.com/2016 /04/30/this-weekend-only-south-phillys-le-virtu-serves-a-49-ingredient -minestrone.
2. Brette Warshaw, "Profiles in Obsession: Francis Cretarola & Cathy Lee," *Lucky Peach*, March 13, 2015, http://luckypeach.com/profiles-in-obsession-francis-cratil-cretarola -cathy-lee.
3. "About the Restaurant," Le Virtù, accessed January 3, 2017, http://levirtu.com/the -restaurant.
4. Francis Cratil Cretarola, "Merigan: 20 January 2015: Rispetto . . . ," *Brigantessa*, January 21, 2015, http://brigantessaphila.com/merigan-20-january-2015.
5. "The 9th Street Italian Market," Fante's Kitchen Shop, accessed May 6, 2016 , https:// www.fantes.com/italian-market.
6. Marc Cappelletti, "A Sample, a Good Story and a Smile: The Evolution of Di Bruno Bros," Di Bruno Bros, May 12, 2014, http://blog.dibruno.com/2014/05/12/a-sample -a-good-story-and-a-smile-the-evolution-of-di-bruno-bros.
7. "12 Old School Di Bruno Bros Food Finds," Di Bruno Bros, May 6, 2014, http://blog .dibruno.com/2014/05/06/12-old-school-di-bruno-bros-food-finds.
8. Anna Wolfe, "Building a Legacy," *Gourmet Retailer*, December 2011, http://www .gourmetretailer.com/article-building_a_legacy-2379.html.
9. "Farmland Preservation," Pennsylvania Department of Agriculture, accessed May 8, 2016, http://www.agriculture.pa.gov/Encourage/farmland/Pages/default.aspx.

CHAPTER ELEVEN: LOOK FOR THE HOG AT THE OAK

1. United States Department of Agriculture, *Yearbook 1922* (Washington, DC: Government Printing Office, 1923).
2. "Corn Production," Iowa Corn Promotion Board, accessed February 18, 2016, https:// www.iowacorn.org/corn-production.
3. Herb Eckhouse, email to the author, March 1, 2016.
4. Herb Eckhouse, email to the author, March 4, 2016.
5. "Our Farmers," La Quercia, accessed March 3, 2016, http://laquercia.us/about_our _farmers.
6. United States Department of Agriculture, "Organic Survey," 2007, https://www .agcensus.usda.gov/Publications/Organic_Survey.

CHAPTER TWELVE: DON'T WE JUST FLY OVER IT?

1. Bret Thorn, "Charcuterie, Egg Most Buzzed-About Menu Items," *Nation's Restaurant News*, February 11, 2014, http://nrn.com/consumer-trends/charcuterie-egg -most-buzzed-about-menu-items.
2. Cameron Meyer and Leigh Bush, "The Humane Human," *Indiana Food Review*, accessed April 14, 2016, http://www.indianafoodreview.com/archives/issue-1/goose.

3. Ibid.
4. Ibid.

CHAPTER THIRTEEN: MILE-HIGH SALUMI

1. Alex Seidel, personal interview with the author, June 3, 2015.
2. Brian Albano and Bill Miner, personal interview with the author, June 2, 2015.
3. "Salt & Grinder: A Deli Tradition," Salt & Grinder, accessed April 20, 2016, http://www.saltandgrinder.com.
4. Ibid.
5. Lori Midson, "Forked!" *Westword*, March 7, 2013, http://digitalissue.denverwestword.com/display_article.php?id=1337774.
6. Frank Bonnano, personal interview with the author, April 20, 2016.

CHAPTER FOURTEEN: THE PACIFIC RIM

1. Hank Shaw, "About," Hunter Angler Gardener Cook, accessed May 24, 2016, http://honest-food.net/about.
2. David Draper, "A Six Pack with Hank Shaw, Author of 'Hunt, Gather, Cook,'" The Wild Chef, *Field & Stream*, June 29, 2011, http://www.fieldandstream.com/blogs/wild-chef/2011/06/six-pack-hank-shaw-author-%E2%80%9Chunt-gather-cook%E2%80%9D.
3. Martin Cizmar, "Old Salt: 2014 Restaurant of the Year Runner-Up," *Willamette Week*, October 14, 2014, http://www.wweek.com/portland/article-23205-old-salt-2014-restaurant-of-the-year-runner-up.html.
4. Ron Rosenbaum, "Anthony Bourdain's Theory on the Foodie Revolution," *Smithsonian Magazine*, July 2014, http://www.smithsonianmag.com/arts-culture/anthony-bourdains-theory-foodie-revolution-180951848.
5. Ibid.
6. Elias Cairo and Meredith Erickson, *Olympia Provisions: Cured Meats and Tall Tales from an American Charcuterie* (Berkeley, CA: Ten Speed Press, 2015), 8.
7. Paul Redman, "Paul Bertolli: Chef, Author, and Salumi Maker," University of California Berkeley, accessed May 28, 2016, http://digitalassets.lib.berkeley.edu/roho/ucb/text/bertolli_paul.pdf.
8. Ibid.
9. Deborah Grossman, "Paul Bertolli: Curemaster at Berkeley's Fra' Mani," Nosh, *Berkeleyside*, May 5, 2014, http://www.berkeleyside.com/2014/05/05/paul-bertolli-curemaster-at-berkeleys-fra-mani.

EPILOGUE

1. Illtud Dunsford, email to the author, June 12, 2015.
2. Michelle Fabio, "Feast of Sant'Antonio Abate," *Italy Magazine*, January 17, 2014, http://www.italymagazine.com/featured-story/feast-santantonio-abate.
3. "St. Anthony the Abbot," Aquinas & More, accessed May 15, 2016, http://www.aquinasandmore.com/fuseaction/store.patronsaintpage/saint/167.
4. G. K. Chesterton, *The Collected Works of G. K. Chesterton: The Illustrated London News, 1908–1910* (San Francisco: Ignatius Press, 1987), 321.

GLOSSARY

MEAT PRODUCT	DEFINITION	MAIN INGREDIENTS
Andouille	Cajun coarse-ground pork sausage	Smoked shoulder; garlic, black pepper, onions, wine, variety of seasonings
Bacon	Cured pork from belly and loins	Pork, salt, spices, smoke
Batsoà	French boneless fried pigs' feet	Pork trotters dipped in beaten egg, covered in bread crumbs, and fried
Black Forest ham	German dry-cured smoked ham	Pork; combinations of garlic, coriander, pepper, juniper berries, other spices, and smoke
Boudin	Generic term for fresh sausage in France and Louisiana	
Boudin blanc	Cajun fresh sausage with rice filler	Pork, heart and liver, various combinations of spices
Boudin rouge	Cajun fresh sausage with rice filler with blood	Pork, heart, liver, and blood, various combinations of spices
Bratwurst	German fresh beef, pork, and veal sausage; many variations across Germany	Beef, pork, veal
Bresaola	Italian air-dried beef made from top round	Beef, coarse salt, juniper berries, cinnamon, and nutmeg
Brühwurst	Generic term for wide variety of German parboiled (scalded) sausages	Beef, pork, veal of various grinds and seasonings
Bündnerfleisch	Swiss air-dried beef shoulder or thigh	Beef, white wine, salt, onion, and herbs
Capicolla/capocollo/ coppa/capicollo/ capocolla/lonza	Italian dry-cured whole neck muscle, seasoned, and stuffed into a casing	Pork, many variations with or without wine, diverse seasonings

MEAT PRODUCT	DEFINITION	MAIN INGREDIENTS
Charcuterie	French term for prepared pork: bacon, ham, sausage, terrines, pâtés, confit	Pork, myriad variations
Chaurice	Creole fresh pork sausage	Pork, fresh vegetables, spices, and herbs
Chorizo	Spanish cured sausage	Pork, paprika
Confit	French; various meats cooked slowly over low heat in fat	Duck, goose, other meats, salt, fat, herbs
Cotto salami	Italian mild-flavored salami from Tuscany; either cooked or smoked	Pork and beef, garlic, sugar, nutmeg, cardamom, black pepper
Country ham	Southern United States dry-cured ham	Pork, salt, sometimes sugar, and smoke
Culatello	Italian dry-cured filet or loin of the hind leg aged in beef or pork bladder	Pork, salt
Finocchiona	Italian salami, generally southern Tuscany	Pork, salt, fennel
Frankfurter	Austrian and German fresh or smoked finely minced sausage	Beef and/or pork, mild seasonings, occasionally smoked
Guanciale	Italian dry-cured spicy pork cheeks or jowl	Pork, salt, sometimes sugar, black pepper, and ground chiles
Jamón	Spanish dry-cured ham of different quality levels	Pork, salt
Kielbasa	Polish sausage of countless varieties, smoked or fresh	Pork, beef, turkey, lamb, chicken, or veal; diverse seasonings and spices
Kochwurst	German sausage containing precooked ingredients	Countless ingredients including blood, liver, tongue
Lachsschinken	German boneless loin rolled in thin layer of fat, slightly cured and smoked	Pork
Landjäger	German, Austrian, and Swiss dried and smoked sausage	Beef, pork, lard, sugar, red wine, and spices

MEAT PRODUCT	DEFINITION	MAIN INGREDIENTS
Lardo	Italian cured fatback	Pork fat, salt, pepper, rosemary, and other herbs
Lebanon bologna	United States; cooked, semicured, and heavily smoked spicy sausage	Beef, salt, sugar, pepper
Liverwurst	German cooked liver sausage	Pig or calf's liver; occasionally veal, fat, black pepper, marjoram, allspice, thyme, mustard seed, nutmeg.
Lomo	Spanish dry-cured tenderloin	Beef or pork, salt, herbs
Mortadella	Italian large, cooked, finely minced pork with small fat chunks throughout	Pork, whole or ground black pepper, myrtle berries, pistachios
Mortadella di Campotosto	Italian ovoid-shaped, finely ground pork, dry aged, smoked with fat center	Pork, fat, salt, spices
'Nduja	Italian cured spicy, spreadable pork salami; well known in Calabria	Pork fat, shoulder and belly, roasted Calabrese chiles
Pancetta	Italian flat or rolled dry-cured belly	Pork, salt, spices
Pastrami	Romanian origins, now widely produced; brined, spiced, and smoked brisket	Beef, some pork, mutton, or turkey; flavored with garlic, coriander, black pepper, paprika, cloves, allspice, and mustard seed
Pâté	French or Belgian, cooked and minced meat and fat	Numerous meats and spices
Porchetta	Italian boneless pork roast with crunchy skin and tender meat	Pork, diverse variety of herbs and spices
Presunto	Portuguese dry-cured ham	Pork, salt
Prosciutto	Italian dry-cured ham	Pork, salt
Rillettes	French cooked meats, cubed, cooked in fat and salt; used as spreads	Pork or other meats

MEAT PRODUCT	DEFINITION	MAIN INGREDIENTS
Rohwurst	German cured and/or smoked sausage	Pork, salt, nitrates
Salami	Italian fermented and air-dried cured sausage	Pork, salt, diverse spices and herbs
Salumi	Italian term encompassing all cured and precooked meat products	
Sanguinaccio	Italian fresh blood sausage	Fresh pig blood infused with spices, herbs
Saucisse de graisse (grease sausage)	Cajun cooked sausage preserved in lard	Pork, lard, spices
Saucisson rouge	French blood sausage	Pork, blood, salt, spices
Saucisson sec	French dry-cured thick sausage	Pork, fat, salt, sugar, spices, nitrites and/or saltpeter
Soppressata	Italian dry-cured sausage, sometimes pressed	Pork, salt, spices
Speck	Dry-cured, lightly smoked prosciutto from northern Italy	Pork thighs
Tasso	Cajun cured pork shoulder	Pork, salt
Terrine	French meat, fish, or vegetable mixture, cooked and cooled	Wide diversity of ingredients
Thuringer	German minced semidry smoked sausage from Thuringia	Pork, beef, or sometimes veal, salt and pepper, caraway, marjoram, and garlic
Toscano salami	Italian dry-cured small salami flavored with fennel	Pork, salt, fennel, other spices and herbs
Violino di capra	Italian dry-cured, sometimes lightly smoked, goat prosciutto	Goat hind legs, salt, herbs, and spices
Wurst	German generic term for ground or minced meat sausage	Beef, pork, or veal

BIBLIOGRAPHY

Ackerman, Diane. *A Natural History of the Senses*. New York: Vintage Books, 1990.

Albarella, Umberto, Keith Dobney, Anton Ervynck, and Peter Rowley-Conwy, ed. *Pigs and Humans: 10,000 Years of Interaction*. New York: Oxford University Press, 2007.

Allan, John, Nat Alcock, and David Dawson, ed. *West Country Households, 1500–1700*. Woodbridge, UK: Boydell Press, 2005.

Allen, Matthew. "National Sausage Loses Its Skin." Swissinfo.ch. June 13, 2007. http://www.swissinfo.ch/eng/national-sausage-loses-its-skin/52396.

Anderson, Brett. "How Katrina Changed Eating in New Orleans." *New Yorker*. August 28, 2015. http://www.newyorker.com/culture/culture-desk/how-katrina-changed-eating-in-new-orleans-2.

Apple, R. W. "Americana, Salted, Smoked and Sliced Thin." *New York Times*. March 23, 2005. http://www.nytimes.com/2005/03/23/dining/americana-salted-smoked-and-sliced-thin.html.

———. "Sausage Aged for Three Generations." *New York Times*. January 28, 2004. http://www.nytimes.com/2004/01/28/dining/sausage-aged-for-three-generations.html.

———. "The Smoky Trail to a Great Bacon." *New York Times*. February 16, 2000. http://www.nytimes.com/2000/02/16/style/the-smoky-trail-to-a-great-bacon.html.

"Artisan Profile: Scott Bridi of Brooklyn Cured." Nona Brooklyn. December 23, 2010. http://nonabrooklyn.com/artisan-profile-scott-bridi-of-brooklyn-cured.

Baker, Evelyn. "Grove Priory." In *Medieval Archaeology: An Encyclopedia*, edited by Pamela Crabtree, 147–148. New York: Garland Press, 2001.

Bannister, Megan. "Pig Breeder Carl Blake's Mission to Acquaint Iowa Technologists, Farmers." *Silicon Prairie News*. April 18, 2014. http://siliconprairienews.com/2014/04/pig-breeder-carl-blake-s-mission-to-acquaint-iowa-technologists-farmers.

Barboza, David. "Farmers Are in Crisis as Hog Prices Collapse." *New York Times*. December 13, 1998. http://www.nytimes.com/1998/12/13/us/farmers-are-in-crisis-as-hog-prices-collapse.html.

Bauer, Kathleen. "At Old Salt Marketplace, Chef Ben Meyer Makes Whole Animal Butchery His Primary Mission." *Oregonian* (Portland, OR). June 5, 2014. http://www.oregonlive.com/dining/index.ssf/2014/06/at_old_salt_marketplace_chef_b.html.

Bienvenu, Marcelle, Carl Brasseaux, and Ryan Brasseaux. *Stir the Pot: The History of Cajun Cuisine*. New York: Hippocrene Books, 2005.

Binkerd, E. F. and O. E. Kolari. "The History and Use of Nitrate and Nitrite in the Curing of Meat." *Food and Cosmetics Toxicology* 13, no. 6 (1975): 655–661. doi:10.1016/0015-6264(75)90157-1.

Bishop, Isabella L. *The Englishwomen in America*. London: John Murray, 1856.

Bissonnette, Jamie. *The New Charcuterie Cookbook: Exceptional Cured Meats to Make and Serve at Home*. Salem, MA: Page Street Publishing, 2014.

Black, Jane. "Better Cured Meat Begins on the Hoof at Home." *Washington Post*. November 28, 2007. http://www.washingtonpost.com/wp-dyn/content/article/2007/11/27/AR2007112700620.html.

Boehrer, Bruce, ed. *A Cultural History of Animals in the Renaissance*. Oxford: Berg, 2007.

Boetticher, Taylor, and Toponia Miller. *In the Charcuterie: The Fatted Calf's Guide to Making Sausage, Salumi, Pâtés, Roasts, Confits, and Other Meaty Goods*. Berkeley: Ten Speed Press, 2013.

Bowen, Dana. "City of Pork." *Saveur*. August 21, 2007, http://www.saveur.com/article/Kitchen/City-of-Pork.

———. "'Taste My Prosciutto,' He Said with a Drawl." *New York Times*. September 17, 2003. http://www.nytimes.com/2003/09/17/dining/taste-my-prosciutto-he-said-with-a-drawl.html.

———. "The Wonders of Ham." *Saveur*. November 16, 2009. http://www.saveur.com/article/Kitchen/The-Wonders-of-Ham.

Bowers Hilliard, Sam. *Hog Meat and Hoecake: Food Supply in the Old South 1840–1860*. Athens: University of Georgia Press, 2014.

Boyer, Martine. "What No One Told You about Alon Shaya." *GoNOLA*. July 20, 2015. http://gonola.com/2015/07/20/what-no-one-told-you-about-alon-shaya.html.

Boyer, Mike. "Cincinnati's 'Porkopolis' Past Fades as Kahn's Plant Falls." *Columbus Dispatch*. February 18, 2012. http://www.dispatch.com/content/stories/business/2012/02/18/when-hogs-ruled.html.

"Breeding for Taste." EatingWell. Accessed April 9, 2016. http://www.eatingwell.com/food_news_origins/people_perspectives/local_heroes/breeding_for_taste.

"Breeds of Livestock — Danish Landrace Swine." Oklahoma State University Division of Agricultural Sciences and Natural Resources. Accessed March 29, 2016. http://www.ansi.okstate.edu/breeds/swine/danishlandrace.

"Breeds of Livestock — Italian Landrace Swine." Oklahoma State University Division of Agricultural Sciences and Natural Resources. Accessed March 29, 2016. http://www.ansi.okstate.edu/breeds/swine/italianlandrace.

Brizzi, Jennifer. "Jacüterie Brings Sublime Locally Made Sausages to the Hudson Valley." *Almanac Weekly*. January 3, 2014. http://hudsonvalleyone.com/2014/01/03/jacuterie-brings-sublime-locally-made-sausages-to-the-hudson-valley.

Brockman, Terra. "Local Artisan Profile: Greg Latakek, West Loop Salumi." *Edible Chicago*. Spring 2015.

Brown, Ian. "Historic Importance of Salt." In *The Role of Salt in Eastern North American Prehistory*. Baton Rouge: Louisiana Archaeological Survey and Antiquities Commission, 1981.

Burros, Marian. *Cooking for Comfort: More Than 100 Wonderful Recipes That Are as Satisfying to Cook as They Are to Eat*. New York: Simon & Schuster, 2003.

Cairo, Elias, and Meredith Erickson. *Olympia Provisions: Cured Meats and Tall Tales from an American Charcuterie*. Berkeley, CA: Ten Speed Press, 2015.

Cappelletti, Marc. "A Sample, a Good Story and a Smile: The Evolution of Di Bruno Bros." *Di Bruno Bros*. May 12, 2014. http://blog.dibruno.com/2014/05/12/a-sample-a-good -story-and-a-smile-the-evolution-of-di-bruno-bros.

Cappiello, Salvatore. *My Life on Arthur Avenue*. Denver: Outskirts Press, 2011.

Carriker, Robert. *Boudin: A Guide to Louisiana's Extraordinary Link*. Lafayette: University of Louisiana Press, 2012.

———. "Southern Boudin Trail." Southern Foodways Alliance. Accessed May 9, 2016. https://www.southernfoodways.org/oral-history/southern-boudin-trail.

Casey, Nell. "The Secret to Running a 93-Year-Old Butcher Shop in Brooklyn." *Gothamist*. March 3, 2015. http://gothamist.com/2015/03/03/video_a_day_in_the_life_of_ beloved.php.

Chamberlain, Chris. "10 Things We Learned about Charcuterie from the Man Who Literally Wrote the Book." *Food Republic*. July 10, 2013. http://www.foodrepublic.com/2013/07 /10/10-things-we-learned-about-charcuterie-from-the-man-who-literally-wrote-the-book.

"Chef Kristopher Doll — Biography." *StarChefs*. March 2012. https://www.starchefs.com /cook/chefs/bio/kris-doll.

Cheslow, Daniella. "The Jewish History of Pick Salami, Hungary's Most Iconic Pork Product." *Tablet*. June 18, 2014. http://www.tabletmag.com/jewish-life-and -religion/175306/hungary-pick-salami.

Chesterton, G. K. *The Collected Works of G. K. Chesterton: The Illustrated London News, 1908–1910*. San Francisco: Ignatius Press, 1987.

Christman, Carolyn J., D. Phillip Sponenberg, and Donald E. Bixby. *A Rare Breeds Album of American Livestock*. Pittsboro, NC: American Livestock Breeds Conservancy, 1998.

Cizmar, Martin. "Old Salt: 2014 Restaurant of the Year Runner-Up." *Willamette Week*. October 14, 2014. http://www.wweek.com/portland/article-23205-old-salt-2014 -restaurant-of-the-year-runner-up.html.

"Cold." *How We Got to Now*. Television miniseries. Hosted by Steven Johnson. 2014. PBS.

Collins, Glenn. "A Ban on Some Italian Cured Meat Is Ending." *New York Times*. April 29, 2013. http://www.nytimes.com/2013/04/30/dining/ban-on-many-italian-pork -products-to-be-relaxed.html.

Coomes, Steve. *Country Ham: A Southern Tradition of Hogs, Salt & Smoke*. Charleston, SC: The History Press, 2014.

———. "A Different Kind of Cure: Woodlands Approach Yields Ham without the Saltiness." *Edible Louisville and the Bluegrass*. June/July 2015. http://ediblelouisville.ediblecommunities .com/shopdifferent-kind-cure-woodlands-approach-yields-ham-without-saltiness.

"Corn Production." Iowa Corn Promotion Board. Accessed February 18, 2016. https:// www.iowacorn.org/corn-production.

"Corn Uses." Iowa Corn Promotion Board. Accessed February 18, 2016. https://www.iowa corn.org/corn-uses.

"Corner Post Meats." Local Harvest. Accessed April 22, 2016. http://www.localharvest.org /corner-post-meats-M60435.

Cretarola, Francis Cratil. "Merigan: 20 January 2015: Rispetto . . ." *Brigantessa*. January 21, 2015. http://brigantessaphila.com/merigan-20-january-2015.

Crews, Ed. "Ossabaw Island Pigs." *Colonial Williamsburg*. Winter 2010. http://www.history
.org/Foundation/journal/Winter10/pigs.cfm.

Culinary Institute of America and John Kowalski. *The Art of Charcuterie*. New York: Wiley, 2010.

"Cured Meats in Italy." Rustico Cooking. Accessed August 7, 2015. http://www.rustico
cooking.com/curedmeats.htm.

Darlington, Tenaya. "How Pork Becomes Prosciutto." *Madame Fromage*. June 16, 2013.
http://madamefromageblog.com/2013/how-pork-becomes-prosciutto.

Davidson, Alan. *The Oxford Companion to Food*. Oxford: Oxford University Press, 1999.

Day, Cheryl. "8 Things to Consider in Your 2016 Hog Marketing Plan." *National Hog
Farmer*. February 2, 2016. http://nationalhogfarmer.com/marketing/8-things
-consider-your-2016-hog-marketing-plan.

"Descendants of William Newsom." Accessed April 1, 2016. http://www.edebby.com
/genealogy/newsom2.htm.

DeYoung, Jeff. "Iowans Held Key Roles in Genetics History." *Missouri Farmer Today*.
November 6, 2008. http://www.missourifarmertoday.com/news/iowans-held-key
-roles-in-genetics-history/article_120203c5-f5c4-5cfe-8b2f-5ce3624c12e8.html.

Di Gregorio, Sarah. "The Salami Maker Who Fought the Law." *Gastronomica* 7, no. 4 (Fall
2007): 53–57. doi:10.1525/gfc.2007.7.4.53.

Dixon Kavanaugh, Shane. "Brooklyn: Court Street's Shops Defy the Odds." *Crain's New
York Business*. August 5, 2012. http://www.crainsnewyork.com/article/20120805
/REAL_ESTATE/308059997/brooklyn-court-streets-shops-defy-the-odds.

Dolinsky, Steve. "Father and Son Bring Nduja Sausage to the Chicago Masses." ABC
Channel 7 Chicago. September 25, 2015. http://abc7chicago.com/food/father
-and-son-bring-nduja-sasuage-to-the-chicago-masses/1001969.

Donati, Silvia. "Inspired by Parma, Making Award-Winning Prosciutto in Iowa." *Italy
Magazine*. November 13, 2013. http://www.italymagazine.com/featured-story
/inspired-parma-making-award-winning-prosciutto-iowa.

Draper, David. "A Six Pack with Hank Shaw, Author of 'Hunt, Gather, Cook.'" The Wild
Chef. *Field & Stream*. June 29, 2011. http://www.fieldandstream.com/blogs/wild-chef
/2011/06/six-pack-hank-shaw-author-%E2%80%9Chunt-gather-cook%E2%80%9D.

"Duroc." National Swine Registry. Accessed March 22, 2016. http://nationalswine.com
/about/about_breeds/duroc.php.

Edwards, Megan E. "Virginia Ham: The Local and Global of Colonial Foodways." *Food and
Foodways* 19, no. 1–2 (February 2011): 56–73. doi:10.1080/07409710.2011.544175.

Edwards, Sammy. "Virginia Hams and American Independence." Edwards Virginia
Smokehouse. Accessed January 29, 2016. http://blog.edwardsvaham.com/virginia
-ham-american-independence.

Egan, Patrick. "A Meat Store Grandmother Would Love." City Room. *New York Times*.
November 18, 2010. http://cityroom.blogs.nytimes.com/2010/11/18/a-meat-store
-grandmother-would-love.

Eligon, John. "An Iowa Farmer's Quest for No Ordinary Pig." *New York Times*. February 28,
2013. http://www.nytimes.com/2013/03/01/us/with-iowa-swabian-hall-a-farmers
-quest-for-perfect-pig.html.

Ellick, Adam B. "A Health Scare Revives the Smokehouse Blues." Neighborhood Report: East Village. *New York Times*. October 8, 2006. http://www.nytimes.com/2006/10/08/nyregion/thecity/a-health-scare-revives-the-smokehouse-blues.html.

Englert, Stuart. "Smokehouse: Preserving Food and Tradition." *American Profile*. November 2, 2013. http://americanprofile.com/articles/smokehouses-preserving-food-and-tradition-video.

Ervolino, Bill. "Old World Charcuterie and Salumi, Made in Hackensack." NorthJersey.com. July 16, 2013. http://www.northjersey.com/food-and-dining-news/old-world-charcuterie-and-salumi-made-in-hackensack-1.614712.

Essig, Mark. *Lesser Beasts: A Snout-to-Tail History of the Humble Pig*. New York: Basic Books, 2015.

Estabrook, Barry. *Pig Tales: An Omnivore's Quest for Sustainable Meat*. New York: W. W. Norton & Co., 2015.

Evans, Amy. "Ronny and Beth Drennan — Broadbent Country Hams." Southern Foodways Alliance. August 22, 2005. http://www.southernfoodways.org/interview/ronny-and-beth-drennan-broadbent-country-hams.

Evans-Hylton, Patrick. *Smithfield: Ham Capital of the World*. Charleston, SC: Arcadia Publishing, 2004.

Fabio, Michelle. "Feast of Sant'Antonio Abate." *Italy Magazine*. January 17, 2014. http://www.italymagazine.com/featured-story/feast-santantonio-abate.

Fabricant, Florence. "Il Buco Is Selling Its Own Salumi." Diner's Journal. *New York Times*. January 19, 2012. http://dinersjournal.blogs.nytimes.com/2012/01/19/il-buco-is-selling-its-own-salumi.

"Farmland Preservation." Pennsylvania Department of Agriculture. Accessed May 8, 2016. http://www.agriculture.pa.gov/Encourage/farmland/Pages/default.aspx.

"Feet in the Trough." *Economist*. December 19, 2006. http://www.economist.com/node/8345876.

Fehribach, Paul. "Our Story of Meat, Part II." Big Jones. June 6, 2013. http://bigjoneschicago.com/2013/06/06/our-story-of-meat-part-ii.

Fox, Brandon. "Italian-Style Salami, Made with American Pigs, Powers Growth of a Virginia Business." *Washington Post*. September 23, 2014. https://www.washingtonpost.com/lifestyle/food/italian-style-salami-made-with-american-pigs-powers-growth-of-a-virginia-business/2014/09/22/e0ed570a-3ebf-11e4-b03f-de718edeb92f_story.html.

Frame, Andy. "Cured Meat Is In, But Is It Safe?" *Food Safety News*. September 6, 2012. http://www.foodsafetynews.com/2012/09/cured-meat-is-in-but-is-it-safe.

Fritsch, Jane. "Some Prosciutto Fans Turn to Iowa." *New York Times*. August 5, 2013. http://www.nytimes.com/2013/08/07/dining/some-prosciutto-fans-turn-to-iowa.html.

Fusco, Mary Ann Castronovo. "Miracle Cure." Jersey Living. *New Jersey Monthly*. January 16, 2012. https://njmonthly.com/articles/jersey-living/miracle-cure.

Gamble, H. Ray. "Trichinae." USDA. Accessed October 15, 2015. https://www.aphis.usda.gov/vs/trichinae/docs/fact_sheet.htm.

Gill, Dan. "Country Ham." *Pleasant Living*. November/December 2010. http://www.pine3.info/Country%20Ham.htm.

Graham, George. "Alligator Sausage and Creole Red Onions with Beer Gravy over Crab-Boiled Smashed Potatoes." Acadiana Table. September 28, 2015. http://acadianatable.com/2015/09/28/alligator-sausage.

Gray, Liz. "Porkopolis: Cincinnati's Pork-Producing Past." Great American Country. Accessed October 13, 2015. http://www.greatamericancountry.com/places/local-life /porkopolis-cincinnatis-pork-producing-past.

Greer, Denise. "Ancora Pizzeria & Salumeria, New Orleans, LA: Old Is New Again." *Pizza Today*. March 1, 2014. http://www.pizzatoday.com/departments/features/ancora -pizzeria-salumeria-new-orleans-la-old-new.

Grigson, Jane. *Charcuterie and French Pork Cookery*. London: Michael Joseph, 1967.

Grossman, Deborah. "Paul Bertolli: Curemaster at Berkeley's Fra' Mani." Nosh. *Berkeleyside*. May 5, 2014. http://www.berkeleyside.com/2014/05/05/paul -bertolli-curemaster-at-berkeleys-fra-mani.

Havill, Georgiana. "A Quest for Peanuts and Pork in Virginia, South of the James More Than 23,000 Acres of Two Counties' Fields Are Planted with Jumbo Goobers, the Size of a Man's Thumb. In Smithfield, Seat of Isle of Wight County, Five Million Pigs Are Butchered Each Year." *Philadelphia Inquirer*. September 1, 1996. http://articles.philly .com/1996-09-01/news/25634754_1_peanuts-goobers-smith-s-fort-plantation.

He, Juling. "Cured Meat, a Southern Specialty." The World of Chinese. February 2, 2012. http://www.theworldofchinese.com/2012/02/cured-meat-a-southern-specialty.

Hedgepeth, William. *The Hog Book*. Garden City, NY: Doubleday Books, 1978.

Henninger, Danya. "This Weekend Only: South Philly's Le Virtù Serves a 49-Ingredient Minestrone." *BillyPenn*. April 30, 2016. http://billypenn.com/2016/04/30/this -weekend-only-south-phillys-le-virtu-serves-a-49-ingredient-minestrone.

Hinke, Veronica. "Food: A Spicy and Bitter (Greens) Start to 2015." Evanston Review. *Chicago Tribune*. January 19, 2015. http://www.chicagotribune.com/suburbs /evanston/lifestyles/chi-evr-food-a-spicy-and-bitter-greens-start-to-2015-20150128 -story.html.

"History." *Jacob's World Famous Andouille and Sausage*. Accessed November 30, 2015. http:// www.cajunsausage.com/history.htm.

"History and Background on Wild Hogs in Georgia." Black Mouth Cur. Accessed January 26, 2016. http://blackmouthcur.com/ha01.htm.

"History: Prosciutto di Parma." Prosciutto di Parma. Accessed August 6, 2015. http://www .prosciuttodiparma.com/en_UK/prosciutto.

Hogsed, Sarah. "Broadbent's Celebrates 100 Years in the Ham Business." *Kentucky New Era*. September 5, 2009. http://www.kentuckynewera.com/web/news/article_5f97fec1 -8de9-5237-94bb-4eb3714762bf.html.

Horowitz, Roger. *Putting Meat on the American Table: Taste, Technology, Transformation*. Baltimore: Johns Hopkins University Press, 2006.

Hui, Y. H., ed. *Handbook of Animal-Based Fermented Food and Beverage Technology*, 2nd edition. New York: CRC Press, 2012.

Ingrassia, Michele. "BRONX BANQUET These Days, the Population Is More Diverse, but Arthur Ave. Still Offers the Best Italian Fare This Side of Tuscany." *New York Daily News*. March 4, 2001. http://www.nydailynews.com/bronx-banquet-days-population -diverse-arthur-ave-offers-best-italian-fare-side-tuscany-article-1.907250.

Kaminsky, Peter. *Pig Perfect: Encounters with Remarkable Swine and Some Great Ways to Cook Them*. New York: Hyperion, 2005.

Katz, Sandor Ellix. *The Art of Fermentation: An In-Depth Exploration of Essential Concepts and Processes from around the World*. White River Junction, VT: Chelsea Green Publishing, 2012.

Kenniff, Sean. "'Nduja and Campanilismo in Chicago." *StarChefs*. May 2015. http://www.starchefs.com/cook/savory/nduja-and-campenalismo-chicago.

Kinsella, John, and David T. Harvey. *Professional Charcuterie: Sausage Making, Curing, Terrines, and Pâtés*. New York: Wiley, 1996.

Kostioukovitch, Elena. *Why Italians Love to Talk about Food*. Translated by Anne Milano Appel. New York: Farrar, Straus, and Giroux, 2006.

Kurlansky, Mark. *Salt: A World History*. New York: Walker & Co., 2002.

Kutas, Rytek. *Great Sausage Recipes and Meat Curing: The Bible of Sausage Making*, 4th edition. Buffalo, NY: The Sausage Maker, Inc., 2008.

"Lachsschinken." Schaller & Weber. Accessed April 11, 2016. http://www.schallerweber.com/product/lachsschinken.

Lake, Deborah. "NEWSOM-L Archives." Roots Web. May 4, 1998. http://archiver.rootsweb.ancestry.com/th/read/NEWSOM/1998-04/0893464524.

Larsen, Janet. "Meat Consumption in China Now Double That in the United States." Earth Policy Institute. April 24, 2012. http://www.earth-policy.org/plan_b_updates/2012/update102.

Latus, Janine. "Edwards Ham." *Distinction Magazine*. November 15, 2014. http://distinctionhr.com/edwards-ham.

LeDuff, Charlie. "At a Slaughterhouse, Some Things Never Die; Who Kills, Who Cuts, Who Bosses Can Depend on Race." *New York Times*. June 16, 2000. http://www.nytimes.com/2000/06/16/us/slaughterhouse-some-things-never-die-who-kills-who-cuts-who-bosses-can-depend.html.

Levine, Ed. "Sausage Making as Art, as Craft, as Family Tradition." *New York Times*. October 7, 1992. http://www.nytimes.com/1992/10/07/garden/sausage-making-as-art-as-craft-as-family-tradition.html.

———. "Unsung Salumi: The Underappreciated Storefront You Might've Missed." *Edible Manhattan*. November 9, 2008. http://www.ediblemanhattan.com/magazine/unsung_alumi.

Lewis, Celia. *The Illustrated Guide to Pigs: How to Choose Them, How to Keep Them*. New York: Skyhorse Publishing, 2011.

Livingston, A. D. *Cold-Smoking & Salt-Curing Meat, Fish, & Game*. New York: Lyons & Burford. 1999.

"Local Heroes." *EatingWell*. Accessed April 9, 2016. http://www.eatingwell.com/food_news_origins/people_perspectives/local_heroes.

Lydecker, Toni H. "Prosciutto — The Pick of the Pork Products." *Washington Post*. July 28, 1982. https://www.washingtonpost.com/archive/lifestyle/food/1982/07/28/prosciutto-the-pick-of-the-pork-products/33707414-d236-4b52-aa0e-3cc56712b684.

MacLeod, Dan. "Sunday Read It and Weep! The Story behind the Cangiano's Dynasty." *Courier Life's Brooklyn Daily*. October 23, 2011. http://www.brooklyndaily.com/stories/2011/42/all_cangianossundayread_2011_10_21_bd.html.

Malcolmson, Robert, and Stephanos Mastoris. *The English Pig: A History*. London and New York: Hambledon and London, 2001.

Marchese, John. "Joseph A. Rigotti." *Philadelphia Magazine*. March 25, 2011. http://www
.phillymag.com/articles/the-di-bruno-s-growing-empire.

Marchetti, Domenica. "Cured Meats a 4th-Generation Family Business." American Food
Roots. February 21, 2013. http://www.americanfoodroots.com/features
/american-made/salami-cured-meats-a-fourth-generation-family-business.

Marianski, Stanley, and Adam Marionski. *The Art of Making Fermented Sausages*, 2nd
edition. Seminole, FL: Bookmagic, 2009.

Marquardt, Deborah. "A War in the Hamlets." *Washington Post*. May 6, 1992. https://www
.washingtonpost.com/archive/lifestyle/food/1992/05/06/a-war-in-the-hamlets
/9682b3dc-673c-428f-9dbc-65c1023c7425.

Mayer, Amy. "Pork Producers Root out Market Niche with Berkshire Pigs." The Salt. *NPR*.
April 29, 2013. http://www.npr.org/sections/thesalt/2013/04/25/179089297/pork
-producers-root-out-market-niche-with-berkshire-pigs.

McDaniel, Rick. *An Irresistible History of Southern Food: Four Centuries of Black-Eyed Peas,
Collard Greens and Whole Hog Barbecue*. Charleston, SC: The History Press, 2011.

McGee, Harold. "Bringing Flavor Back to the Ham." The Curious Cook. *New York Times*.
June 2, 2009. http://www.nytimes.com/2009/06/03/dining/03curi.html.

McNulty, Ian. "Clean Slate." *Gambit*. January 24, 2006. http://www.bestofneworleans
.com/gambit/clean-slate/Content?oid=1245179.

Melamed, Samantha. "Fishtown Butcher Slices through Gender Barrier." Philly.com.
December 8, 2014. http://articles.philly.com/2014-12-08/news/56806987_1
_butcher-shop-whole-animals-small-farmers.

Meyer, Cameron, and Leigh Bush. "The Humane Human." Indiana Food Review. Accessed
April 14, 2016. http://www.indianafoodreview.com/archives/issue-1/goose.

Midson, Lori. "Forked!" *Westword*. March 7, 2013. http://digitalissue.denverwestword
.com/display_article.php?id=1337774.

Mooth, Bryn. "A Passion for Place: Steven Geddes." *Edible Ohio Valley*. October 30, 2013.
http://ohiovalley.ediblefeast.com/food-drink/passion-place-steven-geddes.

Morgan, Margaret. "The Ancient Craft and Tradition of Artisan Charcuterie is Being
Reborn." *Crushbrew*. September 15, 2015. http://crushbrew.com/the-craft-and
-tradition-of-artisan-charcuterie.

Moskin, Julia. "Dry-Cured Sausages: Kissed by Air, Never by Fire." *New York Times*. May
17, 2006. http://www.nytimes.com/2006/05/17/dining/17sala.html.

Muhlke, Christine. "Aging Gracefully." *New York Times*. January 29, 2009. http://www
.nytimes.com/2009/02/01/magazine/01food-t-000.html.

Myers, Sandra. "Trigg Ham Takes Prize." *Kentucky New Era*. August 25, 2000. http://www
.kentuckynewera.com/article_dca6007c-2418-5826-8910-1e333ae78e73.html.

National Pork Board. "The History of Pork." Pork: Be Inspired. Accessed June 21, 2015.
http://www.porkbeinspired.com/about-the-national-pork-board/the-history-of-pork.

———. "The Other White Meat® Brand." Pork: Be Inspired. Accessed June 21, 2015. http://
www.porkbeinspired.com/about-the-national-pork-board/the-other-white-meat-brand.

Neimark, Jill. "The Revival of Lamb Ham: A Colonial Tradition Renewed." The Salt.
NPR. March 31, 2015. http://www.npr.org/sections/thesalt/2015/03/31/396588498
/the-resurrection-of-lamb-ham-a-colonial-tradition-revived.

Ngo, Nancy. "Some Twin Cities Chefs Have Rediscovered the Fine Art of Charcuterie." *Taher*. July 8, 2009. http://www.taher.com/twin-cities-chefs-rediscovered-fine-art-charcuterie.

Nicoletti, Piergiorgio and Amy. "All about Sopresse and Sopressate." Delallo. Accessed May 13, 2015. https://www.delallo.com/article/sopresse-sopressate.

———. "Salumeria: A Triumph of Gastronomical Proportions Italy's Renowned Cured, Preserved and Cooked Meat." Dellalo. Accessed January 30, 2016.

"The 9th Street Italian Market." Fante's Kitchen Shop. Accessed May 6, 2016. https://www.fantes.com/italian-market.

"Nitrate and Nitrite: Health Information Summary." New Hampshire Department of Environmental Services. Accessed May 11, 2016. http://des.nh.gov/organization/commissioner/pip/factsheets/ard/documents/ard-ehp-16.pdf.

O'Connor, John. "In Cajun Country, in Search of the Boucherie." *New York Times*. June 3, 2011. http://www.nytimes.com/2011/06/05/travel/in-cajun-country-in-search-of-the-boucherie.html.

O'Grady, Patrick. "North Country Smokehouse Sold." *Valley News*. March 9, 2015.

Olmert, Michael. "Smokehouses." *Colonial Williamsburg*. Winter 2004–2005. https://www.history.org/Foundation/journal/Winter04-05/smoke.cfm.

"Ossabaw Island Hog." Livestock Conservancy. Accessed April 12, 2016. https://livestockconservancy.org/index.php/heritage/internal/Ossabaw.

"Our Farmers." La Quercia. Accessed March 3, 2016. http://laquercia.us/about_our_farmers.

"Our History." Seltzer's Lebanon Bologna. Accessed April 4, 2016. http://www.seltzerslebanon.com/about-us.

"Our Principles." Home Place Pastures. http://www.homeplacepastures.com/our-principles.

Pagani, P. "The Magical Wisdom of the Early 'Salter.'" Italian Food Excellence. November 7, 2013. http://www.italianfoodexcellence.com/the-magical-wisdom-of-the-early-salter.

Pegg, Ronald B., and Fereidoon Shahidi. *Nitrite Curing of Meat: The N-Nitrosamine Problem and Nitrite Alternatives*. Trumbull, CT: Food & Nutrition Press, 2000.

Pellegrini, Georgia. *Food Heroes: 16 Culinary Artisans Preserving Tradition*. New York: Stewart, Tabori & Chang, 2010.

Pennisi, Elizabeth. "The Taming of the Pig Took Some Wild Turns." *Science*. August 31, 2015. http://www.sciencemag.org/news/2015/08/taming-pig-took-some-wild-turns.

"Pennsylvania Agricultural History Project." Pennsylvania Historical & Museum Commission. August 26, 2015. http://www.phmc.state.pa.us/portal/communities/agriculture.

"Pennsylvania Dutch Meat." Welcome to Lancaster County. Accessed April 4, 2016. http://www.welcome-to-lancaster-county.com/pennsylvania-dutch-meat.html.

Perry, Robert. "Heritage Hog Carcass Yields." University of Kentucky. https://dhn-hes.ca.uky.edu/content/heritage-hog-carcass-yields.

Pols, Mary. "Top Chef Who Walked Away from 'Chaos' Finds Higher Calling among Amish in Unity." *Portland (ME) Press Herald*. January 14, 2016. http://www.pressherald.com/2016/01/13/peripatetic-chef-pursues-his-calling-among-unity-amish.

"Pork History and Lore." American Berkshire Association. Accessed August 18, 2015. http://www.americanberkshire.com/consumers/eating-pork/pork-history-and-lore.

Prichard, Diana. "The Rise and Fall of the Great American Hog." *Modern Farmer*. August 21, 2013. http://modernfarmer.com/2013/08/the-rise-and-fall-of-the-great-american-hog.

Pridmore, Jay. "Italian Odyssey." *Chicago Tribune*. August 14, 1986. http://articles.chicago tribune.com/1986-08-14/entertainment/8602280878_1_tomatoes-abruzzo-region-pasta.

"Production Specifications." Prosciutto di San Daniele. Accessed May 17, 2016. http://www.prosciuttosandaniele.it/en/the-ham/strict-specifications-to-ensure-quality.

"Prosciutto di San Daniele DOP." Academia Barilla. Accessed August 4, 2015. http://www.academiabarilla.com/the-italian-food-academy/meats-charcuterie/prosciutto-daniele.aspx.

"Raven & Boar Farm." Raven & Boar Farm. Accessed April 26, 2016. http://ravenandboar.com/about.

Ray, Frederick K. "Meat Curing." Oklahoma Cooperative Extension Service. Accessed April 4, 2016. http://pods.dasnr.okstate.edu/docushare/dsweb/Get/Document-2055/ANSI-3994web.pdf.

Reddicliffe, Steve. "No More 'Banging on the Shutters.'" *New York Times*. June 7, 2014. http://www.nytimes.com/2014/06/08/nyregion/walters-in-mamaroneck-reopens-its-hot-dog-stand.html.

Redman, Paul. "Paul Bertolli: Chef, Author, and Salumi Maker." University of California, Berkeley. Accessed May 28, 2016. http://digitalassets.lib.berkeley.edu/roho/ucb/text/bertolli_paul.pdf.

Regan, Caleb D. "Home Meat Curing." *Grit*. November/December 2011. http://www.grit.com/departments/home-meat-curing.

Roberts, Jeffrey P. *Vermont Dry-Cured Meat Marketing Study*. Montpelier: Vermont Housing and Conservation Board, 2012.

Rogers, Craig. "Lamb Ham." Lowcountry Rice Culture Group, Facebook post. January 15, 2015.

Romfoody. "Mititei Sau Mici." *Romanian Food Blog*. March 26, 2012. http://romanianfood blog.blogspot.com/2012/03/mititei-sau-mici.html.

Rosenbaum, Ron. "Anthony Bourdain's Theory on the Foodie Revolution." *Smithsonian Magazine*. July 2014. http://www.smithsonianmag.com/arts-culture/anthony-bourdains-theory-foodie-revolution-180951848.

Rountree, Helen C. "Uses of Domesticated Animals by Early Virginia Indians." *Encyclopedia Virginia*. May 30, 2014. http://www.encyclopediavirginia.org/Domesticated_Animals_During_the_Pre-Colonial_Era.

Ruhlman, Michael, and Brian Polcyn. *Charcuterie: The Craft of Salting, Smoking, and Curing*. New York: W. W. Norton & Company, 2013.

———. *Salumi: The Craft of Italian Dry Curing*. New York: W. W. Norton & Company, 2012.

Russo, Kristin. "Award-Winning Flavor." *Valley Breeze*. February 24, 2015. http://www.valleybreeze.com/2015-02-24/features/award-winning-flavor.

"Salt & Grinder: A Deli Tradition." Salt & Grinder. Accessed April 20, 2016. http://www.saltandgrinder.com.

Sausage Obsession. "The History of Sausage." Accessed March 2, 2015. http://www.sausage obsession.com/history_of_sausage.

Sawtelle, Hank. "Cured Meat, Explained." Culinate. April 5, 2010. http://legacy.culinate
.com/content/273960/index.html.

Schulz, Dana. "Back to the Butchers." Greenwich Village Society for Historic Preservation.
December 1, 2011. http://gvshp.org/blog/2011/12/01/back-to-the-butchers.

Schwarcz, Joe. "Is Celery Juice a Viable Alternative to Nitrites in Cured Meats?" McGill
University. April 4, 2013. http://blogs.mcgill.ca/oss/2013/04/04/is-celery
-juice-a-viable-alternative-to-nitrites-in-cured-meats.

Seichrist, Tony. *Meat. Salt. Time. Salumi Master Cristiano Creminelli*. Atlanta, GA: PC
Press, 2010.

Severson, Kim. "Young Idols with Cleavers Rule the Stage." *New York Times*. July 7, 2009.
http://www.nytimes.com/2009/07/08/dining/08butch.html.

Shaheen, Troy. "Pig Tattoos Lead to Pennsylvania, Questions over Born-in-Vermont Brand
Claims." *VT Digger*. March 15, 2015. http://vtdigger.org/2015/03/15/pig
-tattoos-lead-to-pennsylvania-questions-over-born-in-vermont-brand-claims.

Shapiro, Stephanie. "A Slice of History." *Baltimore Sun*. November 9, 2005. http://articles
.baltimoresun.com/2005-11-09/news/0511080137_1_lebanon-bologna-lebanon
-county-weaver.

Shaw, Hank. "About." Hunter Angler Gardener Cook. Accessed May 24, 2016. http://
honest-food.net/about.

———. *Buck, Buck, Moose: Recipes and Techniques for Cooking Deer, Elk, Antelope, Moose, and
Other Antlered Things*. Glendale, CA: H&H Books, 2016.

———. *Duck, Duck, Goose: Recipes and Techniques for Cooking Ducks and Geese, Both Wild and
Domesticated*. Berkeley: Ten Speed Press, 2013.

———. *Hunt, Gather, Cook: Finding the Forgotten Feast*. Emmaus, PA: Rodale Books, 2011.

Shire, Bernard. "The 'Working' CEO." *Meat & Poultry*. March 17, 2015. http://www.meat
poultry.com/Writers/Bernard-Shire/The-working-CEO.aspx.

Slatalla, Michelle. "ONLINE SHOPPER; Country Ham, as Close as the Keyboard." *New
York Times*. December 12, 2002. http://www.nytimes.com/2002/12/12/technology
/online-shopper-country-ham-as-close-as-the-keyboard.html.

Smith, J. Russell. *Tree Crops: A Permanent Agriculture*. New York: Harcourt, Brace, 1929.

"Smoking Goose." Smoking Goose. Accessed November 16, 2015. http://www.smoking
goose.com.

Sombke, Laurence. "The Wurst of New York." *New York Magazine*. February 3, 1986.

"St. Anthony the Abbot." Aquinas & More. Accessed May 15, 2016. http://www.aquinas
andmore.com/fuseaction/store.patronsaintpage/saint/167.

Stannard, Paul. "Dry-Cured Sausage: A Brief History." Fortuna's Sausage Company.
Accessed August 13, 2015. http://www.fortunasausage.com/Soupy-Supri-s/40.htm.

Stern, Gary. "How One Old-Fashioned Pork Store Survived and Thrives." *New York
Business Journal*. December 7, 2015. http://www.bizjournals.com/newyork/news/2015
/12/07/schaller-weber-new-york-city-pork-store.html.

Stolberg, Sheryl Gay. "Fire at Virginia Smokehouse Leaves Pork-to-Table Movement
Reeling." *New York Times*. February 1, 2016. http://www.nytimes.com/2016/02/02/us/
from-smoked-ham-to-a-charred-culinary-institution-in-virginia.html.

Sula, Mike. "The Charcuterie Underground." *Chicago Reader*. November 26, 2009. http://
www.chicagoreader.com/chicago/the-charcuterie-underground-outlaw-bacon
-curers-and-sausage-grinders/Content?oid=1241681.

———. "Ghosts in the Ham House." *Eater*. October 29, 2010. http://www.eater.com
/2014/10/29/7080059/feature-newsoms-country-hams.

———. "Meet Billy Pork, the Father of Chicago's Charcuterie Revolution." *Chicago
Reader*. November 13, 2014. http://www.chicagoreader.com/chicago/charcuterie
-haccp-billy-nolen-consultant-publican-quality-meats-health-department-permit
/Content?oid=15602901.

———. "One Bite: Kulen." *Chicago Reader*. December 22, 2009. http://www.chicago
reader.com/Bleader/archives/2009/12/22/one-bite-kulen.

Svoronos, M. Jean. "The Origins of Coinage." *American Journal of Numismatics* 44, no. 1
(January 1910): 16. https://www.jstor.org/stable/43583557.

Swenson, Ben. "Pork of Yore." *Distinction Magazine*. October 4, 2014. http://distinctionhr
.com/pork-of-yore.

"Swine in China. Empire of the Pig." *Economist*. December 17, 2014. http://www
.economist.com/news/christmas-specials/21636507-chinas-insatiable-appetite-pork
-symbol-countrys-rise-it-also.

"Tasso." Nitty Grits. Accessed December 9, 2015. http://sofab.wikia.com/wiki/Tasso.

Taylor, Joe Gray. *Eating, Drinking, and Visiting in the South: An Informal History*. Baton
Rouge: Louisiana State University Press, 1982.

Thorn, Bret. "Charcuterie, Egg Most Buzzed-About Menu Items." *Nation's Restaurant
News*. February 11, 2014. http://nrn.com/consumer-trends/charcuterie-egg-most
-buzzed-about-menu-items.

"Today's Farm." Becker Lane Organic. Accessed March 6, 2016. http://beckerlaneorganic
.com/todays-farm.

"Todd Family of Smithfield, Virginia." Ancestry.com. Accessed March 22, 2016. http://
freepages.genealogy.rootsweb.ancestry.com/~jganis/toddfamily.html.

Towne, Charles W., and Edward N. Wentworth. *Pigs from Cave to Corn Belt*. Norman:
University of Oklahoma Press, 1950.

Trillin, Calvin. "Missing Link." *New Yorker*. January 28, 2002. http://www.newyorker.com
/magazine/2002/01/28/missing-links.

"12 Old School Di Bruno Bros. Food Finds." Di Bruno Bros. May 6, 2014. http://blog
.dibruno.com/2014/05/06/12-old-school-di-bruno-bros-food-finds.

United States Department of Agriculture. "Organic Survey." 2007. https://www.agcensus
.usda.gov/Publications/Organic_Survey.

———. *Yearbook 1922*. Washington, DC: Government Printing Office, 1923.

Vann, Mick. "A History of Pigs in America." *Austin Chronicle*. April 10, 2009. http://www
.austinchronicle.com/food/2009-04-10/764573.

Vecchio, Francois Paul-Armand. *Charcutier. Salumiere. Wurstmeister*. Delaware: Self-
published, 2013.

Voltz, Jeanne, and Elaine J. Harvell. *The Country Ham Book*. Chapel Hill: University of
North Carolina Press, 1999.

Ward, Logan. "The New Frontier of Country Ham." *Garden and Gun*. December 2010/
   January 2011. http://gardenandgun.com/article/new-frontier-country-ham.
Warren, Wilson J. *Tied to the Great Meatpacking Machine: The Midwest and Meatpacking*.
   Iowa City: University of Iowa Press, 2007.
Warshaw, Brette. "Profiles in Obsession: Francis Cretarola & Cathy Lee." *Lucky Peach*. March
   13, 2015. http://luckypeach.com/profiles-in-obsession-francis-cratil-cretarola-cathy-lee.
Watson, Lyall. *The Whole Hog: Exploring the Extraordinary Potential of Pigs*. Washington,
   DC: Smithsonian Books, 2004.
Weigl, Andrea. "Sam Suchoff Woos Locavores, One Country Ham at a Time." *News &
   Observer*. March 13, 2015. http://www.newsobserver.com/living/food-drink/article
   14017100.html.
Weinstein, Bruce, and Mark Scarbrough. *Ham: An Obsession with the Hindquarter*. New
   York: Stewart, Tabori & Chang, 2010.
Weiss, Jeffrey. *Charcutería: The Soul of Spain*. Chicago: Agate Surrey, 2014.
"Why We Love Cincy." *Cincy Magazine*. August/September 2009. http://cincymagazine
   .com/Main/Articles/Why_We_Love_Cincy_3847.aspx.
Wicks, Amanda. "Q&A with Chef Nick Martin." *Bone & Seed by Dinner Lab*. May 13, 2016.
Wilder, Charlotte. "How an Italian Family Built a Prosciutto Empire in Rhode Island."
   Cook's Illustrated. May 29, 2014. https://www.cooksillustrated.com/articles
   /225-how-an-italian-family-built-a-prosciutto-empire-in-rhode-island.
Wilford, John Noble. "First Settlers Domesticated Pigs before Crops." *New York Times*. May
   31, 1994. http://www.nytimes.com/1994/05/31/science/first-settlers-domesticated
   -pigs-before-crops.html.
Wilson, Carol, and Christopher Trotter. *The Whole Hog: Recipes and Lore for Everything but
   the Oink*. London: Pavilion Books, 2010.
Wise, Victoria. *American Charcuterie: Recipes from Pig-by-the-Tail*. New York: Penguin
   Books, 1987.
Wolfe, Anna. "Building a Legacy." *Gourmet Retailer*. December 2011. http://www.gourmet
   retailer.com/article-building_a_legacy-2379.html.
Wolfe, Benjamin. "A New Mold Species Discovered on Salami." Microbial Foods. January
   17, 2015. http://microbialfoods.org/science-digested-new-penicillium-species
   -discovered-salami.
"Yorkshire." National Swine Registry. Accessed March 22, 2016. http://nationalswine.com
   /about/about_breeds/Yorkshire.php.
Young-Brown, Fiona. *A Culinary History of Kentucky: Burgoo, Beer Cheese and Goetta*.
   Charleston, SC: The History Press, 2014.
Zhen, Wang. "Chinese Ham You Never Know Before." Study in China. Accessed July 15,
   2015. http://www.study-in-china.org/ChinaFeature/Diet/20111014224539102.htm.
Zhou, G.-H., and G.-M. Zhao. "History and Heritage of Jinhua Ham." *Animal Frontiers* 2,
   no. 4 (December 22, 2014): 62–67. doi:10.2527/af.2012-0063.

INDEX

ABOUT THE AUTHOR

Lizzari Photographic

A resident of Montpelier, Vermont, Jeff Roberts is president of Cow Creek Creative Ventures, which is dedicated to developing solutions in the areas of agriculture and food policy, conservation, the environment, and community economic development. He was cofounder and principal consultant at the Vermont Institute for Artisan Cheese at the University of Vermont. His book *The Atlas of American Artisan Cheese* (Chelsea Green, 2007) was the first comprehensive survey of small-scale producers. He is a member of *Guilde Internationale des Fromagers*. He teaches the history and culture of food at the New England Culinary Institute, is a visiting professor at the University of Gastronomic Science, provides consulting services to a wide array of small-scale food producers, and is a frequent speaker in Europe and the United States on artisan food, sustainable agriculture, and the working landscape.

During his career, Jeff was a meteorologist, museum curator and historian, and director of development at the Morris Arboretum in Philadelphia. From 1987 to 1994, he was associate dean at the University of Pennsylvania School of Veterinary Medicine. From 1995 to 1998, he was vice president of external affairs at the Vermont Land Trust.

For more than a decade, Jeff was active in Slow Food International and USA, including service as a director and treasurer of the national board. Locally he served as a director of the Central Vermont Community Land Trust, Vermont Arts Council, and Vermont Fresh Network.

the politics and practice of sustainable living

CHELSEA GREEN PUBLISHING

Chelsea Green Publishing sees books as tools for effecting cultural change and seeks to empower citizens to participate in reclaiming our global commons and become its impassioned stewards. If you enjoyed *Salted and Cured,* please consider these other great books related to food and culture.

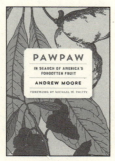

PAWPAW
*In Search of
America's Forgotten Fruit*
ANDREW MOORE
9781603587037
Paperback • $19.95

CHEDDAR
*A Journey to the Heart of
America's Most Iconic Cheese*
GORDON EDGAR
9781603587044
Paperback • $17.95

WILD FERMENTATION
*The Flavor, Nutrition, and Craft of
Live-Culture Foods,*
Updated and Revised Edition
SANDOR ELLIX KATZ
9781603586283
Paperback • $29.95

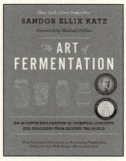

THE ART OF FERMENTATION
*An In-Depth Exploration of
Essential Concepts and Processes
from around the World*
SANDOR ELLIX KATZ
9781603582865
Hardcover • $39.95

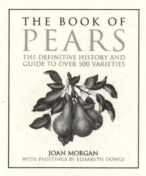

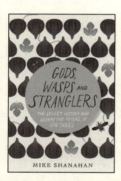